EXPLORER'S GUIDE

SANTA FE
& TAOS

NINTH EDITION

EXPLORER'S GUIDE

SANTA FE & TAOS

SHARON NIEDERMAN

with photographs by the author

THE COUNTRYMAN PRESS
A division of W. W. Norton & Company
Independent Publishers Since 1923

ALSO BY THE AUTHOR:

New Mexico: An Explorer's Guide

New Mexico's Tasty Traditions: Recollections, Recipes, and Photos

Return to Abo: A Novel of the Southwest

*A Quilt of Words: Women's Diaries, Letters,
and Original Accounts of Life in the Southwest 1860–1960*

Signs and Shrines: Spiritual Journeys Across New Mexico

*The New Mexico Farm Table Cookbook: 100 Homegrown Recipes
from the Land of Enchantment*

For information about permission to reproduce selections from this book,
write to Permissions, The Countryman Press
500 Fifth Avenue, New York, NY 10110

For information about special discounts for bulk purchases, please contact
W. W. Norton Special Sales at specialsales@wwnorton.com or 800-233-4830

The Countryman Press
www.countrymanpress.com

A division of W. W. Norton & Company, Inc.
500 Fifth Avenue, New York, NY 10110
www.wwnorton.com

978-1-58157-411-1 (pbk.)

10 9 8 7 6 5 4 3 2 1

Winter Twilight, Canyon Road

Do not say you will come back
When it is warmer
When you have time
When the light is better
When the galleries are open
When the chestnut trees are green
When a woman in red sits on the garden bench
When the blue gate is wide open
When the duende seizes you
When you are not obsessing
When you are not regretting
When you are not counting
Your losses
See the Hunger Moon scale the Sangres
Press the shutter. Now.

—Sharon Niederman

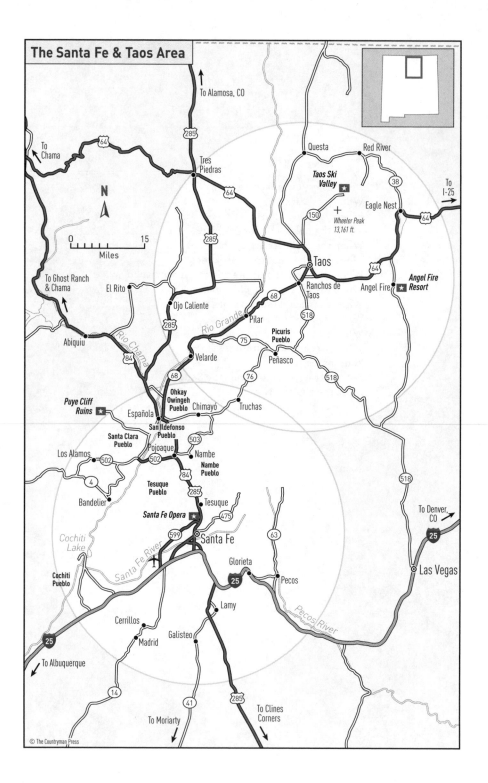

The Santa Fe & Taos Area

CONTENTS

MAPS

INTRODUCTION

I n 1881, New Mexico governor Lew Wallace made the observation, "Every calculation based on experience elsewhere fails in New Mexico." While Wallace meant the statement ironically and that is how it is generally understood, this book is all about the celebration of the 47th state's wondrous, unique qualities.

The vibrant mix of cultures, the variety of languages spoken, and the respect for time-honored customs makes New Mexico an exciting place to be. However, a happy and successful visit to New Mexico requires the appropriate attitude adjustment. Just as you can go from desert to high mountain environments in an hour, you can shift from adventure to luxurious relaxation faster than you can say *mañana*. This book, based on three decades of living, writing, and traveling here, can guide you toward creating the best possible New Mexico experience—for you. Here's what you need to know:

- Always get precise directions before setting out. Travel with adequate maps. Once on the road, you may find a lack of signs, street names, and markers. Historic markers of the Old Spanish Trail and El Camino Real may not be very useful helping you find a restaurant or lodging. In addition, many streets are old and winding, and undergo name changes midway. They were built for burros, not automobiles (this is one aspect of "Santa Fe charm"), so travel can be disorienting. If you stop to ask directions, you may find they are skimpy or given with an assumption of familiarity you do not possess. Locals may be able to tell each other, "It's over there, just past the big cottonwood, turn right at the dip and look for the blue mailbox," while, after half a dozen bumps in a dirt road, you may wonder exactly which "dip" was meant.

- Always call ahead to be sure a restaurant or attraction is open. Although definite hours may be advertised, the reality is that hours of operation are often flexible, based on time of year, family demands, and number of visitors. The place you expected to be open because the website said it was might have its door locked. This situation is particularly true in out-of-the-way locations. To avoid disappointment and unnecessary driving, just call first.

- Santa Fe and Taos are popular destinations. It is not unusual for

THE HISTORY OF NATIVE PEOPLE IS DEPICTED ON MUSEUM HILL IN SANTA FE

ROASTING CHILES SCENT THE AUTUMN AIR

favorite lodgings to be booked for the winter holiday season and Indian Market a year in advance; for many other wonderful B&Bs, six months in advance is common. The sooner you can make your travel plans, the more choices you will have and the fewer compromises you will have to make. Also, booking in advance can help you negotiate more favorable rates.

· Remember you are entering another time zone here. We're not just talking about Mountain Time. *Mañana* does not mean "tomorrow." It may be translated as "not today." The room you booked was supposed to be ready at 2, yet when you arrive you're told it won't be ready until 4. Or the tour you booked is canceled until next week. Patience, courtesy, and flexibility, always a good idea, are the best attitudes to maintain. Pressuring or threats to "talk to the manager" or "call the boss" will be counterproductive. New Mexico is not the place to throw your weight around. Yes, you are the customer. And you are prepared to pay good money for competent service. But any display of self-importance will only typecast you as an outsider and decrease the chances that you'll get what you want. New Mexicans were isolated for four centuries, and they made up their own rules. Rushing is not efficient here. But you're on vacation anyway, right? So go with the flow. And carry a book with you for times you might have to wait. Taking a "chill" attitude may make the difference between having a good vacation and a terrible time.

· Take care of your health. You've probably heard it before, but here goes: Allow a few days to adjust to the altitude, drink lots of water, wear sunscreen at all times of day, take a hat, dress in layers, give yourself lots of rest stops. The sun is very intense at this altitude, there's less oxygen, and you may very well feel the effects. And whatever the season, it's best to be prepared for sudden changes in weather. When venturing out, be prepared for temperature changes of as much as 40 degrees in a single day—and remember, the weather may change dramatically very suddenly. A day that starts out quite cool may become very warm in the afternoon sun. Dress accordingly. That means pack your layers and wear them.

- The official state question in restaurants is: Red or green? But you will find that the question most commonly asked by outsiders in New Mexico is: Which is hotter, red or green chile? Regardless of the answer, if you are genuinely concerned, it's best to ask for a small taste of each kind of chile before placing your order. It might take you a little while to become accustomed to the taste sensation of chile, but once you do, you will be addicted, eagerly anticipating your next taste. And the touted health benefits of chile are real. Meanwhile, at most restaurants, you can order any dish containing chile with the chile served on the side.
- Even if you are not by nature a shopper, you will find things here so special, so unique that you'll find yourself frequently reaching for your wallet. Art, jewelry, furniture, clothing, crafts—northern New Mexico is a bazaar of the one-of-a-kind and the exquisitely handmade. In Santa Fe, Spanish Market takes place the last weekend in July, while Indian Market is held the weekend of August closest to the 19th, and the wildly popular International Folk Art Festival is the second weekend in July. In fall, artists' studio tours held in the nearby villages of El Rito, Dixon, Abiquiu, and Galisteo offer especially appealing shopping opportunities. Some Pueblo artists sell from their home studios as well. In the case of silver and turquoise jewelry, it is buyer beware, so purchasing from a reputable dealer or museum shop is your best bet. The wares sold at the Portal Program at the Palace of the Governors are juried and certified Indian Handmade, so that is another safe place to shop. The stores described in this book are well-researched, reliable purveyors of original work.

While people speak of off-season and in-season, there really is no clear off-season in New Mexico. Each time of year has its own beauty, to be found on a peaceful desert hike on a dazzling summer morning or cuddling up in front of a sweet piñon fire after a winter afternoon walk through snowy Santa Fe. There's nothing better than a stroll through Taos in early November, when the cottonwoods are still golden and the scent of autumn piñon smoke is in the air. Whatever season you choose for your visit, New Mexico has the power to touch and satisfy your soul. Your chances of finding worthwhile bargains may be found during the quieter times of spring and fall.

Be prepared to be surprised in New Mexico. The sweep of a red earth vista, the sight of a 10-foot, stark white Penitente cross on a hillside, the faded altar paintings of a centuries-old Spanish colonial church, the drumbeats and jangling shells of hundreds of dancers at a Pueblo corn dance, the spontaneous connection

SANTA FE'S INTERNATIONAL FOLK ART FESTIVAL HAS BECOME A MUST-DO SHOPPING OCCASION

with a local grower at the Santa Fe Farmers' Market, the sight of more stars than you've ever seen in the clear night sky—any of thousands of moments have the power to move you deeply and perhaps change your life in some way you could never have predicted.

In this ninth edition of *Explorer's Guide Santa Fe & Taos*, we've included many new restaurants, lodgings, shops, and cultural opportunities, some of which replace enterprises that have moved or closed or repurposed themselves. This content of this book is curated to inform you of a wide range of the best values, opportunities, and experiences in lodging and cuisine. Many fine, newer high-end restaurants have opened in Santa Fe, and they are well known; however, you will find the emphasis in these pages is on the places locals frequent and on revealing the hidden gems your hotel concierge might not tell you about. You can get an excellent meal in Santa Fe that doesn't cost an arm and a leg, and you can save

ALTAR SCREEN AT EL RANCHO DE LAS GOLINDRINAS

up for a splurge at the table of an internationally recognized chef.

Once you visit, you may find a single vacation isn't enough. And no matter how much time you've spent here, it's still possible to make new discoveries. As I travel the state, New Mexico continuously reveals new discoveries, and so I invite you, too, to return to this unique place to learn more, see more, and continue the delightful adventure.

You can take the book with you on your travels and skip around, reading about the places you visit as you go. Or you can read the entire book through from start to finish. For ease of navigation, we've divided information into discrete neighborhoods, so if you are exploring a particular part of town, say, Santa Fe's Canyon Road, you'll find listings of food, art, and shopping grouped together to link accessible destinations in that area. Specific practical information on each listing is organized for easy reference in blocks at the head of each entry. All details given in the information blocks—as well as all phone numbers and addresses in other parts of the book—were checked as close to publication as possible. Even so, such details do change. When in doubt, call ahead.

Santa Fe lodging and dining prices have, no doubt about it, gone up, and they are still going up. Santa Fe is one of the most popular destinations in the world, so the way to economize is to travel in the off-season, make every effort to book your travel well ahead of time, and be adventurous. It is still possible to have a vacation here that will not break the bank, but it must be carefully planned. Every effort has been made to offer information about a range of lodging and affordable dining options that still deliver quality and authenticity. You may need to go a bit out of the way to find them, but the experience is usually rewarding.

Because prices are fluid, we've usually avoided listing specific prices, preferring instead to indicate a range. Lodging price codes are based on a per-room rate, double occupancy, during high season (summer and ski months). Low-season

rates are likely to be 20 percent less. Once again, it's always best to call ahead for specific rates and reservations.

Restaurant prices indicate the cost of an individual meal, including appetizer, entrée, dessert, tax, and tip, but not including alcoholic beverages.

	Lodging	Dining
Inexpensive	Up to $145	Up to $35
Moderate	$150–250	$35–60
Expensive	$250–450	$60–90
Very expensive	Over $450	Over $90

MINIMUM STAY Many higher-priced lodgings in Santa Fe and Taos, including

EL PUEBLO LODGE IS A FAVORITE WITH SKIERS

IT'S JAVA JUNCTION FOR A COFFEE BREAK IN MADRID
WHILE TOURING THE TURQUOISE TRAIL

the B&Bs, require a minimum stay of two or three nights on high-season weekends and busy holidays. During such times, your best bet for a single night's stay is a motel.

DEPOSIT/CANCELLATION To reserve a room in Santa Fe or Taos, you generally must make a deposit to cover the first night, although more is sometimes required—particularly if you're going to be staying for several nights. If you have to cancel a reservation, you'll usually get your deposit back, provided you cancel 10 days to two weeks before your arrival. Be sure to check the particular cancellation policy of your lodging, though, because these regulations vary widely. Some establishments refund the deposit minus a 10 to 15 percent service fee, a few will refund only if your room gets rented, and many don't give refunds at all for cancellations at peak times such as Indian Market weekend or during the Christmas holiday. If you cancel only a few days before your expected arrival, you're most likely to lose your deposit, although sometimes it may be applied to a future stay. During the high season, the demand for lodging often exceeds the supply, so plan well in advance—at least three to six months ahead for the most popular lodgings—so you will not be disappointed.

OTHER OPTIONS There are two telephone area codes for New Mexico: 505 and 575. Santa Fe is 505; Taos is 575. For areas in between, if one does not work, try the other.

The best sources for year-round tourist information are the **Santa Fe Convention and Visitors Bureau** (505-955-6200; 800-777-2489; www.santafe.org; 201 W. Marcy St., Santa Fe, NM 87501) and the **Taos Visitor Center** (575-758-3873; 800-732-8267; www.taos.org; 1139 Paseo del Pueblo Sur, Taos, NM 87571). For specific information on activities near Taos, contact the **Angel Fire Visitor Center** (575-377-6555; 866-668-7787; www.angelfirefun.com; 3365 Mountain View Blvd., #7, Angel Fire, NM 87710); the **Eagle Nest Chamber of Commerce** (575-377-2420; 800-494-9117; 60 W. Therma Dr., Eagle Nest, NM 87718); or the **Red River Visitor Information Center** (575-754-3030; www.redriver.org; 101 W. River St., Red River, NM 87558).

There are several convenient visitor centers within Santa Fe:

Downtown Visitor Information Center
Plaza Galeria
66 E. San Francisco St., Suite 3
Santa Fe, NM 87501
505-955-6215/800-777-2489

Santa Fe Community Convention Center
201 W. Marcy St.
Santa Fe, NM 87501
505-955-6200/800-777-2489

Railyard Visitor Information Center
Santa Fe Depot
410 S. Guadalupe St.
Santa Fe, NM 87501
505-955-6230/800-777-2489

TOWNS IN THE SANTA FE–TAOS AREA Though we focus primarily on Santa Fe and Taos, other towns in the area are worth a visit. Within the circle to the south of Santa Fe, for example, you'll find Golden and Madrid on the road known as the Turquoise Trail, and east of Santa Fe lie Galisteo and Lamy, villages that retain their Wild West and old New Mexico flavor. A few minutes to the north of Santa Fe lies the picturesque village of Tesuque, a favored suburb of Santa Fe with the Santa Fe Opera, Shidoni Gallery, and the gathering spot of the Tesuque Village Market. To the west is Los Alamos, home of the Los Alamos National Laboratory, the birthplace of the atomic bomb, and site of the new Manhattan Project National Historical Park.

Scattered up and down the Rio Grande are 11 Indian pueblos—not towns but individual sovereign nations—each unique in its own way, from ceremonies and dances to crafts and cooking. On the way to Taos via the Rio Grande on NM 68, you'll pass through the little farming and orchard villages of Velarde and Embudo, with the artists' community of Dixon and its La Chiripada Winery a quick side trip east. And if you take the High Road to Taos via NM 76 and NM 518, you'll cruise through more than half a dozen villages dating to the 18th century, where time virtually stands still—Chimayó, with its famous Santuario known for its healing "holy dirt," and Truchas, Peñasco, Vadito, and others that offer everything from wonderful crafts and galleries to venerable Spanish colonial churches and the experience of quieter times.

North of Taos are the old mining towns of Questa, Red River, and Angel Fire, today all hubs of outdoor sports and backwoods places with wild and rustic flavors. West of Taos is Ojo Caliente, site of the famed mineral springs spa. And if you go as far west as Abiquiu, you'll find the home of artist Georgia O'Keeffe. One look at the landscape, with its pink and red cliffs, is explanation enough of the artist's fascination with northern New Mexico and why her work seems so inspired. As she said, "In New Mexico, half your work is done for you." Another journey outside the area, this time 60 miles to the southeast via I-25, will take you to the busy metropolis of Albuquerque with its numerous historical and cultural attractions, including the botanic gardens, aquarium, and zoo that

VINTAGE QUILTS DISPLAYED AT DIXON CAN TELL THE STORY OF NEW MEXICO PIONEER WOMEN

compose the Biopark; the University of New Mexico with its basketball stadium, now called "WisePies Arena"; bustling Nob Hill with its shops and cafés, in 2016 celebrating its 75th anniversary as the first shopping mall to open west of the Mississippi; and the Albuquerque Isotopes baseball stadium.

A NOTE ON THE CUISINE Feeding the soul with a phenomenal amount of history and culture is paramount here, but so is feeding the body. As agricultural communities, Santa Fe and Taos have been bastions of local produce and home cooking for the better part of 400 years. And vendors still sell seasonal fare, from sweet corn and chile to apples and *bizcochitos* (the anise-flavored "state cookie") at roadside stands. During past decades, specialty establishments, including ice cream and candy shops, delis, bakeries, and gourmet markets, have become better established. Farmers' or growers' markets continue to proliferate, offering fresh, locally grown produce in-season and inspiring chefs as well as home cooks. Following are some of the special places and products, both old and new,

that make the modern Santa Fe–Taos area a gastronomic delight. And if you are fortunate to drive past one of the old-time general stores, such as Bode's in Abiquiu, do venture in. It's possible to find gourmet delights, a handmade tamale in the crockpot, or a great bowl of chile amid the pots and pans, hardware, and sacks of beans.

The official state question is: "Red or green?" When dining in a New Mexican establishment, you will inevitably be asked this question by the waitperson. It is remarkable the different spin put on this same essential fruit—for it is a fruit, not a vegetable, technically. You will no doubt wonder which is hotter, but there is no good answer to that question. It all depends on the method of preparation, how much rain has fallen this season, and where the chile was grown. Sometimes green is hotter, sometimes red. When in doubt, you can always ask for your chile on the side. Most places will oblige, but some famously refuse to serve it that way. It may take a while to accustom your palate to chile, but once you do, you will have become just as addicted as the rest of the population.

HISTORY

This was a land of vast spaces and long silences, a desert land of red bluffs and brilliant flowering cactus. The hot sun poured down. This land belonged to the very old Gods. They came on summer evenings, unseen, to rest their eyes and their hearts on the milky opal and smoky blue of the desert. For this was a land of enchantment, where Gods walked in the cool of the evening.
—From *Land of Enchantment: Memoirs of Marian Russell*
    Along the Old Santa Fe Trail

The history of northern New Mexico is one of dramatic change. From hot, turbulent forces that originally shaped the land to social movements that molded its present-day mix of cultures, the area has been embroiled in flux since prehistoric times. The story of the Santa Fe–Taos area is one of an enchanting land and its varied peoples: of hunter-gatherers and modern Pueblo Indians; of Spanish conquistadors and colonists; of American mountain men, French trappers, German merchants, and adventurers of various origins; and more recently of artists, tourists, skiers, and spiritual seekers.

In 2015, during the Santa Fe Fiesta celebration held each September to commemorate the *entrada*, or entrance into the city of conquistadors led by Don Diego de Vargas in 1693, local Native Americans staged the first protest to the accepted, official version of Santa Fe's history. On a brilliant September afternoon, when the Plaza was drenched in autumn sunlight, for the first time the story of the "peaceful reconquest" of Natives by the Spaniards was challenged. Native Americans held signs like flash cards that told an alternative story, peacefully and movingly. They shared the story of conquered Pueblo people as recounted in their history. The power of this peaceful demonstration rocked the city that had been celebrating its life under the flag of Spain for four centuries with parades, reenactments, and the procession of its revered icon, *La Conquistadora*, kept in a private chapel adjacent to Cathedral Basilica of St. Francis of Assisi. The cries of *"Vive La Fiesta!"* took on a different meaning and the

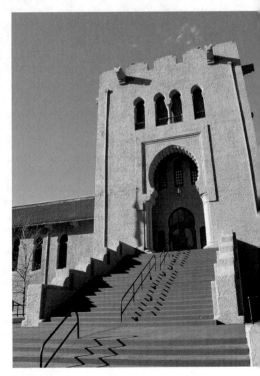

SANTA FE'S SCOTTISH RITE CATHEDRAL IS AS OLD AS THE STATE ITSELF

annual ceremony became more complicated, rousing a range of emotions, much like a family secret revealed at a staid holiday gathering. The demonstration was articulate and historically accurate, but it stabbed the tradition of the city's venerated Spanish identity in the heart. For all its modernity, Santa Fe remains proper and old-fashioned; in a changing world, it holds fast to enduring beliefs.

Even more recently, in 2016, La Fonda, the city's premier historic hotel, underwent a redesign of its lobby and bar. Even though the familiar, beloved bar that was remodeled was built in the 1980s and the 2016 redecoration went back in time to reference the original 1920s Fred Harvey version many locals felt their tradition had been destroyed. Letters to the editor raged, and much of the population remained upset about the controversial redesign.

To begin to understand the complexity of Santa Fe's history, to untangle the roots of the culture's rich cuisine, art, architecture, music, spirituality, and rituals, some historic background is helpful. In 1598, Don Juan de Onate, with 83 oxcarts in a 4-mile-long caravan, traveled up the Camino Real de Tierra Adentro (the Royal Road of the Interior Land) from Mexico, establishing the first enduring European settlement at Ohkay Owingeh Pueblo, which he renamed San Juan. (It has since returned to its original name.) Soon after, Onate moved 25 miles south to the city he named Santa Fe, or "holy faith." A plaza was laid out according to guidelines expressed in the 16th-century Laws of the Indies (*Leyes des Indias*), which governed New World Spanish colonies and dictated the construction of cities, including those in its northern province, the location of Santa Fe. Then, in 1680, led by Popé, the Tewa Indian from Ohkay Owingeh, the Pueblo Revolt rose against the oppressive behavior of the Spanish, who, in their quest for gold and souls, cruelly used the Native population for their own purposes.

In their rage, the local population burned churches, murdered priests, and drove the Spanish out of New Spain 400 miles down the Camino Real to El Paso del Norte. After 12 years in the south in exile, Don Diego de Vargas brought the colonists back north, and the reconquest succeeded. And here is where the story told by the protestors diverges from the official version. The reconquest was not peaceful. It was, in fact, marked by violence and terror. The Natives did not submit willingly, or happily, to the returning Spanish. And by the time Fiesta 2015 rolled around, the "rest of the story" demanded a hearing.

That story was heard on the plaza that day. It reverberated throughout the media and in every bakery, barbershop, and nail salon in the city. With grudging acceptance, it was agreed the official fiesta text, recited by fiesta reenactors fully outfitted as priests and conquistadors, and which had assumed the sanctity of a holy text, would have to be altered to include Native voices and Native participants. It was as though a dysfunctional family finally admitted its long-held forbidden secrets and began the process of healing.

✳ The Tricultural Myth

At the beginning of the 20th century, Santa Fe's town fathers, concerned about the economic welfare of the city, invented the myth of Three Cultures to describe its varied population—and attract tourists. They did this around the same time they established what they called the "New-Old Santa Fe Style," an architectural idiom also known today as "Santa Fe Style." The construction of the Museum of Fine Arts (now known as the New Mexico Museum of Art) in 1917 established the city's distinctive architectural brand. That architecture, also called Spanish-Pueblo Revival, melds elements like vigas—supports of tree trunks interlaced with *latillas,* branches or twigs laid at an angle, with the carved wooden corbels, uses adobe mud as a building material, and features sheltered portals around the buildings with Native elements to produce a distinctive look both well-weathered and resonant with historical significance.

Not only Santa Fe, but all of New Mexico, as they promoted it, was unique because of its three cultures: Spanish, Indian, and Anglo. The myth conveniently ignores the variety of cultures that also settled here. They arrived as Buffalo Soldiers, as merchants and traders on the Santa Fe Trail, and they sought prosperity to be gained through homesteading, mining, trade, and later, the railroad. They included African American, Italian, German, Basque, Mexican, Italian, and Jewish immigrants.

In truth, Spanish and Native societies coexisted in this part of the world peaceably for centuries, intermarrying, becoming godparents to each other's children, sharing knowledge of architecture, cooking, agriculture, astronomy, water, and land stewardship, in effect borrowing each other's tools. But there is a deeper, darker side to the story. The legend of La Llorona, the Weeping Woman, persists. It is used to frighten young children into good behavior. La Llorona can be heard at night crying in the bosque, the cottonwood forest by the river, looking for her lost children, after she has been abandoned by her Spanish lover. That is the origin of the mestizo, the half-Native, half-European who now populates the New World.

In truth, today's Santa Fe is far richer than the definition of itself that limits it to three cultures. The millions of visitors who come to Santa Fe annually arrive from all over the world. Any day, Spanish, French, Japanese, German, Chinese, and Scandinavian languages are heard on the Plaza. Just as visitors observe and are impacted by Santa Fe, the influx of travelers in turn influences the city to shine. Artists, musicians, and performers from many countries come to Santa Fe to experience the inspiration the city offers. New Mexico is a land that, through the centuries, has continuously been "discovered"—first by wandering bands of indigenous people, then, four centuries ago, by the Spanish, and successively by 19th- and 20th-century pioneers determined to build a better life. Each new group of discoverers brought and added its own perspective and customs to the mix. The area's remoteness from major population centers, extreme weather, scarce water, and challenging terrain have proven both blessing and curse. Isolation protected and strengthened Native cultures and built an ethos of self-sufficiency among Spanish farmers and villagers. Simultaneously, New Mexico was cut off from innovation and economic growth. It wasn't until the 19th century, with the coming of the Santa Fe Trail, the railroad, and successive waves of people, trade, and ideas that New Mexico opened up to the outside world.

✳ Natural History

If we could compress 2 billion years into a few minutes, we would see the New Mexico landscape as it was shaped and reshaped. The invasion and retreat of inland seas, the rise and fall of great mountain ranges, the shifting of subterranean plates, the cracking of mantle and crust, the explosions of volcanoes, the seeping of magma, the shifting of sands, and the continual erosion by wind and water—each of these forces has left its mark on the modern landscape.

More than 100 million years ago, great dinosaurs roamed this land, as evidenced by their remains on display at Ghost Ranch Conference Center in Abiquiu. At the same time, colorful sands and silts from the ancestral Rockies formed pink and red cliffs, and volcanoes spewed ash over the landscape. As the modern Rockies rose to the north, the dinosaurs mysteriously disappeared, giving way to the mammals.

A MUST-DO FOR LOVERS OF GEORGIA O'KEEFFE'S WORK IS THE GHOST RANCH LANDSCAPE TOUR THAT COMPARES HER PAINTINGS WITH THE ACTUAL SITES THAT INSPIRED HER

To the east of Santa Fe and Taos, the Sangre de Cristo Mountains began to rise near the end of the Mesozoic. Later, about 30 million years ago, an upswelling in the earth's mantle created a pair of massive fault lines, and the land between them caved in, resulting in the Rio Grande Rift, a trench up to 5 miles deep. It filled with debris and water from the mountains, creating a long chain of basins. Finally, about 2.5 million years ago, the Rio Grande became a continuous river flowing 1,800 miles to the Gulf of Mexico. Thereafter, volcanic activity on the west side of the Rio Grande created basaltic mesas and broad volcanic tablelands, including the present-day Taos Plateau.

The Jemez (HAY-mess) Mountains west of Santa Fe are the remains of a composite volcano that geologists believe was once almost as high as Mount Everest. About 50,000 to 60,000 years ago, the volcano blew its top and caved in, forming what is called a caldera; it sits on top of much older calderas. The explosion, 600 times more powerful than the 1980 eruption of Mount St. Helens, left a crater 15 miles wide and buried much of the land with ash up to 1,000 feet thick. Later, some of that volcanic tuff became home to the Ancient People as they migrated toward the Rio Grande. Their cave dwellings may be viewed at the bases of canyon walls at nearby Bandelier National Monument, and the Valles Caldera National Preserve recently was named a new national park.

During more recent ice ages, lava seeped into the foothills and glaciers scoured the mountains. Heavy snows and rains formed lakes and created wide, sloping foothills. As the weather warmed, these areas sprouted new vegetation, from scrub brush and small pines in the lowlands to lush aspens and evergreens in the mountains.

Such was the landscape discovered by the first human inhabitants of the Santa Fe–Taos area some 12,000 years ago. Today it is essentially the same: the wide, fertile Rio Grande Valley flanked by spectacular sets of mountains. To the east lies the Sangre de Cristo range, where, in good years, the snow is a joy for skiers and outdoor enthusiasts, stretching north to the Colorado Rockies, while to the west lie the volcanic Jemez.

From north of Taos, the Rio Grande rushes through a 50-mile stretch of basalt, the gorge providing year-round fishing and summer thrills and chills for whitewater rafting enthusiasts. Likewise, the Chama River, flowing north of the Jemez into the Rio Grande, offers some of the most spectacular wild and scenic excursions in the state. Flowing south through the fertile farms and orchards of Velarde, the Rio Grande eventually meanders through the ancient Pueblo lands north of Santa Fe and the hills and valleys to the west. This vast country was named Rio Grande del Norte National Monument in 2013.

Elevations in the area range from less than 6,000 feet in the valley to 13,161 feet at the top of Wheeler Peak, the highest point in the state. The air is clear and dry, with sunny skies 300 days of the year. A 14-inch average annual rainfall leaves a desert-like setting in the lowlands, while winter storms can dump snow generously on the lush mountain areas of Taos Ski Valley and the Enchanted Circle towns of Red River and Angel Fire.

These factors make for a diversity of life zones and an especially rich flora and fauna. Santa Fe and Taos have wonderful shade trees, the most prominent being the giant willows and cottonwoods that grace municipal plazas and downtowns. Juniper and piñon pines dominate the dry lower elevations, giving way to scrub oak and thicker forests of ponderosa pine, and finally to high-alpine forests with a spectacular mix of fir, aspen, and spruce. Spring and summer wildflowers, especially in the mountains, make a colorful spectrum, from Indian paintbrush and wild iris to columbine, buttercups, and alpine daisies.

Northern New Mexico is a haven for animals large and small. The *arroyos* (dry gullies or washes) and foothills are dominated by mice, prairie dogs, jackrabbits, and cottontails and by the coyotes, foxes, and bobcats that feed on them. Muskrat and beaver paddle through some rivers and streams, and signs of river otter can be found on secluded parts of the Rio Grande. A herd of sure-footed and shy bighorn sheep roam parts of the Sangre de Cristo around Taos, Questa, and Red River, while pronghorn antelope are common on the plains. The mountains are home not only to snowshoe hares and various species of squirrels, but also to herds of mule deer, elk, and a fair number of black bears. Mountain lions also are sighted with increasing frequency in these parts. Recovery from severe forest fires in Los Alamos and above Taos is transforming the ponderosa pine–dominated ecology to open green meadows and young aspen stands inhabited by an increasing diversity of birds and wildflowers.

Birds fill every available avian niche, from seed-eating finches and bug-eating swallows to breathtakingly beautiful bluebirds, the chatty black and white magpies of Taos, and large, winged predators. Eagles and hawks soar above canyons, while quail, dove, and roadrunners (the state bird) skitter through the brush below. Lowland wet and

THE ASPENS REALLY DO SHIMMER GOLD IN AUTUMN ALONG THE ENCHANTED CIRCLE

THE CHAMA RIVER OUTSIDE ABIQUIU IS A STREAM OF SILVER SERENITY

marsh areas play host to ducks, geese, and shorebirds, while the mountains are home to a wide range of species.

✳ Social History

EARLY HUMAN INHABITANTS The first human inhabitants of the Santa Fe–Taos area were Stone Age hunters who followed herds of giant bison and mammoth more than 12,000 years ago. As the centuries passed they became less nomadic, gathering fruits, nuts, and greens in the lowlands, hunting deer and elk in the mountains, and trapping small game. By around 5500 B.C. these hunter-gatherers were living season-ally in what is today the Santa Fe–Taos area, mostly in caves and other natural shelters. Soon afterward, they began to plant corn and other crops and to make baskets. Even-tually, they constructed circular pit houses, which centuries later gave way to abo-veground dwellings of stone and adobe. Around 200 B.C. they began making pottery.

From A.D. 900–1300, great Ancestral Puebloan complexes flourished at Chaco Can-yon and Mesa Verde to the west and north. (Although the word *Anasazi* was used to refer to these people for many years, it is no longer an acceptable term. *Ancestral Pueb-loan* is used instead.) These centers were marked by extensive roadways and huge, multitiered complexes of stone. The people performed sophisticated ceremonies, irri-gated extensive farmlands, and accurately predicted the movements of the sun and moon. Another group of Ancestral Puebloans developed a similar complex in Frijoles (free-HOLE-ace) Canyon about 30 miles northwest of Santa Fe in what is now Bande-lier National Monument. However, by A.D. 1300, most of these great centers had been abandoned. It is widely believed that the "ancient ones" were some of the ancestors of present-day Pueblo people.

Sometime during the Ancestral Puebloan era, a number of stone and adobe vil-lages sprang up in the Santa Fe area. The largest of these, called Ogapoge or Kuapoge (meaning "dancing ground of the sun"), once occupied part of Santa Fe. Scores of other small settlements, including the beginnings of present-day Taos Pueblo and other pueblos north of Santa Fe, were built along the Rio Grande.

Ogapoge and other settlements around Santa Fe were abandoned around A.D. 1425 during the worst drought in 1,000 years. Others remained and continued to flourish, including Pecos Pueblo to the southeast and the present-day pueblos of Tesuque, Pojoaque, Nambé, San Ildefonso, Santa Clara, San Juan, Jemez, Picuris, and Taos to the north. When the first Spaniards arrived in New Mexico, the Pueblo Indians (*pueblo* is Spanish for "village") were well established in some 150 adobe villages, large and small, scattered along the Rio Grande and its tributaries. In New Mexico today, 19 Indian pueblos, each a sovereign state, carry on their ancestral customs.

Before the arrival of the Spaniards, the Pueblos lived a life of ceremony in accordance with the seasonal cycles of hunting and planting. They cultivated corn, beans, and squash and gathered greens, berries, fruits, and seeds. They hunted wild game, from prairie dogs, rabbits, and turkeys to deer, elk, and antelope. They made clay pottery; wove baskets and mats from corn, cattail, and yucca leaves; and fashioned blankets from feathers and animal hides. Although they traveled exclusively on foot, they not only maintained close ties with each other but also had trade links with the Plains Indians, the Pacific Coast Indians, and tribes in Mexico.

The ancient Pueblos, like their modern counterparts, spoke several different languages. They continuously honored the Great Spirit and the forces of nature. Underground, they built circular chambers called kivas, adaptations of their ancestral pit houses that served as centers for prayer and teaching. They also developed elaborate ceremonial dances that expressed their sense of oneness with nature. With the exception of raids by neighboring Plains tribes, their lives were generally tranquil until the arrival of the Spaniards from Mexico.

TAOS PUEBLO IS A 1,000 YEAR-OLD WORLD HERITAGE SITE

THE SPANISH INFLUENCE One of the first Spaniards to come to New Mexico, then known as New Spain, was Fray Marcos de Niza, a Franciscan friar who arrived in 1539 after hearing fabulous accounts of the New World Seven Cities of Cibola, supposedly made of gold. Speculation has it that the "gold" was actually the rays of sunshine on the adobe city. De Niza never visited these cities himself, but he embellished the stories he heard. His own overblown reports of riches spurred a massive expedition in 1540, in which Francisco Vasquez de Coronado rode north from Mexico City with 300 soldiers. Cibola turned out to be nothing more than the little pueblo of Zuni, which Coronado and his men conquered and subjugated. Other pueblos to the north were similarly invaded, yet neither Coronado nor those who followed him found gold. Thereafter the Spanish crown turned its focus toward colonization, while the Spanish Church attempted to reeducate the "souls" of the native population and make them believers.

The first official colonizer of the area was Juan de Oñate. In 1598, with 129 soldier-colonists and their families, 10 Franciscan friars, and thousands of cattle, sheep, horses, and mules, he set out to establish the first permanent Spanish settlement in New Mexico. Many horses escaped, eventually providing Plains Indians and the rest of North America with a new form of transportation.

Oñate chose a spot across the Rio Grande from Ohkay Owingeh Pueblo, about 25 miles north of present-day Santa Fe, near Española. The settlement, called San Gabriel, was beset with problems from the beginning. Some settlers were apparently still under the illusion that they would find easy riches. Others balked at the hard labor and difficult living conditions, still others at the difficulty of converting the Indians to Catholicism. By 1600, almost half the settlers had given up and gone back to Mexico. A few years later, referring to the stories of fantastic riches and abundance in the area, the viceroy of New Spain wrote to the king from Mexico City, "I cannot help but inform your majesty that this conquest is becoming a fairy tale. . . . If those who write the reports imagine that they are believed by those who read them, they are greatly mistaken. Less substance is being revealed every day."

Many Spaniards thought the most reasonable alternative was to leave New Mexico altogether. However, after long debate, they decided to stay, partly to maintain their claim to the huge territory west of the Mississippi, but primarily because the friars were so reluctant to abandon the Indians to paganism. A new governor, Pedro de Peralta, was appointed and sent to New Mexico to found a permanent settlement. He chose a spot south of San Gabriel that offered more water and better protection. The result was La Villa de Santa Fe—the City of Holy Faith. (In 1823, St. Francis became its patron saint, hence its current name: the Royal City of the Holy Faith of St. Francis of Assisi.) In 1610, a decade before the arrival of the Pilgrims at Plymouth Rock, the Spanish settlers laid out their new plaza in accordance with the Laws of the Indies that governed all Spanish colonies. They began building the Palace of the Governors, today the oldest continuously occupied public building in the United States, constructed in 1610. That same year, supplies began moving northward to Santa Fe along the newly opened Camino Real (meaning "royal road") from Chihuahua, Mexico. A caravan might take three years to make the journey, stopping at *posadas* (inns) along the way to trade.

Over the years, the settler-soldiers built adobe houses and dug a network of *acequias*, or irrigation ditches, to divert water from the Santa Fe River. They cultivated fields of beans, squash, corn, and wheat with handheld plows and wooden hoes. Accompanied by Franciscan friars, they ranged far and wide, subjugating the Pueblos, building churches, and trying to convert the Indians to Catholicism. By 1625 the Spaniards had built some 50 churches in the Rio Grande Valley with forced Indian labor, and more than half the original pueblos had disappeared.

One that continued to thrive was Taos Pueblo, about 70 miles north of Santa Fe. (*Taos* is the Spanish version of a Tewa phrase meaning "place of the red willows.") The first Spanish settlers moved there with Fray Pedro de Miranda in 1617. They settled near Taos Pueblo, even moving within its walls during the 1760s for protection against the Comanches. Taos Pueblo, a World Heritage Site, has existed for approximately 1,000 years in the same location, and today those who live there live according to the old way, as much as possible, without electricity and running water. So long as the Pueblo is not closed for ceremonies, it is open to the public; a photo permit may be purchased if the photos to be taken are not of spiritual festivals and images are for personal use only. Photography and videography of feast days and special events is strictly forbidden. The rights to the Sacred Blue Lake, the Pueblo's water source, were returned to the Pueblo in 1970, and this pure, sacred water source runs through the Pueblo today.

DRESSED AS COMANCHES, TAOSEÑOS COMMEMORATE THEIR PLAINS INDIAN HERITAGE EVERY NEW YEAR'S DAY

The Indians objected to Spanish encroachment. All through the Rio Grande Valley, Pueblo spiritual and political leaders were routinely treated harshly, in many cases abusively, while others were forced to build churches, work in the fields, and weave garments for export to Mexico. Conflicts between Spanish civil and religious authorities fueled the discontent. Over a 75-year period, the Indians attempted a number of revolts, most stemming from attempts to outlaw their religious ceremonies. None was successful. Rebellions at Taos and Jemez Pueblos in the 1630s resulted in the deaths of several priests and were met with even more brutality and repression from the Spaniards. While some governors allowed the Indians to continue their dances, most supported the Franciscans in their attempts to stamp out all remnants of Pueblo ceremony.

One of the most brutal of these attempts came in 1675, when Governor Juan Francisco de Trevino charged 47 Pueblo religious leaders with sorcery and witchcraft and sentenced them to death or slavery. An Ohkay Owingeh leader named Popé, who was frequently flogged because of his religious influence, secretly vowed revenge. For several years he hid at Taos Pueblo, quietly plotting and sending out runners to orchestrate a revolt of all the pueblos. Runners communicated the exact time of the revolt by carrying and counting knotted cords called quipus, each knot signifying another day.

The revolt took place on August 10, 1680. At break of day, Indians in pueblos from Taos in the north to Acoma in the south and Hopi in the west suddenly turned on the Spaniards, killing men, women, children, and priests and setting mission churches ablaze. In Santa Fe, about 1,000 settlers holed up in the Palace of the Governors. When Governor Otermín learned of the widespread devastation, he and the others loaded their belongings onto mules and wagons and abandoned Santa Fe on August 21.

The refugees eventually made their way to El Paso del Norte, near the site of present-day Juarez, Mexico, where they lived in exile for 12 years. Meanwhile, Indians took over the Palace of the Governors.

✳ A Note on the Area as Spiritual and Arts Center

"You can feel it, the atmosphere of it, around the pueblos. Not, of course, when the place is crowded with sightseers and motor-cars. But go to Taos Pueblo on some brilliant snowy morning and see the white figure on the roof; or come riding through at dusk on some windy evening, when the black skirts of the silent women blow around the wide boots, and you will feel the old, old root of human consciousness still reaching down to depths we know nothing of."
—D. H. LAWRENCE, "Mornings in Mexico"

Events during the early decades of the 20th century contributed to Santa Fe's reputation as a center for the arts. Dr. Edgar Lee Hewett, director of the Museum of New Mexico, and other arrivals organized the first Indian Market in 1922, which, now grown into the world's largest market for Indian wares, continues annually on the third weekend of August. Three years later, Mary Austin and others founded the Spanish Colonial Arts Society to encourage a revival of Hispanic folk art. The annual Spanish Market celebration of traditional Spanish crafts like woodcarving and straw weaving is held the last weekend of July. In 1926, Will Shuster created Zozobra, an effigy of "Old Man Gloom" that each year since has been set ablaze to touch off the annual Fiesta de Santa Fe. At the same time, Indian potters such as Maria Martinez of San Ildefonso began to achieve popularity. The Santa Fe Concert Series was founded in 1936, followed by the opening of the Wheelwright Museum of the American Indian, founded by Bostonian Mary Cabot Wheelwright and Navajo medicine man Hosteen Klah. It was also during the 1930s that the dedicated Dorothy Dunn began nurturing a new generation of artistic talent at the Santa Fe Indian School.

World War II brought more changes. One of the most profound was the 1943 purchase of the Los Alamos Ranch School for Boys, a place where Robert J. Oppenheimer had spent time as a boy, and its conversion into Los Alamos National Laboratory, birthplace of the atomic bomb. Since the war, the lab has been a focal point for defense research, from hydrogen bombs to Star Wars technology.

A lesser-known fact is that during the war there was a Japanese detention camp in Santa Fe. Surrounded by barbed wire and located in the Casa Solana area, the camp imprisoned more than 4,500 Japanese American men from the East and West coasts who, by virtue of their ethnicity, were considered "dangerous enemy aliens."

After the war, Santa Fe and Taos were again "discovered." As artists and tourists continued to arrive, the first galleries began to sprout in the cities. During the latter half of the 1950s, the newly opened Taos Ski Valley spurred tourism in the area, as did the Santa Fe Opera and the

THE CRYSTAL LIGHT OF NORTHERN NEW MEXICO CALLS TO ARTISTS

PIGS FLY AS VISITORS DELIGHT IN QUIRKY ARROYO SECO EN ROUTE TO TAOS SKI VALLEY

Museum of International Folk Art. Festivals and exhibitions such as Indian Market and the International Folk Art Market routinely bring as many as 50,000 to 100,000 visitors to town.

At the same time, Santa Fe and Taos became known as spiritual power centers, attracting individuals and groups that have promoted everything from Asian philosophies and healing to Shamanism, American Indian, and New Age thought. The Santa Fe Institute brings Nobel laureates and other top thinkers together, resulting in intriguing public presentations. During the 1960s and 1970s, Indians and Hispanic farmers accommodated thousands of hippies and experimenters in alternative living. Non-Hispanics now outnumber Hispanics. Today, both Santa Fe and Taos have large alternative-healing communities offering everything from massage and acupuncture to herbology, Ayurveda, and past-life regression. In recent years, the area has also attracted the film industry, and numerous well-known movie stars have taken up at least part-time residence here. Star spotting has become a popular spectator sport around Santa Fe and Taos, particularly with the current strength of the movie industry. Whatever the future holds for the Santa Fe–Taos area, it will be shaped by a combination of factors, including the national economy, the availability of water, and the will of the people. If trends are any indication, it will continue not only as a fascinating tourist destination but also as an ongoing stage for the interactions among the many diverse cultures that have shared in the area's rich and turbulent past.

New Mexico is home to a remarkable variety of spiritual paths. From Christian to Buddhist to Sikh, all have found the high mountains and desert expanses an inspiration to faith and practice. Contemporary spiritual seekers resonate with ancient Native American traditions, ongoing for thousands of years and still very much alive in New Mexico. The generations have imparted to the land itself a sense of the sacred, with the continuity of spiritual practice. Meditation, prayer, and song are performed in time with the cycles of the year and hours of the day. Here people of all faiths are inspired to solitary contemplation as well as participation in community gatherings.

New Mexico also has a tradition of pilgrimage. Each Holy Week, pilgrims may be seen walking the roads and highways to the Santuario de Chimayó, long considered a site of miraculous healing. Catholic roots go five centuries deep into the land.

THE CAROUSEL KNOWN AS TIO VIVO WAS HAND-PAINTED BY MEMBERS OF THE TAOS SOCIETY OF ARTISTS

Worship often extends outside the church or kiva into the plaza, streets, and homes of the community. Prayer is more often than not accompanied with feasting, music, and dance, considered vital elements of the ceremony. Gatherings, such as the Matachines Dances performed in the Hispanic villages as well as on the Indian pueblos, are often open to the public. Any slightly-more-than-casual observer will be struck not only by the depth of religious observance involving the entire community, but also by the shared traditions, such as the mixtures of Catholic and Indian ceremony, that occur here as well as throughout Mexico and Latin America. Such sharing is a natural evolution for cultures that have lived side by side for centuries.

But sacred sites in New Mexico encompass more than shrines and altars built by human hands. Many believe the ancient ruins that stand on this land occupy power or holy spots. Some of these ruins contain places that in the past were used for prayer and ritual. Many consider certain natural wonders to be their own personal power spots, reminders of the power of the Creator, where they are able to feel a connection with the divine.

Whatever your own spiritual path, you need not travel far in northern New Mexico to receive inspiration and revitalization. Because of the variety of spiritual paths

HAUNTING 1820S PECOS RUINS EMBODY THE HISTORY OF NEW MEXICO'S SPANISH AND INDIGENOUS ANCESTRY AND IS SACRED TO BOTH PEOPLES

that have found a home here, northern New Mexico also offers a spiritual "educational opportunity" not generally available elsewhere. Whatever sacred sites you choose to visit, you will be joined in spirit to the many others who have stood there before you.

✳ Architecture

Adobe architecture, as much as the landscape, gives New Mexico a distinctive identity. In a nation where many places look the same, the Santa Fe–Taos area still displays its unique identity.

For a look at the old adobe architecture, stroll around the Santa Fe Plaza, along East De Vargas Street, and up Canyon Road. Or explore Taos Plaza and its intriguing side streets. The soft, rounded adobe structures appear to have grown right out of the earth.

As centuries passed, people adapted their techniques and materials. For example, mud walls were built up a handful at a time, a technique called puddling. Or they were laid with "bricks" of mud cut from streambanks. Ruins such as those at Chaco Canyon and Bandelier National Monument reveal sophisticated use of natural sandstone and other rock for the construction of four- and five-story apartment-type buildings. The stone walls were mortared with mud.

When Spanish settlers arrived in the early 1600s, the Pueblo Indians quickly adopted the newcomers' adobe-brick-making techniques. The Spaniards' knowledge of adobe construction can be traced back to the Middle East and Mesopotamia, as can their use of the *horno* (OR-no), a beehive-shaped outdoor oven originally acquired from the Moors.

Twentieth-century architects Isaac Hamilton Rapp and John Gaw Meem embraced the Spanish-Pueblo Revival style that was originally inspired by the Laguna and Acoma Pueblos. The style found early expression in sites such as La Fonda Hotel and the Museum of Fine Arts.

To get a feel for the city's early adobe residences, visit the oldest house in the United States at 215 East De Vargas Street in Santa Fe. The cavelike interior features a corner fireplace of Spanish origin. The oldest parts of the walls are of puddled adobe. Contrast this humble home with the modern, five-story Eldorado Hotel at 309 West San Francisco Street to see how flexible the idea of mud construction can be. The Eldorado is a recent expression of the Santa Fe style, or Spanish-Pueblo Revival style, which has been in vogue since the 1920s. Like most newer buildings in Santa Fe, however, the Eldorado is not real adobe; it simply wears an adobe-style stucco veneer.

Santa Feans were especially proud of their new state capitol. Dedicated in 1900, with a rotunda and an Ionic-columned portico, it was a fine example of the classical style then in vogue in the United States—and totally out of place in New Mexico. This structure was completely redesigned in the 1950s to make it consistent with Spanish-Pueblo Revival style.

A group of artists, archaeologists, and civic activists, alarmed by the loss of the city's architectural heritage, dedicated themselves to preserving older Spanish structures and searching for a new regional building style. This group staged an exhibit in 1912 called "The New-Old Santa Fe Exhibition" to awaken interest in preserving the old Santa Fe and to promote Santa Fe as the "unrivaled tourist center of the Southwest." It was this second goal that eventually won over the city's business community. The city fathers realized that in order to attract tourists, Santa Fe must remain unique.

Success did not come overnight. One of the key battles took place over the Palace of the Governors three years before the exhibition. Progressives wanted to demolish this symbol of New Mexico's Hispanic past and put up a proper "American" courthouse.

THE BLUE GATES OF SANTA FE AND TAOS ARE ENDLESSLY FASCINATING

But in 1909, the conservatives—Dr. Edgar Lee Hewett, director of the Museum of New Mexico, and his followers—persuaded the legislature to preserve the palace as a historical museum. In the restoration that followed, the building's Territorial-style portal and brick coping were replaced with a Spanish-Pueblo portal and vigas. These renovations were intended to evoke the building's early history, and they helped establish the emerging Santa Fe style.

The Museum of Fine Arts across from the palace, designed by Isaac Hamilton Rapp, was another milestone that helped establish the "new-old" style Hewett and others wanted to achieve. Building the structure of brick rather than adobe, Rapp nevertheless incorporated many elements of Hispanic Mission-style churches for the museum design. Though the museum was built in 1916 and 1917, its evocative design makes it appear far older.

Two commercial buildings designed by Rapp to boost the Santa Fe style can still be seen: the Gross, Kelly & Co. Almacen, a warehouse near the railroad tracks on Guadalupe Street, and La Fonda, off the southeast corner of the Plaza. The warehouse, though in poor condition, still clearly displays its Spanish-style towers, portals, vigas, and *canales.*

As a result of accolades for the museum and the palace, the city adopted the Santa Fe style (called Spanish-Pueblo Revival), carried on by enthusiasts like John Gaw Meem and writer Oliver La Farge. Meem, who like many in his day believed New Mexico's climate to be a cure for tuberculosis, stayed in Santa Fe to become the most eloquent architect of Santa Fe style. One of the most memorable of his dozens of buildings is the Cristo Rey Church (see "Sites, Parks, and Museums", page 110–111). This massive structure, built in 1940 with 150,000 adobe bricks, bespeaks the architect's love for New Mexico's early mission churches.

The look of Santa Fe's downtown Plaza also owes much to Meem, who remodeled several Victorian and commercial buildings there, among them the former Woolworth building, the Franklin store, the Renehan building, and the old Masonic Lodge. In 1966 he also designed the portals that run along three sides of the Plaza.

In 1957, after six years of study, the city council adopted the Historic Zoning Ordinance and established Santa Fe's Historic District, which roughly encompasses the downtown area and Canyon Road. The ordinance gave an official stamp to two architectural styles: Spanish-Pueblo Revival and Territorial. The first is characterized by massive walls, rounded parapets, and hand-hewn woodwork. Territorial style is recognized by brick coping atop adobe walls, milled woodwork, and decorative pediments on doors and windows. A number of fine Victorian buildings from New Mexico's Territorial days still survive in Santa Fe (for example, the First Ward School at 400 Canyon Road); however, that style was deemed a diversion from the vernacular in 1957 and remains so today.

Anglicization came somewhat later to Taos, which lost many of its original buildings to "progress" in the 1920s and 1930s. In 1984, the Taos Town Council approved a Historic Design Review Ordinance that included many elements borrowed from Santa Fe's ordinance. The Historic District includes the Plaza and several clusters of buildings within Taos's 3 square miles.

Though Spanish-Pueblo Revival style borrows some important features from Pueblo architecture, such as rounded contours, large blank surfaces, and stepped-back levels, the philosophy and purposes of the two styles are quite different. To feel the difference, visit the older sections of some of the pueblos.

Santa Clara Pueblo native and architectural consultant Rina Swentzell writes: "Landscaping, or the beautification of outdoor spaces, was a foreign concept. The natural environment was primary, and the human structures were made to fit into the hills and around boulders or trees. In that setting, planting pretty flowers that need watering was ridiculous. Decoration for decoration's sake was unnecessary." In that Pueblo world, she concludes, "All of life, including walls, rocks and people, were part of an exquisite, flowing unity."

TRANSPORTATION

Santa Fe and Taos are beautiful auto destinations—which is a good thing, because neither is directly accessible by train or by major commercial airline. The nearest train station is in the hamlet of Lamy, 18 miles southeast of Santa Fe. A shuttle service coordinates its runs with the arrival of trains, so this is one relatively easy way to reach Santa Fe without a car. Shuttles run frequently from Albuquerque International Sunport and between Taos and Santa Fe. The majority of visitors, however, simply drive straight from their homes or fly into Albuquerque and rent a car. Currently, American Airlines operates four nonstop jet flights daily between Santa Fe and Dallas/Fort Worth or Phoenix. (Flights to California are seasonal; check with the airline.) United Airlines operates daily nonstop jet service between Santa Fe and Denver or Phoenix.

By whatever means you arrive, once you're here you need a car, because towns in New Mexico tend to be far apart. Also, driving northern New Mexico's back roads through centuries-old Hispanic villages, Indian pueblos, and magnificent desert and mountain scenery is an experience you won't forget. You'll be happiest if you pace your own tour through this part of the world.

For your convenience, a host of details about Santa Fe–Taos transportation follows.

✳ Getting to Santa Fe and Taos

BY CAR

FROM ALBUQUERQUE

The quickest route to Santa Fe is I-25 north (65 miles). A more scenic route is I-40 east to Cedar Crest, then north along NM 14, known as the Turquoise Trail, which meanders through several old mining villages: Golden, the site of the first gold rush west of the Mississippi; Madrid, a coal town turned arts-and-crafts center; and Cerrillos, a once bustling mining camp and subsequent film setting that is now a photogenic, sleepy town with plenty of Old West character. Whichever way you go, you'll be struck by the crystal-clear air and expansive views.

The most direct way to get to Taos from Santa Fe is to take US 84/285 north to Española, then NM 68 up the Rio Grande, a 47-mile drive. This is scenic all the way, but the last part, through the Rio Grande Gorge and up onto the expansive

ALL ABOARD THE RAIL RUNNER EXPRESS FROM DOWNTOWN SANTA FE ALL THE WAY TO ALBUQUERQUE

Taos Plateau, is particularly magnificent. Two of the greatest views in the world are available on this route: the sweep of piñon-studded desert as you crest Opera Hill north of Santa Fe and the unforgettable unfolding of the Taos Plateau as you approach Taos while driving out of the gorge. Also a beautiful drive, but at least an hour longer, is the High Road to Taos, which winds its way along the Sangre de Cristo range, passing through 17th-century Hispanic villages, including Truchas, the setting for Robert Redford's film, *The Milagro Beanfield War*. Don't miss the church in Las Trampas, a masterpiece of Spanish Colonial architecture built in 1763.

To absorb the true flavor of old northern New Mexico, a tour of the High Road is a must. To follow this route, take NM 76 east out of Española 11 miles to Chimayó. Go another 17 miles to Truchas, then go east for a few miles on NM 75 to Penasco, then north on NM 518. This highway eventually hooks up with NM 68, the main route to Taos. Taos is 70 miles from Santa Fe and 135 miles from Albuquerque. The best way to go would be to take the winding road through Taos Gorge, also known as the River Road, one way and the High Road the other.

THE VENERABLE PICKUP TRUCK IS A NEW MEXICO ICON

FROM DALLAS

Another long haul. Take I-20 west through Fort Worth, then go northwest on US 84 through Lubbock, Clovis, and Fort Sumner to Santa Rosa, where you'll take I-40 to Clines Corners. Then go north on US 285 to I-25 and south on I-25 to Santa Fe. Distance: 718 miles.

FROM DENVER

A beautiful drive along Colorado's rugged Front Range. It's simple, too: Just go south on I-25; after 386 miles you'll be in Santa Fe.

FROM LAS VEGAS

Take US 95 to Hoover Dam, US 93 to I-40, then proceed according to I-40 travel directions to Albuquerque and I-25 north to Santa Fe. Distance: 625 miles.

FROM LOS ANGELES

This is a two-day drive at minimum. Flagstaff is a good halfway point. The quickest and easiest route is to take I-15 northeast to Barstow, then I-40 east all the way to Albuquerque, where you'll take I-25 north to Santa Fe. Distance to Santa Fe: 850 miles.

A SUNNY AUTUMN DAY IS THE TIME FOR A DRIVE ALONG THE RIO GRANDE TO TAOS

FROM PHOENIX

Take I-17 to Flagstaff, then proceed as in directions for I-40 travel to Albuquerque. Distance: 525 miles.

FROM SALT LAKE CITY

There is no direct route from Salt Lake City to Santa Fe. One option is to take I-15 south to I-70, then I-70 east through the heart of the Rockies to Denver, then I-25 south to Santa Fe for a journey of 879 miles. A shorter and more scenic route, albeit more complicated, is to cut through the southeastern corner of Utah (magnificent canyons) and the southwestern edge of Colorado (equally magnificent mountains) before entering northern New Mexico. Or drive a little farther south into northeastern Arizona and see the Navajo and Hopi Indian reservations. There are any number of interesting ways to go; consult a map to help you choose.

FROM TUCSON

Take I-10 east to Las Cruces, then I-25 north up the Rio Grande Valley to Santa Fe. Distance: 636 miles.

BY BUS **Greyhound Lines** (505-243-7922; 505-243-4435; 800-231-2222; www.greyhound.com/en/contactus.aspx; 320 First St. S.W., Albuquerque). Serves Albuquerque from outside the state.

FROM DALLAS (19 HOURS)

Two buses depart daily to Albuquerque from the Greyhound station at 205 S. Lamar St. (214-849-6831). The 2016 one-way fare was $120; round-trip, $232.

FROM DENVER (9 HOURS)

Two buses run daily to Albuquerque from the station at 1055 19th St. (303-293-6555). One-way ticket prices in 2016 were $46; round-trip, $92.

FROM EL PASO (8 HOURS)

Greyhound has three buses leaving for Albuquerque every day from its station at 200 W. San Antonio Ave. (915-532-5095). A one-way ticket in 2016 cost $27; round-trip, $55.

FROM LAS VEGAS (16 HOURS)

Two buses run daily to Albuquerque from the Greyhound station at 200 S. Main St. (702-383-9792). In 2016, one-way tickets cost $105; round-trip, $209.

FROM LOS ANGELES (20 HOURS)

Three buses depart daily to Albuquerque from the downtown station at 1716 E. Seventh St. (213-629-8401). The 2016 one-way fare was $114; round-trip, $233.

FROM PHOENIX (12 HOURS)

Buses leave three times a day for Albuquerque from the station at 2115 E. Buckeye Rd. (602-389-4200). The 2016 one-way fare was $76; round-trip, $156.

FROM SALT LAKE CITY (20 HOURS)

Two buses run daily to Albuquerque from the station at 300 South 600 West (801-355-9579). One-way tickets in 2016 cost $148; round-trip, $292.

FROM TUCSON (13 HOURS)

Seven buses run daily to Albuquerque from the Greyhound station at 471 W. Congress St. (520-792-3475). The 2016 one-way fare was $134; round-trip, $268.

SHUTTLE SERVICE The following shuttle service companies provide transportation between Santa Fe and Albuquerque and Santa Fe and Taos.

ABQ Ride (505-768-2000; www.cabq.gov/abqride). To get from the Rail Runner train to the Sunport, take ABQ Ride Route 250, the Sunport Express, from the Alvarado Transportation Center at Central Avenue and First Street Northwest in downtown Albuquerque. Fare is $1 (exact change needed), seniors 35 cents.

New Mexico Rail Runner Express (866-795-RAIL [7245]; www.nmrailrunner.com). Provides train service from the Alvarado Transportation Center to Santa Fe. Tickets are approximately $9 one-way.

RoadRunner Shuttle and Charter (505-424-3367; www.roadrunnershuttleand charter.com; reservations required). Shared rides from airport to most Santa Fe hotels. Tickets are $32 one-way.

Sandia Shuttle Express (505-474-5696; 888-775-5696; www.sandiashuttle.com; reservations required). Provides 15 round-trip runs daily between the Albuquerque airport and downtown Santa Fe. It also drops off and picks up guests at all hotels, motels, and B&Bs in Santa Fe. The 2016 one-way fare was $30; round-trip, $55.

Twin Hearts Express & Transportation (575-751-1201). Provides four buses from 11:30 AM–5:30 PM each day to the major hotels in Taos from the Albuquerque airport. The cost of a round-trip ticket in 2016 was $60 one-way and $110 round-trip.

Taos Ski Valley Airport Shuttle (575-776-2291 ext. 2384). Daily year-round service between airports in Santa Fe and Albuquerque and Taos Ski Valley.

BY TRAIN Getting to Santa Fe and Taos by train can be fun and relaxing. The nearest train station is in the little village of Lamy, 18 miles southeast of Santa Fe. Road Runner Shuttle runs twice a day from Lamy and will pick up Amtrak passengers at hotels in Santa Fe. Service to Taos, White Rock, and Los Alamos is also available. The 2016 cost is $40 one-way to Santa Fe. Another way to get into town is to call a cab. **Capital City Cab Co.** (505-438-0000) is the only taxi service in Santa Fe. The 2016 fare from Lamy to the Plaza is approximately $80.

Santa Fe cannot be reached by passenger train from either Dallas or Denver, but you can take the Amtrak (800-872-7245) train from Chicago, Los Angeles, or New York:

FROM CHICAGO

Amtrak also runs a daily train from Chicago; the Southwest Chief takes approximately 26 hours. The 2016 fares started at $114–$275 in coach, one-way. Sleepers are priced at $262–$1,271, one-way.

FROM LOS ANGELES

Amtrak has a train leaving downtown LA each evening and arriving in Lamy the following afternoon. One-way rates in 2016 ranged from $65–$156 for coach. Sleepers, depending on time of year, go from $196–$936 one-way.

FROM NEW YORK

The train ride from New York takes two days. Fares in 2016 ranged from $186–$455 for coach and $971–$2,302 for sleeper, one-way.

BY PLANE If you're like most people, you'll get to Santa Fe and Taos by flying into the Sunport, as the Albuquerque airport is known. As you disembark and head for the baggage-claim area, take note of the southwestern décor, the pastel colors, the outstanding regional artwork on the walls, and the huge cast-metal sculpture of a soaring Indian clutching an eagle. The airport commissioned works by 93 major New Mexico artists, including 30 Native Americans. If you have doubts about New Mexico's reputation as a land apart, they'll begin to evaporate in the Sunport.

The **Santa Fe Municipal Airport** (SAF) is open to private aircraft, American Airlines, and United Airlines. American Airlines offers non-stop flights to and from Dallas with seasonal flights to California and United offers flights from Denver.

Shuttle service is available from the Albuquerque airport, the Santa Fe airport, and the train station in Lamy about 20 miles from Santa Fe.

✳ Getting around Santa Fe and Taos

Given the relatively long distances between towns in the Santa Fe–Taos region, the best way to see the area is by car. However, there are other options.

Santa Fe Trails (505-955-2001) is Santa Fe's first and only widespread public transportation system. Operations began in 1993, and the attractive tan buses provide service along 10 routes covering most parts of the city, including Rail Runner stops. Descriptions of routes and schedules can be picked up at city hall (200 Lincoln Ave., two blocks north of the Plaza), the public library (145 Washington Ave., one block north of the Plaza), and most supermarkets. The buses run 6 AM–10 PM on weekdays and 8 AM–8 PM on Saturday. There is 8:30 AM–6:30 PM service on Sunday. Fares are $1 for adults and 50 cents for seniors and kids under 18.

The very handy Santa Fe Pickup is a free shuttle that runs 10 AM–5:30 PM daily along two routes: One stops at major historical sites and the other goes from the state Capitol up Museum Hill and down Canyon Road.

Faust's Transportation (575-758-3410). They'll pick you up or drop you off at almost any motel or hotel in Taos. All transportation is private hire. Rates are approximately $300 one-way to Albuquerque Sunport; $200 to Santa Fe. They provide taxi service throughout Taos.

The Taos bus service is known as the **Chile Line** (575-751-4459) and offers transportation seven days a week. The in-town Red Route and University of New Mexico routes are free. You can take the Chile Line to Taos Ski Valley (Dec.–Apr.) and Santa Fe as well as around town, primarily along Paseo del Pueblo Norte and Sur; ADA van service is available. Taos Express operates between Taos, Española, and Santa Fe on weekends at fares of $5–$7 each way and is designed to connect with the Rail Runner at Santa Fe, which then offers access to Albuquerque. Please visit taosexpress.com for schedule and pickup points.

BY TAXI Maybe you just need a good old-fashioned taxi to get you from point A to point B as quickly as possible.

SANTA FE

Capital City Cab Co.: 505-438-0000

TAOS

Faust's Transportation Service: 575-758-3410

BY RENTED CAR Perhaps the simplest thing to do if you arrive by air is to rent a car at the Albuquerque airport. Virtually all major car rental agencies are based there:

Advantage: 800-777-5524
Avis: 800-633-3469
Budget: 800-404-8033
Dollar: 800-800-3665

Once you're in Santa Fe and Taos, you can also rent a car from one of the following companies:

Avis: 505-471-5892; 121 Aviation Dr.
  Budget: 505-984-1596; 1946 Cerrillos Rd.

TAOS

Enterprise: (575) 758-5553; 1350 Paseo del Pueblo Sur.

Most rental cars come equipped with air conditioning for summer weather and all-terrain tires for winter conditions. Virtually all the agencies listed above also rent a limited number of four-wheel-drive trucks or jeeps for bumpy dirt roads. Ski racks can also be requested, usually at a small additional cost.

BY BICYCLE Northern New Mexico, with its abundant open space and miles of dirt roads, is prime mountain biking territory. In 2016, a mountain bike rental in Santa Fe runs $60–$75 a day. For further information, see "Bicycling" on page 44.

ON FOOT Perhaps the best way to see Santa Fe and Taos is on foot. Good walking maps can be found from TOURISM Santa Fe at the **Santa Fe Community Convention Center** (505-955-6200; 800-777-2489; www.santafe.org; 201 W. Marcy St.). Also try the **Santa Fe County Chamber of Commerce** (505-988-3279; 1644 St. Michael's Dr.). In Taos, the **Taos Convention and Visitors Bureau** (575-758-3873; 800-732-8267; www.taos.org; 1139 Paseo del Pueblo Sur) is most helpful. There are also hundreds of miles of superb hiking trails in the Santa Fe and Carson National Forests outside Taos. For further information on walking, see "Hiking and Climbing" on page 50; "Guided Tours" on page 74; or Elaine Pinkerton's book, *Santa Fe on Foot*.

❊ Neighbors All Around

Near Santa Fe and Taos are 10 Indian pueblos (see "Pueblos" on page 76); three ancient Indian ruin sites; and a score of old Hispanic villages, all in a marvelous desert-mountain setting that offers endless recreational opportunities. Listed below are some of the things to do and places to see within the area.

NEAR SANTA FE

Santa Fe is flanked by two mountain ranges, the Sangre de Cristo to the east and the Jemez to the west. Both offer hiking, cross-country skiing, downhill skiing, fishing, car camping, and backcountry camping—all within less than an hour's drive. There are a number of Indian pueblos to visit, as well as three major Indian ruins: **Pecos National Historical Park** (28 miles east of Santa Fe), **Bandelier National Monument** (45 miles west of Santa Fe), and **Puye Cliffs** (45 miles northwest of Santa Fe). For a taste of the rich cultural traditions of rural Hispanic New Mexico, you can do no better than to visit the old village of **Chimayó** (25 miles north of Santa Fe on the High Road to Taos), known for its historic church and its tradition of fine Spanish weaving. If you have a hankering for the Old West, check out the old mining towns of **Cerrillos** and **Madrid** (20 to 25 miles southwest of Santa Fe).

SANTA FE–TAOS ACCESS

The chart below will tell you about how long a drive it is from the following cities to Santa Fe. Times do not include stops and are calculated to the nearest hour at the posted speed limit. Allow more time for bad weather.

City	Time	Miles	City	Time	Miles
Albuquerque	1 hr.	59	Las Vegas, NV	12 hrs.	625
Amarillo	7 hrs.	348	Los Angeles	15 hrs.	850
Cheyenne	9 hrs.	481	Oklahoma City	10 hrs.	607
Dallas	13 hrs.	718	Phoenix	10 hrs.	525
Denver	7 hrs.	385	Reno	21 hrs.	1,078
El Paso	6 hrs.	330	Salt Lake City	14 hrs.	680
Flagstaff	7 hrs.	375	San Antonio	16 hrs.	952
Houston	17 hrs.	959	Wichita	13 hrs.	754

NEAR TAOS

Taos is surrounded by natural and human-made environmental marvels. **Ojo Caliente Hot Springs**, a curative bathing spot for ancient Indians—and today a delightful spa offering mud baths, salt glows, and massages, in addition to four kinds of mineral waters—lies some 70 miles to the west. About 30 miles south of Taos is San Jose de Gracia **Las Trampas Church**, which dates from the early 1800s, and **Picuris Pueblo**, the

WINTER RESIDENTS OF BANDELIER NATIONAL MONUMENT

only pueblo in the mountains (the rest are in the Rio Grande Valley or on the Taos Plateau). Less than an hour's drive north from Taos you'll find the Taos and Red River ski areas. Deep in the Sangre de Cristo Mountains, 60 miles to the northeast, shimmers **Eagle Nest Lake**, a prime fishing and boating spot, and **Angel Fire Ski Resort**, along the "Enchanted Circle." To the west of Taos, the Rio Grande cuts a dramatic gash in the Taos Plateau known as the Rio Grande Gorge, a playground for boating and fishing enthusiasts.

OUTSIDE THE AREA

A little outside the area to the west on US 84 sits the Hispanic village of **Abiquiu**, where artist Georgia O'Keeffe lived. You'll see why when you get a look at the landscape with its spectacularly colored cliffs and mesas. A few miles up the road, you'll come to spacious Abiquiu Lake. The nearby Chama River, a federal Wild and Scenic River, flows through some of the most gorgeous desert scenery on the planet. Farther north, during warm weather, you can take a trip on the Cumbres and Toltec scenic railroad, an old-fashioned, steam-powered narrow gauge that runs between Chama and Antonito in southern Colorado. Snaking back and forth along the border through the San Juan Mountains, it's a wonderful way to see spectacular mountain scenery and fall color from the comfort of a railroad car. Beyond the Sangre de Cristo to the east, at the edge of the Great Plains, stands historic Cimarron, one of the major way stations along the Santa Fe Trail. A few hours' drive to the west and north will take you to Chaco Canyon and Mesa Verde, two of the most spectacular Ancestral Pueblo sites.

IF TIME IS SHORT

The more time you spend in New Mexico, the more you will want to see. If your time is limited, however, you won't want to miss these attractions. The suggestions here are but a few personal favorites, each with its own distinctive flavor. If you must make your visit brief, try to come back soon and create your own list of favorites.

✳ Lodging

SANTA FE

Inn of the Five Graces (505-992-0957; fivegraces.com; 150 E. de Vargas St., Santa Fe, NM 87501). The place to stay to be indulged with luxury and superb service. Pet friendly, too. A Relais & Châteaux property.

Inn on the Alameda (888-984-2121; 304 E. Alameda St.). The **charms** of a small European hotel.

TAOS

Old Taos Guesthouse (575-758-5448; 1028 Witt Rd., Taos, NM 87571). A beautiful, relaxing, family-run inn with fine hospitality. A bit removed from the hustle and bustle of town.

Mabel Dodge Luhan House (575-751-9686; 240 Morada Ln., Taos, NM 87571). Set on 5 acres at the edge of a vast open tract of Taos Pueblo land, this rambling, three-story, 22-room adobe hacienda *is* Taos history. Savor time standing still in the elegant home of Taos's most notorious patron of the arts.

✳ Cultural Attractions

SANTA FE

Georgia O'Keeffe Museum (505-946-1000; 217 Johnson St.). View the evolution of the artist's vision in an elegant setting she would have approved of.

SANTA FE'S MOST LUXURIOUS LODGING, THE INN OF FIVE GRACES, IS WALKING DISTANCE TO THE PLAZA

Museum of International Folk Art (505-476-1200; 706 Camino Lejo). You simply cannot visit Santa Fe and skip this rich, colorful treasure trove.

Santuario de Chimayó (505-351-4889; 6 Santuario Dr., Chimayó, 26 miles northeast of Santa Fe on NM 76). Nowhere can you get a better understanding of the spirit of northern New Mexico than at this holy shrine.

TAOS

Harwood Museum (575-758-9826; 238 Ledoux St.). Excellent overview of the Taos Modern painters, plus an Agnes Martin wing.

Martinez Hacienda (575-758-1000; 2 miles south of the Plaza on NM 240). The best place to get a feel for Spanish colonial life is at this well-preserved hacienda.

Millicent Rogers Museum (575-758-2462; 1504 Millicent Rodgers Rd., El Prados, 4 miles north of Taos on NM 522). The best all-around collection of Native American jewelry, pottery, painting, and textiles, including the Martinez family's collection of Maria's pottery.

✳ Recreation

TO RELAX Bandelier National Monument (505-672-3861; 15 Entrance Rd., Los Alamos, 46 miles west of Santa Fe). Hike and climb amid cliff dwellings and view village ruins and ceremonial kivas through Frijoles Canyon. If you can, schedule a Night Walk with a ranger.

THE SANTUARIO DE CHIMAYÓ IS A PILGRIMAGE SITE, KNOWN AS THE LOURDES OF AMERICA

Rafting the **Rio Grande Gorge**, specifically, the Taos Box (see page 58), can be an unforgettable whitewater adventure.

Ojo Caliente Hot Springs (505-583-2233; ojospa.com; 50 Los Banos Dr., Ojo Caliente). With four kinds of mineral waters and a variety of heated pools, this is the place to soak and unwind.

Ten Thousand Waves (505-982-9304; tenthousandwaves.com; 21 Ten Thousand Waves Way, Santa Fe). Pamper yourself in this Japanese spa with private tubs overlooking the city.

✳ Restaurants

SANTA FE

The Shed (505-982-9030; 113½ E. Palace Ave., Santa Fe, NM 87501). Located in an adobe dating to 1692, The Shed serves flavorful hot red chile—order your enchiladas "burnt" if you like extra-hot—as well as alternative dishes like grilled salmon for non-chile eaters and homemade hot fudge sundaes.

Cafe Pasqual (505-983-9340; 121 Don Gaspar Ave., Santa Fe, NM 87501). People still line up here for breakfast, with good reason, so best time to go is during off-hours. Cafe Pasqual serves delicious lunch and dinner in a unique fusion of Mexican, Latin American, and New Mexican flavors.

TAOS

Love Apple (575-751-0050; 803 Paseo del Pueblo Norte, Taos). Locally sourced small-ish menu includes steak, vegetarian, New Mexican offerings; funky-romantic candlelit former chapel is the real Taos deal.

Rancho de Chimayó (505-351-4444; around the bend from Santuario de Chimayó). A renovated 1880s ranch house that lives and breathes the traditions of northern New Mexico. A must for first-time visitors. Dine alfresco on the terrace.

Taos Diner (575-758-2374; 908 Paseo del Pueblo Norte, Taos). Hang with the locals! My go-to place for big, fresh salads, huevos rancheros smothered in red chile, and the best burger, locally sourced.

RECREATION

With high-mountain terrain, clear blue skies, and several million acres of forestlands, the Santa Fe–Taos area offers a bountiful backdrop for year-round outdoor fun. Fishing, hunting, camping, golfing, boating, biking, horseback riding, running—every sport has its place and season. In spring, rafters buck the frothing rapids of the Rio Grande and balloonists float high over scenic hills. Summer hikers roam backcountry trails between 7,000 and 13,000 feet, while windsurfers sweep across the choppy waters of wide-open lakes. In fall, hunters and anglers take to rivers and hills with visions of lunker trout, kokanee salmon, and trophy deer and elk. The winter mountains become a snowy wonderland, offering world-class ski areas, myriad cross-country trails, and challenging snowmobile highways. The area boasts one new national park, the Valles Caldera Preserve near Los Alamos, and the Rio Grande del Norte National Monument, encompassing the Rio Grande Gorge country in Taos County.

BALLOONING For a blessedly quiet bird's-eye view of the Santa Fe–Taos area, there's nothing better than hopping in a basket and casting your fate to the wind. In Santa Fe, the place to call for a ride May–Oct. is **Santa Fe Balloons** (505-699-7555), available at $285 per person, including pickup and drop-off at your hotel. **Soaring Adventures of America** (800-764-7464) charges approximately $200 per person for a three-hour ride with discounts available.

In Taos, **Pueblo Balloon Company** (575-751-9877) is available to take you aloft, offering Rio Grande Gorge flights for $250 ($220 cash).

BICYCLING From smooth country highways to rugged mountain trails, you can't beat the Santa Fe–Taos area for road biking and knobby-tired mountain bike adventures. If your heart is set on road biking, try to bring your own bike, but if you don't, or if you want to be spontaneous, please see the shops listed below. And if you're mountain biking, remember: (1) Mountain bikes are not allowed in wilderness areas; (2) be considerate of hikers and those on horseback; (3) trails are usually steeper and more difficult than forest roads; and (4) trail conditions change markedly with the weather.

SANTA FE AREA

One of the best ways to start pedaling in Santa Fe is to get hold of a **Santa Fe Bicycle Map** in the **Public Works office** at City Hall (505-995-6949; 120 S. Federal Pl., Santa Fe, NM 87501) or at one of the bicycle dealerships listed below. This map, compiled by the members of the Sangre de Cristo Cycling Club, shows both recreational and utilitarian routes in and around the city. Other good publications are the *New Mexico Bicyclist's Guide* compiled by the state highway department and *Santa Fe on Foot: Walking, Running and Bicycling Routes in the City Different* by Elaine Pinkerton. Both are available at most local bookstores and sports shops.

There are some great mountain biking trails minutes from downtown Santa Fe and a

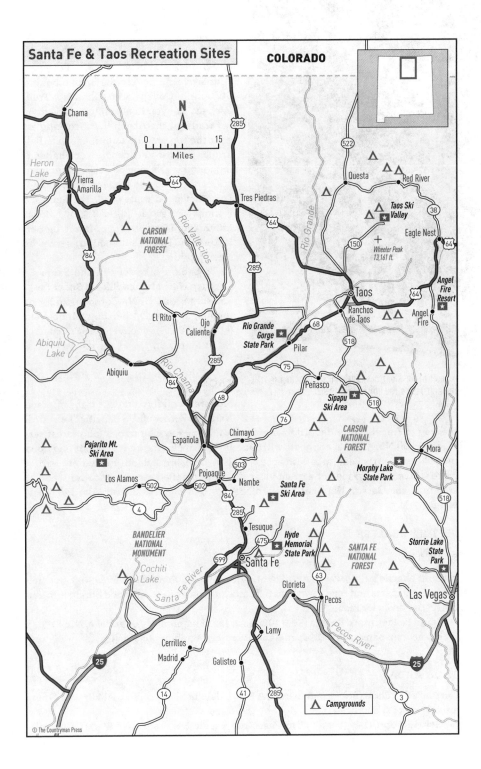

Santa Fe & Taos Recreation Sites

COLORADO

N

0 |||||| 15
Miles

Chama

Heron Lake

Tierra Amarilla

285

522

Questa

Red River

Taos Ski Valley ★

38

64

64

Rio Grande

Tres Piedras

285

Rio Vallecitos

CARSON NATIONAL FOREST

84

Eagle Nest

Wheeler Peak 13,161 ft.

150

64

Angel Fire Resort ★

El Rito

Ojo Caliente

Rio Grande Gorge State Park ★

Pilar

68

Taos

Ranchos de Taos

Angel Fire

Abiquiu Lake

Rio Chama

Abiquiu

84

285

68

75

518

Peñasco

Sipapu Ski Area ★

518

Pajarito Mt. Ski Area ★

Española

Chimayó

76

CARSON NATIONAL FOREST

Mora

Los Alamos

502

503

Pojoaque

502

Nambe

84

Santa Fe Ski Area

Morphy Lake State Park ★

518

4

285

Tesuque

475

Hyde Memorial State Park ★

SANTA FE NATIONAL FOREST

Storrie Lake State Park ★

BANDELIER NATIONAL MONUMENT

Cochiti Lake

599

Santa Fe

Santa Fe River

63

Glorieta

Pecos

Las Vegas

25

Cerrillos

Madrid

Galisteo

Lamy

Pecos River

25

14

41

285

3

△ Campgrounds

© The Countryman Press

couple of places to rent the sturdy-framed, low-geared contraptions. Camino La Tierra accesses a number of easy trails on city-owned land close to town. For more aggressive riding, try the arroyo behind St. John's College, the Chamiso Trail, Pacheco Canyon Road, or any of the myriad trails off the Aspen Vista parking lot near the top of Ski Basin Road. Dale Ball Trails, praised as rideable yet challenging for all levels, can be accessed in town at Cerro Gordo and Upper Canyon Road. For other good routes, call the Santa Fe National Forest at 505-438-5300. *Mountain Biking Northern New Mexico* by Bob D'Antonio (Falcon Publishing) serves as a good guide.

To book a bike tour in the Santa Fe area, try **New Mexico Bike N Sport** (505-820-0809; 524-C W. Cordova Rd.). For rentals, at $60–$75 per day, **Mello Velo** (505-995-8356) is conveniently located at 132 E. Marcy St.

IF YOU'RE NOT IN GREAT SHAPE, YOU WILL BE BY THE TIME YOU BIKE ALONG THE HONDO RIVER TO TAOS SKI VALLEY

TAOS AREA

Mountain biking trails in the Carson National Forest off US 64 will take you all the way to Angel Fire. A favorite route for families is Rio Chiquito, a long forest service road off NM 518 that connects with Garcia Park, including beaver ponds and good picnicking. Picuris Peak, also with access off NM 518, is a good intermediate-to-expert route with a steep grade but a great view. For more detailed recommendations, call or stop in at the Carson National Forest office (575-758-6200; 208 Cruz Alta Rd., Taos, NM 87571).

BICYCLE DEALERS

SANTA FE

rob and charlie's (505-471-9119; 1632 St. Michael's Dr., Santa Fe, NM 87505). Specialists in retail parts and repair, with more than 4,000 parts in stock; good biking info and BMX stud bikes for kids.

    Santa Fe Mountain Sports (505-988-3337; 1221 Flagman Way, Santa Fe, NM 87505). Offers new suspension bikes; open daily. Rents ski equipment as well.

TAOS AREA

Cottam's Ski Shop (800-332-8267; 207A Paseo del Pueblo Sur, Taos, NM 87571). Offers a selection of specialized bikes, right by the Plaza.

    Gearing Up (575-751-0365; 616 Paseo del Pueblo Sur, Taos, NM 87571). Centrally located sales and service; mountain, road, hybrid, and tandem bike rentals; books, maps, and info. Geared toward general bike users.

Taos Mountain Outfitters (575-758-9292; 113 N. Plaza, Taos, NM 87571). Helpful staff and top brands to furnish a missing detail or make an investment to upgrade your outdoor experience.

Mudd N Flood (575-751-9100; 103 Bent St., Ste. A, Taos, NM 87571). Well stocked sporting good store with gear specific to Taos outdoor recreation, excellent shopping advice and convenient Bent St. location.

BOATING See "Water Sports" on page 68–70.

CAMPING See also "Hiking and Climbing" on page 50.

Many first-time visitors are surprised and delighted to find a land of lush mountain wilderness, including scores of idyllic campsites. Public, vehicle-accessible sites in national forest and state park areas are usually open May–Oct. and available on a first-come, first-served basis. There are also myriad backcountry campsites for those on the trail (usually requiring overnight permits), plus a number of private camping areas that offer trailer hook-ups and tent sites with all the amenities. For maps and specifics on public areas, contact the government agencies listed under "Hiking and Climbing." For information and reservations at private RV campgrounds, contact the following.

PRIVATE CAMPGROUNDS

NEAR SANTA FE

Los Campos Recreation Vehicle Park (505-473-1949; 3574 Cerrillos Rd., Santa Fe, NM 87501, only five minutes from the Plaza). One of two full-service RV parks within the city limits, with 94 full hook-ups, four tent sites, restrooms, shower, laundry, swimming pool, and car rentals.

Rancheros de Santa Fe Camping Park (505-466-3482; 736 Old Las Vegas Hwy., Santa Fe, NM 87505, Exit 290 off I-25, 1 mile east on Old Las Vegas Highway). Wooded and open sites for tents, trailers, and motor homes with pool, showers, restrooms, groceries, hiking trail, laundry, and propane. Camping cabins also available. Open mid-Mar.–Nov. 1.

NEAR TAOS

Golden Eagle RV Park (575-377-6188; 800-388-6188; P.O. Box 458, Eagle Nest, NM 87718, 50 W. Therma Dr., off US 64 in Eagle Nest). A 531-space RV park, including 29 pull-throughs, restrooms, cabins, showers, RV supplies, propane, and game room. Open year-round. $39.95 nightly.

Questa Lodge (575-586-9913; 80 Lower Embargo Rd., Questa, NM 87556, 0.25 mile off NM 522 in Questa, on the Red River). Motel and RV park with 26 full-service hook-ups, six cabins, tent sites, Laundromat, restrooms, children's playground, and a pet park. Open year-round.

Road Runner RV Resort (575-754-2286; 1371 E. Main St., Red River, NM 87558). Camping for 150 vehicles with 89 full hook-ups, laundry, showers, tennis court, restrooms, cable TV, playground, barbecue area, picnic tables, fire ring, tepees, WiFi, and gazebo. $45 nightly.

Red River RV Park & River Retreat Cabins (575-754-6187; 100 High Cost Trail, Red River, NM 87558). Pet friendly, open year-round, WiFi, cable, full hook-ups, three yurts, three cabins, river fishing. $36–$39 nightly; prices go up to $45 a night Nov. 1–April 1.

Taos Valley RV Park and Campground (575-578-4469; 120 Este Es Rd., Taos, NM 87571). Complete commercial campground, including 35 full hook-ups, 75 water and electric hook-ups, 18 tent sites, playground, rec room, showers, phones, convenience store, and Laundromat. Open year-round. $42 nightly.

CASINOS You can't drive very far in northern New Mexico without running into an Indian-run gambling casino. While the pros and cons of gambling are hotly debated on the streets and in the courts, the casinos remain up and running, with packed parking lots. If you yearn to try your luck without going all the way to Las Vegas, Nevada, just join the crowd. Many also serve lavish, low-cost buffets.

Buffalo Thunder Resort and Casino (505-455-5555; 30 Buffalo Thunder Trail, on US 84/285 north of Santa Fe). The newest and most exciting place to try and win your fortune.

Camel Rock Casino (800-GO-CAMEL; 17486A US 84/285, 10 minutes north of downtown Santa Fe). Run by Tesuque Pueblo, Camel Rock offers slots, blackjack, bingo, roulette, and a restaurant.

Cities of Gold Casino (505-455-3313; 10-B Cities of Gold Rd., on US 84/285, 15 miles north of Santa Fe). Cities of Gold is run by Pojoaque Pueblo and has more than 700 slot machines in addition to other games, an extravagant 24-hour buffet spread, and simulcasting.

Ohkay Casino (505-747-1668; 68 New Mexico 291, along US 84/285, just north of Española in Ohkay Owingeh). Operated by Ohkay Owingeh Pueblo, this popular casino is well known for its breakfast buffet.

Taos Mountain Casino (575-737-0777; 700 Veterans Hwy., Taos). The only nonsmoking casino in the state, Taos Mountain offers 200 slots, a restaurant, gaming tables, and a smoke shop.

FITNESS CENTERS Whether it's weight training, aerobics, racquetball, stretching, swimming, or yoga, rest assured there are plenty of gyms available. Most of them also employ fitness experts who are ready and eager to help you with a program tailored to meet your needs. Membership rates vary. It's to your advantage to shop around. Most offer day and month passes.

SANTA FE

Bulldog Gym (505-988-5117; 909 Early St., Santa Fe). Specializes in one-on-one personal fitness training.

Carl and Sandra's Physical Conditioning Center (505-982-6760; 153-A Paseo de Peralta, in the DeVargas Center). Run by Olympic trainer Carl Miller and his wife, this gym specializes in individualized personal weight training, aerobics, nutrition, stress management, and exercises for pregnant women.

Club International Family Fitness Center (505-473-9807; 1931 Warner Ave., Santa Fe). Separate rooms specialize in yoga, martial arts, free weights, aerobics (including bench step), and cardiovascular exercise. Also offers lap pool with water exercises, six racquetball courts, treadmills, StairMasters, Lifecycles, Bio Cycles, CombiCycles, whirlpool, individualized fitness programs, sauna, steam room, and child care.

Fitness Plus (505-473-7315; 1119 Calle del Cielo, Santa Fe, off Cerrillos Rd.). A club for women only, with varied fitness classes, free weights, toning tables, and more.

Fort Marcy Recreation Complex (505-955-2500; 490 Bishops Lodge Rd., Santa Fe). The city's major sports complex, with gym, weight room, jogging course, racquetball courts, aerobic and workout room, pool, water aerobics, and classes galore. Best bargain gym in town.

Mandrill's Gym (505-988-2986; 708 W. San Mateo Rd., Santa Fe). A serious weight-training center with free weights, Flex machines, aerobics, women's body-shaping classes, and sports massage.

Santa Fe Spa (505-984-8727; 786 N. St. Francis Dr., Santa Fe). Includes free weights, Nautilus and Cybex equipment, treadmills, yoga classes, individual training, sauna and steam rooms, plus an extensive schedule of classes. A local's favorite. $15 day rate.

TAOS AREA

Northside Health and Fitness (575-751-1242; 1307 Paseo del Pueblo Norte, El Prado). A friendly, accessible, community-oriented fitness center with indoor and outdoor pools, four tennis courts, Cybex weight equipment, aerobics classes, a cardiovascular room with Cybex rowers and NordicTrack skiers, physical therapy, kids' activities, and great drumming classes!

Taos Spa & Tennis Club (575-758-1980; 111 Dona Ana Dr., Taos, across from Sagebrush Inn). Includes racquetball, tennis, indoor and outdoor pools, aerobics, weight room with free weights and machines, personalized instruction, hot tubs, sauna, steam rooms, and child care.

GOLF Many people don't think of New Mexico as a golf haven, but the sport is becoming increasingly popular in these parts. Local courses, varying between 6,000 and 8,600 feet in elevation, offer some of the highest fairways in the world, with terrain ranging from brushy plains to rolling hills thick with conifers. Most clubs hold seasonal tourneys, with schedules available at the pro shops.

GOLF CLUBS

SANTA FE

Santa Fe Country Club (505-471-0601; 3950 Country Club Rd., Santa Fe). Designed by one of the first PGA members more than 50 years ago, this 18-hole, semiprivate, par-72 course open to the public that features tree-shaded golfing close to town. Usually open Mar.–Nov., it has four sets of tees with distances between 6,703 and 7,091 yards, and a ladies' course measuring 5,955 yards. It also features a driving and chipping range and a practice putting green. Resident greens fees $38 weekdays, $48 weekends. The pro on duty is Dave Nowall.

NEAR SANTA FE

The Cochiti Lake Golf Course (505-465-2230; 5200 Cochiti Hwy., Cochiti Lake) is rated fifth in the state and among the top 25 public courses in the country. Set against a stunning backdrop of red-rock mesas and steep canyons, this Robert Trent Jones course features an 18-hole, par-72 course of 6,450 yards along with a driving range, putting green, pro shop, and restaurant complete with green chile cheeseburgers. The pro on duty is Travis Pecos. Greens fees $55 weekdays, $68 weekends; both include a cart. Open all year, weather permitting.

Los Alamos Golf Course (505-662-8139; 4250 Diamond Dr., Los Alamos). This course is 18 holes, par 71, 6,500 yards, with three tees of various skill levels. It includes a driving range, putting green, bar, and a new restaurant, Cottonwood on the Greens. The pro on duty is Donny Torrez. Greens fees $31–$35.

Pendaries Village Golf & Country Club (505-425-6076; 1 Lodge Rd., Sapello). About an hour and a half out of Santa Fe, on the north side of Las Vegas. With a well-deserved reputation as one of the state's most beautiful golf courses, Pendaries is an 18-hole, par-72 mountain course at 7,200 feet. Greens fees $53 weekdays, $63 weekends, with cart. Has a pro shop, snack bar, and restaurant with bar. The pros on duty are Larry Webb and Suzy Valypek. Open Apr. 15–Oct. 15.

NEAR TAOS

Angel Fire Golf Course (575-377-4488; Angel Fire Resort, 10 Miller Ln., Angel Fire). At 8,600 feet, this is one of the highest and most lushly wooded regulation courses in the world. Usually open mid-May–mid-Oct., it's an 18-hole, par-72 course with driving range and putting greens, club and cart rentals, and a restaurant, snack bar, and bar. The clubhouse is glorious. Greens fees for resort guests, including cart, are $95.

HIKING AND CLIMBING Cradled by mountains containing two national forests and numerous wilderness areas and state parks, north central New Mexico offers more than 3 million acres of public forestland with hundreds of miles of lakeshores and cold mountain streams. Most of this land is truly wild and forested. It is also laced with more than 1,000 miles of well-maintained trails that vary from a half-hour guided nature walk to a two-week pack trip. There are more excellent hikes in town, along the Ski Basin Road (Hyde Park Road) in Tesuque, and in the national forests and monuments, each with their own character, than can be covered in this space.

The primary recreation areas are the Santa Fe and Carson National Forests. A few of the gems within these two massive preserves include the 223,333-acre Pecos Wilderness, east of Santa Fe, with magnificent aspen and evergreen forests; the 5,200-acre Dome Wilderness in the volcanic Jemez Mountains to the west; the 41,132-acre San Pedro Parks Wilderness with rolling, spruce-studded mountaintops and open meadows; and the rugged Wheeler Peak and lake-strewn Latir Peak Wilderness Areas northeast of Taos. The new Valles Caldera Preserve National Park offers great wildlife viewing, especially of elk.

BOOKS, MAPS, AND ORGANIZATIONS For an excellent introduction to some of the fine trails in the Santa Fe–Taos area, we suggest you contact the **Santa Fe (The Northern Group) Sierra Club** (505-983-2703; 1807 Second St., Unit 45, Santa Fe, NM 87501). During spring and summer months, they run two or three trips of varying difficulty every weekend. Visit their Facebook page for the most up-to-date information about hiking meetups. They've also published a book, *Day Hikes in the Santa Fe Area*, detailing numerous short hikes, many of which can be made into overnight journeys. Another good hiking contact is the **Randall Davey Audubon Center** (505-983-4609; 1800 Upper Canyon Rd., Santa Fe, NM 87501). There, right in town, you can access the excellent Dale Ball Trails system. Relevant books are for sale and tours of Davey's home are available.

You can also get topographical maps of the northern New Mexico area at the **Public Lands Information Center** (877-276-9404; 301 Dinosaur Trail, Santa Fe, NM 87508). At the same address, the **Bureau of Land Management** (505-954-2000) has an invaluable series of 1:100,000 scale maps based on the USGS series showing roads, trails, and landownership by color.

TAOS AREA

In Taos, one of the best wilderness contacts is **Taos Mountain Outfitters** (575-758-9292; 113 N. Plaza, Taos, NM 87571). In addition to routes and rentals, most of their salespeople are avid hikers and climbers. They also have a little publication called *Taos Rock*, which will steer you toward the best rock climbing in the area. Another good bet is **Cottam's Rio Grande Rafting** (800-322-8267; 1335 Paseo del Pueblo Sur, Taos, NM 87571), which rents backcountry gear and offers a variety of wilderness treks, including combo trips of rafting with rock climbing, mountain biking, and horseback riding. **Sipapu Ski & Summer Resort** (800-587-2240; 5224 NM 518, Vadito, NM 87579) offers year-round fun with disc golf, fly-fishing, and alpine adventures, in addition to skiing and snowboarding. Very family friendly.

NATIONAL FOREST OFFICES

SANTA FE AREA

Santa Fe National Forest (505-438-5300 supervisor's office; 11 Forest Ln., Santa Fe, NM 87508). Contact this office for general information, maps of the Santa Fe National Forest, and detailed topo maps of Pecos and San Pedro Parks Wilderness Areas.

Coyote Ranger District (505-638-5526 in Santa Fe; HC 78 Box 1, Coyote, NM 87012). Handles San Pedro Parks Wilderness Area.

Española Ranger District (505-753-7331; 1710 Riverside, Española, NM 87532, or P.O. Box 3307, Española, NM 87533, corner of Santa Clara St. and Los Alamos Hwy.).

Jemez Ranger District (575-829-3535; P.O. Box 150, Jemez Springs, NM 87025, between Los Alamos and Jemez Springs on NM 4).

Pecos/Las Vegas Ranger District (505-757-6121; P.O. Drawer 429, Pecos, NM 87552, Exit 299 for Glorieta/Pecos to NM 50).

TAOS AREA

Carson National Forest (575-758-6200 supervisor's office; 208 Cruz Alta Rd., Taos, NM 87571). Call the supervisor's office for information on the districts below.

El Rito Ranger District: 575-581-4554; P.O. Box 56, El Rito, NM 87530, at the junction of NM 110 and NM 96.

Peñasco Ranger District: 575-587-2255; 15160 State Rd. 75, Peñasco, NM 87553.

Questa Ranger District: 575-586-0520; P.O. Box 110, Questa, NM 87556, 2 miles east of Questa on NM 38. Handles 20,000-acre Latir Peaks Wilderness Area north of Red River.

Tres Piedras Ranger District: 575-758-8678; P.O. Box 38, Tres Piedras, NM 87577, 1 mile west of the junction of US 64 and US 285.

NATIONAL MONUMENTS

NEAR SANTA FE

Pecos National Historical Park (505-757-7241; www.nps.gov/peco; National Park Service, P.O. Box 418, Pecos, NM 87552, 2 miles south of Pecos off NM 63). It includes a handicapped-accessible, self-guided trail through the ruins of the old Pecos Pueblo and Spanish mission church. A very interesting intermingling of Native American and Spanish culture.

Fort Union National Monument (505-425-8025; P.O. Box 127, Watrous, NM 87753). Here find Civil War reenactments and much about the Santa Fe Trail. The fort was an important destination on the trail, where all the branches met. Tours of Glorieta Battlefield, the "Gettysburg of the West," leave from here as well.

Bandelier National Monument (505-672-3861, ext. 517; www.nps.gov/band; 46 miles west of Santa Fe: take US 285 north to Pojoaque, west on NM 502, south on NM 4; open daily year-round, visitors center summer 9 AM–6 PM, winter 9 AM–5 PM closed Christmas and New Year's; ruins trails open dawn–dusk; $20 per vehicle; campsites $12 per night and $35 per night for groups of 10-20 people; gift shop, snack bar.) (Access is by shuttle only from the White Rock visitor center between 9 AM and 3 PM from last week of May through second week of Oct.; other times you may enter through the park's main Visitor Center.) Once a lush little Shangri-La tucked in a deep canyon on the Pajarito (pa-ha-REE-toe) Plateau, home to the ancestors of some Pueblo tribes between A.D. 1100 and 1550. The residents irrigated their corn, beans, and squash with water from Frijoles Creek and made their homes from the plentiful volcanic rock. You can visit cliff dwellings and view the village ruins and ceremonial kivas. The loop trail of the main Frijoles Canyon ruins takes about an hour. More agile visitors can climb ladders, as the residents once did, to enter Bandelier's restored dwellings—including a spectacular ceremonial cave with kiva. Ancestral Pueblo petroglyphs are visible on many trails. In summer, visitors can take ranger-led tours of the ruins after dark on special night walks.

Bandelier's 33,000 acres are federally designated wilderness, with 70 miles of maintained trails that go up onto mesas, down into volcanic canyons, and through high-altitude pine forests. Those in good physical condition can take day hikes to more remote ruins. The visitors center and Frijoles Canyon ruins tend to be crowded, but solitude can be yours if you're willing to walk a bit. (See also "Hiking and Climbing," page 50.) Call for current conditions of backcountry trails. No pets on trails.

Puye Cliff Dwellings (505-753-7326; www.puyecliffs.com; NM 30 and Santa Clara Canyon Road; call for directions and hours; $5 per adult). About 40 miles northwest of Santa Fe, near Española, the Puye Cliffs are home to Santa Clara Pueblo. The tribe welcomes visitors, who can walk to the top of a mesa where a village once stood and take in the magnificent views, although access has been somewhat limited due to the Las Conchas fire of 2011, which destroyed much of the pueblo. Here you will find cliff dwellings dating from the 1200s. This ancient pueblo, built 1450 to 1475, was once the center of numerous villages on the Pajarito Plateau. Many of the designs found on pottery here focus on a plumed serpent figure who guarded the springs, which provided life-giving water. The tourism office of Santa Clara Pueblo offers tours here, the only and best way to see the site. Ask for information at the gas station at the intersection above.

Tsankawi Ruin Trail (505-672-3861; open daily; closed Christmas and New Year's Day; free). To get to the trail, go about 30 miles west of Santa Fe on US 84/285 to NM 502, then get on NM 4 on the way to Bandelier, immediately south of White Rock. Look for sign and gate on the west side of NM 4, just south of Y-shaped stoplight intersection of east Jemez Rd. An easy walk to unexcavated ruins, a visit to the Tsankawi section of Bandelier National Monument offers a spectacular panoramic view across the Rio Grande Valley to Santa Fe and the Sangre de Cristo Mountains. Tsankawi is a simplification of the Tewa Indian name *saekewikwaje onwikege*, which means "village between two canyons at the clump of sharp, round cactus." The enclave protects an important Rio Grande ruin of the Anasazi, a prehistoric Puebloan people. Take the 1.5-mile loop trail that begins at the parking area along NM 4. Descendants of the Chaco Canyon Ancestral Puebloan people lived here about A.D. 1300–1580. Faint petroglyphs and hand- and toeholds of the original Tewa-speaking dwellers are visible along the climb, aided in places by ladders. Please do not disturb the shards of black-on-cream pottery lying on the ground

Pecos National Historical Park (505-757-7200; www.nps.gov/peco/index.htm; 1 Peach Tree Lane, Pecos, 28 miles southeast of Santa Fe, off I-25; open daily, 8 AM–4:30 PM

Labor Day–Memorial Day, 8 AM–6 PM Memorial Day–Labor Day, closed Christmas; free; bookstore). In 1540, before the Spaniards arrived, Pecos was a thriving Pueblo Indian village with apartment-like houses four or five stories high. In their green river valley, the Pecos people traded with other Pueblo villages and the Plains Indians to the east. Coronado's men visited in 1541, and by the early 1620s the Franciscans had arrived to build a mission and convert the Indians to the Spanish way of life. The Franciscans also enlisted the Indians to help build a church, 150 feet from altar to entrance, with walls 22 feet thick in places. The foundations can still be seen, but the church and the Franciscans' efforts were destroyed in the Pueblo Revolt of 1680 (see page 25). A smaller church built atop the ruins in 1717 also lies in ruins.

What happened to the thriving village? Historians believe Pecos was decimated by European diseases and Comanche raids in the 17th century. The last residents left in 1838 to live with relatives at Jemez Pueblo, across the Rio Grande Valley. Today a 1.25-mile trail on gentle terrain rings the mission and pueblo ruins and includes a ceremonial kiva playing recorded Indian chants.

STATE PARKS

SANTA FE

New Mexico State Parks Division (505-476-3355; 888-667-2757; nmparks@state.nm.us; www.emnrd.state.nm.us/nm parks; 1220 S. St. Francis Dr., Santa Fe, NM 87504).

NEAR SANTA FE

Hyde Memorial State Park (505-983-7175; 740 Hyde Park Rd., Santa Fe, NM 87571, 12 miles northeast of Santa Fe via Hyde Park Rd.). Offers 350 acres of mountains and streams with trails, camping, and picnic areas.

Santa Fe River Watershed Association (505-820-1696; 1413 S. Second St., Santa Fe, NM 87501). Includes 5 narrow acres of greenery with a few picnic tables along Alameda Street, a few blocks from the center of town. Offers scheduled hikes.

TAOS AREA

Cimarron Canyon State Park (575-377-6271; P.O. Box 28869, US Highway 64, Eagle Nest, NM 87718, 3 miles east of Eagle Nest via US 64). A 33,000-acre mountainous preserve with numerous wonderful trails and camping and picnic areas.

Kit Carson Memorial Park (575-758-8234; 115 Civic Plaza Dr., Taos, NM 87571). Offers short walks and a playground on 22 acres.

Rio Grande Gorge State Park (575-751-8800; 16 miles southwest of Taos on NM 570). Includes shelter, barbecues, trails, drinking water, and campgrounds along the road by the river, as well as boating at Orilla Verde.

Vietnam Veterans Memorial State Park (34 Country Club Rd., Angel Fire, NM 87710). Established in 1968 by Dr. Victor Westphall and his wife, Jeanne, to honor their son David, killed in Vietnam in 1968.

Eagle Nest State Park (575-377-1594; 42 Marinam Way, Eagle Nest, NM 87718). Located along the Enchanted Circle in the Moreno Valley, the lake here is stocked with salmon and trout. Boating, wildlife viewing, camping—it's a cool, pristine, high mountain refuge in summer, ringed by mountains.

OUTSIDE THE AREA

Chaco Culture National Historical Park (505-786-7014; www.nps.gov/chcu; open daily dawn–dusk, closed Christmas; visitors center open 8 AM–5 PM; $4 per individual, $8 per vehicle; campsites $10 per night, no hook-ups, no showers).

To get to this historical park, go 60 miles south of Bloomfield in northwest New Mexico, via CR 7900 (approximately 3 miles east of Nageezi Trading Post). From NM 57, go 21 miles north on unpaved road. All roads into the park are unpaved for the final 20–26 miles. Known as the Stonehenge of the West, Chaco is believed by many to be one of the great "power spots" on the globe. It is one of three United Nations World Heritage Sites in New Mexico. Humans have inhabited the area for 6,000 or more years. About A.D. 900 the Anasazi (now referred to as Ancestral Puebloan) culture began to flower, and Chaco Canyon was its crowning achievement: six large pueblos and as many as 75 smaller towns, all built in a relatively short time. The largest, Pueblo Bonito, was a community of four-story masonry apartment buildings with solar orientation, hundreds of rooms, and dozens of kivas. The Chacoan people farmed with an elaborate irrigation and terracing system and created stunning pottery and turquoise jewelry. They built an astonishing 400 miles of arrow-straight roads connecting the canyon with outlying settlements, and they traded with the people of Mesoamerica. Then, sometime around A.D. 1200, this thriving culture suddenly faded away. The inhabitants are believed to be the ancestors of today's Pueblo people.

The ruins were known to Spaniards and Indians in the region at least as far back as 1840, and the first archaeological excavations were started in 1896. Today, you can spend a couple of days or more exploring the ruins along the Chaco Wash. There are even more ruins atop the mesas. Rangers are available for guided walks, and the visitor center offers a good introduction with films and displays. The ruins are in surprisingly good condition, so it's easy to imagine Chaco Canyon alive again with the laughter of children and the sounds of men and women at work in the courtyards and fields.

Note: Consult a good map before setting out and call the park to check on road conditions, as roads can become impassable during rain or snow. Also, there's no lodging, gasoline, or food at the park; the nearest town, Bloomfield, is 60 miles away. Staples are available on weekdays at Blanco Trading Post or convenience stores on US 550. Campsites tend to fill quickly on weekends and most days during summer. The 9-mile auto tour is a good way to get an overview of the park.

HORSEBACK RIDING See also "Hunting and Fishing" on page 55.

Horse travel may not be as common today as it was in the days of yore, but it's definitely alive and well. You can still get a whiff of the Old West as you saddle up and head on out, whether for a few turns around the corral, a picnic ride, or a weeklong pack trip. Following are some local outfitters.

SANTA FE AREA

Bear Creek Adventures (505-757-6229; P.O. Box 705, Pecos, NM 87552). A variety of horseback and horse-drawn experiences, from trail rides to sleigh rides and hayrides. Weddings, too!

The Bishop's Lodge (505-819-4013; 1297 Bishops Lodge Rd., Santa Fe, NM 87507). Approximately two-hour guided trail rides within the lodge's 1,000-acre grounds. Special wrangler rides for children under 8. Call for reservations and fees. Grounds open during renovation of Bishop's Lodge. Following renovation, the lodge will re-open Spring 2018.

Broken Saddle Riding Co. (505-424-7774; 26 Vicksville Rd., Cerrillos, NM 87010, 26 miles from Santa Fe Plaza in Cerrillos). Enjoy 360-degree views along the Turquoise Trail.

Four Seasons Resort Rancho Encantado Santa Fe (505-946-5890; 198 NM 592, Santa Fe, NM 87506, about 8 miles north of Santa Fe off NM 592). Fifty-seven acres bordering the Santa Fe National Forest. Trail rides for guests only.

Terrero General Stores and Riding Stables (505-431-1132; P.O. Box 12A, Terrero, NM 87573). Owner Hugh Ley runs sight-seeing and photography trips, as well as seasonal hunting, fishing, and pack trips into the Santa Fe National Forest and the Pecos Wilderness. The last stop for campers heading into the Pecos Wilderness.

TAOS AREA

Cieneguilla Stables (575-751-2815; 2961 HC 68, NM 68, near the village of Pilar, 13 miles south of the Taos visitors center). Custom rides available, or ride to the miner's cabin in Rio Grande Gorge canyon country.

THE BISHOP'S LODGE, ONCE THE SANCTUARY OF ARCHBISHOP LAMY, IS THE PLACE TO FIND SERENITY

Nancy Burch's Roadrunner Tours (575-377-6416; one hour west of blinking light on US 64; Angel Fire). The ultimate "City Slicker" experience. Lessons, one-hour to all-day rides, sleigh rides, romantic wedding, and engagement rides into the Carson National Forest and along the Enchanted Circle.

HUNTING AND FISHING The Santa Fe–Taos area is a hunting and fishing paradise. Gun or bow hunters can bag not only deer, elk, squirrels, game birds, and waterfowl, but also wild turkey, antelope, elk, bighorn sheep, and javelina—even exotic species such as ibex and oryx. Lake fish include bass, perch, catfish, and walleye. Kokanee salmon (introduced from the Pacific Coast) and five species of trout abound in stocked lakes and streams.

Before you go, be sure to get licenses and current rules and regulations from the **New Mexico Department of Game and Fish** (505-476-8000; www.wildlife.state.nm.us/contact; One Wildlife Way, Santa Fe, NM 87504) or from a local sporting goods store. You may also call or write them for their list of registered guides and outfitters. For information on hunting and fishing on Indian lands, see "Pueblos" on page 76–81. You don't need a license to hunt or fish there, but you must have written permission and an official tribal document showing legal possession of any game or fish taken.

For information on conditions and places to go, talk to any local guide or outfitter. They can take you to prime fishing and hunting territory, both public and private. If you decide to use a guide, check with the National Forest Service or the Bureau of Land Management to make sure the outfit has proper permits and insurance. Prices for guides and outfitters vary widely, depending on the quarry and kind of hunting, the destination and accommodations, and the length of time. Prices range from $220 for a day of fishing to around $4,000 for a five-day elk hunt, with the most luxurious trips going as high as $15,000.

GUIDES AND OUTFITTERS

SANTA FE

High Desert Angler (505-988-7688; 453 Cerrillos Rd., Santa Fe, NM 87501). This is the fly-fishing center of Santa Fe, including instruction and guide service, rentals, equipment sales, and expert, friendly advice. It's the opposite of intimidation.

Known World Guide Service (505-983-7756; 825 Early St., Santa Fe, NM 87505). This service takes you to the Wild and Scenic Rio Grande, Red River, Pecos River, and Santa Fe National Forest.

Oshman's Sporting Goods (505-473-3555; 4250 Cerrillos Rd. (in Santa Fe Place Mall), Santa Fe, NM 87501). Here you'll find everything from spinning and fly rods to rifles and shotguns with all the eggs, lures, flies, and accessories you'll ever need.

Outdoorsman of Santa Fe (505-983-3432; 530 N. Guadalupe St., Santa Fe, NM 87501). An archery and bow-hunting headquarters with an indoor archery range.

The Reel Life (505-995-8114; 526 N. Guadalupe St., Santa Fe, NM 87501). One-stop shopping for the clothing, equipment, guide service, instruction, and travel information you need to make your next fly-fishing adventure a memorable one.

Ron Peterson Guns (505-471-4411; 509 Airport Rd., Santa Fe, NM 87505). Guns, ammo, rods, reels, bows, black powder, scopes—the works. Also the home for Imperial Taxidermy, which does game heads, fish, reptiles, and life-sized animals.

Santa Fe Flyfishing School & Guide Service (713-502-1809; 79 Camino Rincon, Pecos, NM 87552). Learn how it's done on the glorious Pecos. Special classes for couples.

NEAR SANTA FE

Bear Creek Adventures (505-757-6229; P.O. Box 705, Pecos, NM 87552). Hunting and fishing trips into the Sangre de Cristos for all experience levels.

TAOS

Los Rios Anglers Fly Shop & Guide Service (575-758-2798; 126 W. Plaza Dr., Taos, NM 87571). The professional fly-fishing guides here are some of the best in the state. A complete fly-fishing shop offering gear, information, and year-round pack-and-float trips—including trips into the Rio Grande Gorge and isolated fishing on private lands.

Solitary Angler (575-758-5653; 226C Paseo del Pueblo Norte, Taos, NM 87571). To book a guided trip on local public water or on the Solitary Angler's 11 private miles of Culebra Creek or the Cimarron Holy Water, give a call. There's also a club for serious fisher people.

NEAR TAOS

Mountain View Cabins and Eagle Nest Marina (575-377-6941; US 64, Eagle Nest, NM 87718). They offer fishing equipment and trips for cutthroats, rainbows, cohos, and kokanee during all seasons at Eagle Nest Lake, including ice fishing in winter.

Rio Costilla Park (575-586-0542; 72 NM 196, House #72, Costilla, NM 87524). Fishing and hunting trips on a 79,000-acre private reserve in the Latir Lakes area about 40 miles north of Taos. Trespass fee required for private hunting; call to arrange for guided trips.

PARKS IN TOWN Following is a list of parks in Santa Fe and Taos that offer open space, quiet, and recreational opportunities for everyone. For maps and further information, contact the **Santa Fe Parks and Recreation Division** (505-476-3355; 1220 S. St. Francis Dr., Santa Fe, NM 87501) or the **Taos Parks and Recreation Department** (575-758-8234).

SANTA FE

Amelia White (Old Santa Fe Trail and Corrales Rd.). A small, natural park with pleasant sitting spots, walking paths, and access for the handicapped.

Ashbaugh (Cerrillos Rd. and San Jose Ave.). A long, narrow finger of green next to the Santa Fe Indian Hospital. Includes picnic tables, tennis court, baseball and soccer fields, walking paths, basketball court, and access for the handicapped.

Cathedral (Palace Ave. and Cathedral Pl.). A quiet, fence-enclosed lunch spot with picnic tables a block east of the Plaza.

Fort Marcy-Magers Field (Washington Ave. and Murales Rd., north of Paseo de Peralta). A major facility complete with picnic tables, restrooms, grills, tennis court, baseball field, indoor swimming pool, fitness room, gymnasium, playground, walking paths, par course, and handicapped access.

Gen. Franklin E. Miles (Siringo Rd. and Camino Carlos Rey). Many square blocks' worth of sports fields and fun, including restrooms, picnic tables, shelter, softball field, indoor swimming pool, paths, playground, and handicapped access.

Larragoite (Agua Fria Rd. and Potencia St., near Larragoite Elementary School). A neighborhood park offering picnic tables, tennis courts, and a softball field.

The Plaza The city's oldest and most used facility, with benches and trees in the very heart of town.

Ragle (W. Zia Rd. and Yucca St.). Many acres of athletic fields near Santa Fe High School, offering picnic tables, grills, shelter, restrooms, baseball fields, pathways, playground, and handicapped access.

Randall Davey Audubon Center (see "Books, Maps, and Organizations," page 50).

Salvador Perez (Alta Vista and Letrado Sts.). A square block of open, green playground with picnic tables, restrooms, tennis courts, a softball field, indoor swimming pool, horseshoe pit, racquetball, volleyball, fitness room, trails, and handicapped access.

Santa Fe River (along Alameda St.). A refreshing sliver of green with picnic tables bordering the Santa Fe River. Trails have been recently upgraded, and the river usually has water running in it, thanks to watershed restoration.

Frank S. Ortiz Dog Park (160 Camino de las Crucitas). Acres of off-leash heaven for pets and their human companions to hike, visit, and explore. Fabulous views of the city and the Sangre de Cristos. Moderate to easy trails.

Washington (Washington Ave. and S. Federal St.). A quiet, landscaped park with benches and big shade trees right next to the post office and courthouse. A great picnic spot.

TAOS

Filemon Sanchez (slightly outside the south side of town). Includes baseball diamonds and other recreation facilities.

Fred Baca Memorial (575-758-8234; 301 Camino del Medio, just outside the town limits). A 4-acre municipal park with picnic tables, restrooms, two tennis courts, a basketball court, soccer field, volleyball court, and playground.

Kit Carson (575-758-8234; 115 Civic Plaza Dr., a block from the Plaza). A 20-acre park with bike and walking path, picnic tables, grills, a playground, tennis court, basketball court, amphitheater, and ice skating. Includes the graves of Kit Carson, Mabel Dodge Luhan, Padre Martinez, and other famous Taoseños.

RAFTING, CANOEING, KAYAKING Northern New Mexico's wild, scenic waters provide some of the best whitewater thrills in the country. The best time for such trips is usually late May through late July, but stretches along the Rio Grande from the Colorado border all the way to Cochiti Dam are negotiable all year. You can also float several stretches of the Pecos River between Cowles and Las Vegas. For current information on river flows, go to waterdata.usgs.gov/nm/nwis/rt. For maps and information on permits, seasons, and conditions, contact the **Bureau of Land Management** (575-758-8851; 226 Cruz Alta Rd., Taos, NM 87571). The BLM maintains a website with information on public lands, including those in New Mexico, at www.nm.blm.gov. Please be aware of the potential serious danger that may occur on raft trips, particularly when the water is high.

Most commercial float companies provide half-day, full-day, and overnight rafting trips on the Rio Grande and the Chama. A relatively serene float, ideal for families, is the Lower Rio Grande Gorge. Two of the most popular whitewater stretches are the Racecourse and the Taos Box on the Upper Rio Grande, with foaming Class IV waters that are bound to awaken your wild side. With increasing restrictions on river use, early booking is advised.

COMMERCIAL FLOAT TRIPS AND RENTALS

SANTA FE

Kokopelli Rafting Adventures (800-879-9035; www.kokopelliraft.com; 802 Early St., Santa Fe, NM 87501).

New Wave Rafting Company (505-984-1444; www.newwaverafting.com; 1101 Cerrillos Rd., Santa Fe, NM 87506). One of the largest and most reputable rafting outfitters in the area. For Rio Chama float trips call 800-984-1444.

Santa Fe Detours (505-983-6565; 800-338-6877; www.sfdetours.com; 54 E. San Francisco St., Santa Fe, NM 87501). Books tours with numerous rafting companies.

Santa Fe Rafting (505-988-4914; www.santaferafting.com; 1000 Cerrillos Rd., Santa Fe, NM 87505).

TAOS

Cottam's Rio Grande Rafting (800-322-8267; www.cottamsriogra03nderafting.com; 207 Paseo del Pueblo Sur, Taos, NM 87571).

Los Rios River Runners (575-776-8854; www.losriosriverrunners.com; P.O. Box 2734, Taos, NM 87571). In business more than 40 years.

RODEOS The Santa Fe–Taos area has its roots in the Old West. No event emphasizes this more clearly than the rodeo, which harks back to the 19th century, when much of New Mexico was dominated by the cattle industry and its rough-and-tumble cowboys.

In late June, you can attend the **Rodeo de Santa Fe** (505-471-4300), with some of the best riding and roping anywhere. A downtown parade of riders from all over the country kicks off the festivities.

Toward the end of July, you can drift on down to the **Rodeo de Galisteo**, a somewhat smaller though no less exciting Wild West event. Up north toward the end of June take in the **Rodeo de Taos** (575-937-0851) at the Taos County Fairgrounds.

RUNNING Runners here enjoy an exceptional variety of terrain and unusually clean, clear skies. From mountain highways and trails to secluded city byways, there's no better place to develop your legs and lungs while enjoying the unspoiled open spaces. For a comprehensive listing of races throughout the state, contact **New Mexico USA Track and Field** (505-908-8996; www.newmexico.usatf.org/About/Contact-Us.aspx).

SANTA FE

The **Santa Fe Striders** running club (505-231-6166; www.santafestriders.org; P.O. Box 1818, Santa Fe, NM 87504) starts fun runs from the Plaza every Wednesday at 6 PM in summer months. Contact them for information on seasonal running events. A few good running spots in Santa Fe include the east side, the banks of the Santa Fe River along Alameda Street, the Old Santa Fe Trail, and the St. Catherine's cross-country course. For more information on these and other good routes, consult Striders or *Santa Fe on Foot* by Elaine Pinkerton. For longer jaunts, try the Ski Basin Road and some of the routes listed under "Bicycling" on page 44.

TAOS

Each year, Taos hosts at least one 10-km race, plus a triathlon in fall and a marathon in June. Because there's no organized running club, your best bet is to check for dates and times with the **Taos County Chamber of Commerce** (575-751-8800; 1139 Paseo del Pueblo Sur, Taos, NM 87571). For training runs, the outskirts of Taos quickly lead to fairly flat, wide-open spaces, particularly toward the north, east, and west.

SKIING

DOWNHILL SKIING

The Santa Fe–Taos area is a skier's paradise, boasting half a dozen areas with some of the most popular world-class slopes in the country. Many of the ski areas start at 9,000 to 10,000 feet and rise to 12,000 or more, making for vertical drops in excess of 2,500 feet with annual snowfalls of up to 300 inches.

A few hardy souls began skiing at the Santa Fe Ski Basin shortly after World War II, and Lloyd and Olive Bolander set up the first rope tow at Sipapu in 1952. The sport really began to take off in 1955, when pioneer Ernie Blake began carving out a mountain niche for families at the Taos Ski Valley. Other spots such as Red River and Angel Fire followed during the 1960s. Since then, lifts, lodges, lounges, snowmaking, and myriad cross-country trails have created a major resort area that now draws skiers from all over the world.

In general, you can count on some of the beginner and intermediate runs to be open by late November, the remaining runs by the middle of December. Snowmaking usually creates a number of good trails by Thanksgiving at Angel Fire, Red River, Santa Fe, and Taos Ski Valley. All areas are open daily 9 AM–4 PM with the exception of Pajarito Mountain near Los Alamos, which is open only on Wednesday, weekends, and federal holidays. Rates quoted are for one full day unless otherwise stated; check ski area websites for full details on special rates and packages.

SIPAPU IS A FAVORITE WITH LOCAL SNOWBOARDERS

For New Mexico ski information, visit **New Mexico Snow Report** (www.onthesnow.com or www.skinewmexico.com/snow-report) for the most up-to-date information.

NEAR SANTA FE

Pajarito Mountain Ski Area (505-662-5725 information; 505-662-SNOW snow report; www.skipajarito.com; 7 miles west of Los Alamos via NM 502 and FR 1; 10,441 feet peak elevation; 1,200-foot vertical drop; 153 inches average snowfall; no snowmaking; 37 downhill trails [20 percent beginner, 50 percent intermediate, 30 percent advanced]; no cross-country trails; lifts: 5 chairlifts [3 double, 1 triple, 1 quad], 1 rope tow; terrain park; $49 adults, $39 half-day, $42 teens and seniors, $34 children, free for ages 6 and younger and 70 and older). Pajarito was started in 1957 by a group of Los Alamos National Laboratory employees who wanted a convenient place to ski. The area is owned and operated by the Los Alamos Ski Club, whose members are mainly Los Alamos employees or residents; however, it's also open to the public.

With 40 trails and 300 skiable acres, Pajarito is geared toward the serious day skier. Its runs are steeper, shorter, and rougher than most areas, which can be frustrating for beginners. On the other hand, some experts consider its runs the most challenging in the state. "If you can ski bumps, you're in heaven," says one of our friends. "If you're a novice who gets stuck on a bumpy run or goes into the trees, it's just hell." In recent years, there's been an effort to increase grooming to accommodate all levels of skiers.

There's no resort atmosphere at Pajarito—you won't find bars, lounges, or day-care for the kids—but you will find a three-story lodge with ski rentals and a nice cafeteria. You'll also find one of the rarest pluses of any ski area: no lift lines. Also, with only three skiing days a week, the snow at Pajarito lasts a relatively long time. Because of this and its small-town family atmosphere, many consider it an undiscovered gem.

Ski Santa Fe (505-982-4429 information; www.skisantafe.com; 2209 Brothers Rd., Ste. 220, Santa Fe, NM 87505, 15 miles northeast of Santa Fe via NM 475 [Ski Basin Rd.]; 12,053 feet peak elevation; 1,703-foot vertical drop; 225 inches average snowfall; snowmaking 50 percent of area; 79 downhill trails [20 percent beginner, 40 percent intermediate, 40 percent advanced]; no cross-country trails; lifts: 4 chairlifts [1 quad, 1 triple, 2 double], 1 poma, 2 Mitey Mites; $75 adults, $60 half-day, $52 ages 13–20, $43 seniors and children, free for ages 72 and older). Ski Santa Fe got its start in the 1930s with sheep and Indian trails as the basis for runs. The first ski area was developed a few miles down from its present site, at Hyde Park. By 1947, two dogleg rope tows with Cadillac engines lugged a few hardy skiers to the top of a nearby hill. In the early 1950s, the first chairlift was built at the present site, using Army Air Corps surplus seats from a B-24 bomber and a 50-year-old cable from a nearby mine.

Currently, five modern lifts ferry skiers to 12,000 feet, the second highest slope in the country. At the top of the triple chair, you can take in 80,000 square miles of awe-inspiring views. You'll also find relatively short lift lines and some of the best family skiing in the state. Beginner and intermediate skiers can always find comfortable slopes, while advanced stretches such as Parachute and Wizard—not to mention Tequila Sunrise and Big Rocks, with their deep powder and ungroomed moguls—provide challenges and thrills for the very best.

The ski school at the basin, which includes telemark and snowboard classes, will take children as young as 3. For adaptive ski lessons, contact 505-954-1224 or visit www.adaptiveski.org. You can get daycare for younger children if you arrange for it in advance. There's also La Casa Lodge at the base of the mountain, updated to meet your every need and including a food court, a boutique, and more than 1,000 pairs of rental skis. In addition, a terrain park is open to the public.

NEAR TAOS

Angel Fire Resort (575-377-6401; 800-633-7463 information, snow report, and reservations; www.angelfireresort.com; 10 Miller Lane, Angel Fire, NM 87710, 22 miles east of Taos via US 64 and NM 434; 10,677 feet peak elevation; 2,077-foot vertical drop; 210 inches average snowfall; snowmaking 52 percent of area; 80 downhill trails [21 percent beginner, 56 percent intermediate, 23 percent advanced]; 15 km groomed cross-country trails; lifts: 5 chairlifts [2 high-speed quads, 3 doubles, 2 SunKid Wonder Carpets]; $71 adults, $56 half-day, $61 ages 7–12, free for ages 6 and younger and 70 and older; sightseers may purchase a single lift ride to the summit for $20). Texan Roy H. Lebus started Angel Fire Resort in 1967 with little more than a dream and a handful of dedicated workers. Today, it is known as a family resort and a "cruiser's mountain," featuring a variety of long, well-groomed trails (the longest is 3.5 miles). Angel Fire is predominantly tailored to beginning and intermediate skiers; however, it also offers a number of outstanding expert runs, including the addition of a new expert trail called C-4. A short 15-minute hike from the top of the Southwest Flyer chairlift, C-4 will top the adventurous skier's or boarder's must-hit list on any fresh powder day. And they are so confident of their conditions and snowmaking machines that, if you are dissatisfied, they will automatically return your ticket within one hour if you want to come back another day. Widespread snowmaking guarantees 2,000 vertical feet of skiing even in the driest of years, and only in the very busiest of times does the lift line require more than a 5- or 10-minute wait. Another plus is the large picnic pavilion on the mountain that can accommodate several hundred skiers at a time.

Night skiing, too.

With 3,000 beds, Angel Fire has one of the largest, most affordable lodging bases in the state. The resort also boasts more major (and offbeat) events than almost any other area—for example, the world shovel race championships, featuring the wild antics of riders careening down the mountain at more than 60 miles an hour on scoop shovels.

Angel Fire Resort has also bolstered its freestyle parks with exciting new features, helping to cement Angel Fire's position as the snowboarding capital of the state. They have added more than a dozen high-quality freestyle rails and fun box features, including the most popular flat rails, rainbows, double-kinks, C-rails, tabletops, and a few surprises—open challenges to freestyle skiers as well as boarders. Angel Fire Resort has been the site of the USASA Snowboard Nationals, and Liberation Park was picked as the 2008 Terrain Park of the Year in North America by *On The Snow*. Now with three terrain parks and the Polar Coaster tubing hill.

The Angel Fire Resort Nordic Center offers 10 kilometers of groomed classic and skate cross-country ski trails, plus snowshoeing lanes and a family snow play hill for sledding. Lessons, equipment rental, retail, and pull-sleds are available in the full-service winter sports shop downstairs. When you're done playing outside and need to warm up, come into the Club, grab a hot chocolate, and enjoy the beautiful views of the Sangre de Cristo Mountains. Snowboarding lessons are available at the ski school.

Red River Ski Area (575-754-2223 information, snow report; www.redriverskiarea. com; P.O. Box 900, Red River, NM 87558, 37 miles north of Taos via NM 522 and NM 38; 10,350 feet peak elevation; 1,600-foot vertical drop; 214 inches average snowfall; snowmaking 85 percent of area; 57 downhill trails [32 percent beginner, 38 percent intermediate, 30 percent advanced]; cross-country trails available nearby at Enchanted Forest; 7 lifts [1 double chair, 3 triple chairs, 2 surface tows]; rates in peak and non-peak times are: $73-70 adults, $55-53 half-day, $67-65 teens, $57-55 children and seniors, free for seniors over 70 and children under 3). Red River was started in 1961 by a well-loved oilman and character named John Bolton, and its first lift consisted of used derricks and cables Bolton imported from an oil field in Texas. Located in the northern arc of the Enchanted Circle, Red River is another family-friendly ski area, a great place to learn, with extensive snowmaking and numerous wide beginner and intermediate trails. Runs such as Kit Carson and Broadway allow plenty of room for everybody to fall down, while expert speedways like Cat Skinner and Landing Strip are enough to get anyone's adrenaline pumping. The area rents about 1,000 pairs of skis, with another 2,000 pairs available in Red River. It also hosts on-slope bars and restaurants.

The Pioneer Flyer, an accelerated reverse chairlift newly opened in 2015, is a thrill akin to bungee jumping. It pulls you backward, then releases you to fly over some of the most spectacular scenery in the West. And the new Emerald Quad will virtually eliminate lift lines at Summit Camp by doubling the uphill capacity and traveling at nearly twice the speed of the current lift.

Red River features a 4,500-bed lodging base less than a block from the ski area. During February's Mardi Gras in the Mountains, the whole town turns to cooking Cajun food and dressing in festive Southern garb. There's a moonlight ski and snowshoe event, and a Spring Break Torchlight Parade & Fireworks show. Red River has a Kinderski school for ages 4 to 10 and Buckaroo Child Care for ages 6 months to 4 years.

Sipapu Ski and Summer Resort (800-587-2240; www.sipapunm.com; 5224 NM 518, Vadito, NM 87579, 25 miles southeast of Taos via NM 68 and NM 518; 9,225 feet peak elevation; 1,055-foot vertical drop; 190 inches average snowfall; snowmaking 70 percent of area; 31 downhill trails [20 percent novice, 40 percent intermediate, 25 percent advanced]; cross-country trails available in nearby Carson National Forest; lifts: 1 triple chair, 2 pomas, 1 Magic Carpet, new quad and quad trail; $44 adults, $33 half-day, $37 ages 12 and younger, $29 ages 65–69, free for seniors 70 and older; ask about the new Power Pass). Sipapu was started by Lloyd and Olive Bolander, who first brought a small portable rope tow to the area in 1952. The next year they offered 30 pairs of rental skis with bear-trap bindings. Now, more than 50 years later, Sipapu is many times its original size. The area's laid-back atmosphere helps everyone feel at home, and the terrain parks are a haven for locals.

This refreshingly small, quiet ski area focuses mainly on beginner and intermediate fun, though they have added trails to appeal to experts, too. It is also known as a telemark mountain. Lots of times after a pleasant run, you can jump right back on the lift with no wait at all. The area includes a restaurant and a snack bar, about 750 pairs of rental skis, on-slope lodging for nearly 200, and another 375 beds nearby. Delightful Sipapu is just about custom-made for families on a budget.

Taos Ski Valley (575-776-2291; 866-968-7386; www.skitaos.com; P.O. Box 90, Taos Ski Valley, NM 87525, 18 miles northeast of Taos via US 64 and NM 150; 11,819 feet peak elevation; 2,612-foot vertical drop; 305 inches average snowfall; snowmaking 100 percent; 110 downhill trails [24 percent beginner, 25 percent intermediate, 51 percent advanced]; no cross-country trails; lifts: 15 chairlifts [4 quad, 3 triple, 5 double], 3 surface lifts; $98 adults, $81 ages 13–17 and 65–79, $61 children). Dreaming of his own resort, the indefatigable founder of Taos Ski Valley (TSV), Ernie Blake, spent countless hours flying his small plane over the Sangre de Cristo Mountains, scouting for the perfect site. The valley he finally located got an inauspicious start as a ski resort, with unreliable investors and near inaccessibility. But Blake persevered. When TSV opened as a fledgling family ski area in 1955, a 300-foot, diesel-driven T-bar was its first lift. TSV has never looked back. A long-standing dilemma was resolved a few years back, for good or not, depending on your point of view, when snowboarding was finally allowed at TSV.

The tradition at TSV is service, and that begins with excellent engineering and design. From lift-line management to trail marking, cafeteria food, and ski school programming, the pattern is consistently high quality. Even with a record-breaking abundance of snow and people, the whole system usually works flawlessly. Exceptions are the parking lots, which because of the lay of the valley tend to be long and narrow.

Lowlanders will definitely feel the elevation here. Drink plenty of water (no alcohol) and take frequent rests. The views across the valley and over to neighboring Kachina Peak (12,481 feet) are worth a pause. The skiing is challenging, even for experts, but there are plenty of intermediate and novice slopes as well, including a few from the very top. The combination of trails called Honeysuckle, Winklereid, and Rubezahl can bring even a first-day skier down safely from the peak. If you're into pushing the envelope, you'll do no better than to bump and pump your way down such mogul-studded trails as the infamous Al's Run (under the #1 lift), or to try the steep trails off the West Basin Ridge.

Amenities are provided at midstation snack bars (Phoenix and Whistlestop) and in numerous lodges and restaurants at the base. Families are efficiently accommodated, with daycare for tots ages 6 weeks and up, ski school for the kids, convenient lockers and storage baskets, and a most welcome addition: ski patrollers who actually patrol the slopes and slow traffic down in tight quarters. In or near the base lodge, you'll find about 2,000 pairs of rental skis, lodging for more than 1,000 skiers, all manner of books and souvenirs, and numerous festive events.

WHERE TO BUY AND RENT SKI EQUIPMENT All the ski areas listed offer a good supply of on-slope rental equipment. You can also find ski rentals, sales, and service at numerous shops in Santa Fe, Taos, and other towns near the ski areas.

SANTA FE

Alpine Sports (505-983-5155; 127 Sandoval St., Ste. B). Downhill and cross-country sales and rentals.

REI (505-982-3557; 500 Market St.). Everything you could want for hiking, bicycling, kayaking, camping, and more.

rob and charlie's (505-471-9119; www.robandcharlies.com; 1632 St. Michael's Dr.). Snowboard sales and rentals, skateboards, bikes.

Skier's Edge (505-983-1025; 1836 Cerrillos Rd.). Downhill, cross-country, and snowboard rentals. Cross-training machine and other cutting-edge equipment.

Ski Tech Ski Rentals (505-983-5512; 905 S. St. Francis Dr.). Cross-country rentals, all ski equipment, fast computerized service.

NEAR SANTA FE

Cottam's Ski Rentals (505-982-0495; 740 Hyde Park Rd.). Downhill and cross-country rental and accessories, snowboards, inner tubes, and sleds.

TAOS

Adventure Ski Shops (575-758-1167; www.adventureskishops.com; 1337 Paseo del Pueblo Sur). Downhill and cross-country sales, service, and repairs.

Cottam's Ski Shops (800-322-8267; 207-A Paseo del Pueblo Sur). Downhill and cross-country rentals and service, snowboards too.

Taos Mountain Outfitters (575-758-9292; 114 S. Plaza). Largest independent outdoor gear shop in New Mexico. Hiking, paddling—whatever you need, they've got.

Mudd N Flood (575-751-9100; 103A Bent St.) Specializing in sales, rentals, custom service, and more. This is the place to come and get oriented.

NEAR TAOS

Cottam's Ski Shops (575-776-8719, 101 Sutton Pl., Taos Ski Valley). Rentals, gear, and services.

High Country Ski Rentals (575-377-6424; 3453 Mountain View Blvd., Angel Fire).

Terry Sports (575-776-8292; 11 Ernie Blake Rd., Taos Ski Valley). Downhill and cross-country sales, rentals, and repair.

Winter Sports Ski Shop (575-377-6612; 12 Aspen St., Angel Fire). A complete selection of sophisticated gear for skiers.

Angel Fire Resort (575-377-4290; located next to the Village Haus on the base area deck). All the gear you need for a day on the slopes.

DOWNHILL RENTALS AND SERVICE Mickey's Ski Rental (575-377-2501; 375 E. Therma Dr., Eagle Nest). Downhill ski rentals and repair. Open 7:30 AM–7 PM every day during ski season; specializing in convenience.

Millers Crossing Ski & Sportswear (575-754-2374; 417 W. Main St., Red River). Cross-country sales, service, rentals, and lessons. The old reliable.

Mountain Sports (575-377-3490; 3375 NM 434, Angel Fire, next to Valley Market). Downhill ski sales and rentals, boots, clothing, snowboards.

Nancy Burch's Roadrunner Tours (575-377-6416; one hour west of blinking light on US 64; Angel Fire). The ultimate "City Slicker" experience. Lessons, one-hour to all-day rides, sleigh rides, and romantic wedding and engagement rides into the Carson National Forest and along the Enchanted Circle.

DOWNHILL SKI AND CLOTHING RENTALS Sitzmark Sports & Lodge (800-843-7547; 416 Main St., Red River). Downhill ski and snowboard sales, rentals, repair, and clothing.

Wild Bill's Ski and Snowboard Shop (575-754-2428; 325 W. Main St., Red River). Downhill ski and snowboard rentals and repair, equipment sales, apparel, and gear.

CROSS-COUNTRY SKIING If you're looking for solitude and the quiet sound of skis sliding over backcountry trails, take a break from the lift lines and go touring or Nordic. Depending on the seasonal snowfall, almost anytime Dec.–Mar. you can find myriad snow-covered trails lacing national forests and wilderness areas, plus countless public trails and a few privately groomed trails within the area. For current snow conditions and maps, contact the national forest offices listed below or www.nmroads. com. Some of the more popular books on the subject include: *Ski Touring in Northern New Mexico* by Sam Beard; *Skiing the Sun* by Jim Burns and Cheryl Lemanski; and *Cross-Country Skiing in Northern New Mexico* by Kay Matthews.

SANTA FE AREA

Some of the best ski touring in the Santa Fe area is in the **Santa Fe National Forest** (Santa Fe office 505-438-5300; 11 Forest Lane, Santa Fe, NM 87501). A few of the more popular trails include those starting from Black Canyon Campground, about 9 miles from town via the Ski Basin Rd.; Borrega and Aspen Vista Trails about 13 miles up the Ski Basin Rd.; and Winsor Trail just off the Ski Basin parking lot. These and other trails in the area are administered by the Española Ranger District (505-438-5300). Ask for recreation staff.

In the Jemez Mountains, Peralta Canyon Rd., the East Fork of the Jemez, and Corral Canyon are all good touring areas, as are Fenton Hill and Jemez Falls in the Jemez Ranger District (575-829-3535). Some areas have been damaged by fire and may be restricted.

TAOS AREA

The **Carson National Forest** offers numerous public ski-touring trails, some of them located right next to the Taos, Red River, and Sipapu ski areas. One of the more popular areas in the Camino Real Ranger District (575-587-2255) is **Amole Canyon** off NM 518 between Taos and Sipapu. Here the national forest, in cooperation with the Taos Norski Club, maintains set tracks and signs along a 3-mile loop that's closed to snowmobiles and ideal for skating. There are also 6- and 7-mile unmaintained loop trails at the same location. Another popular snowmobile-free route off NM 518 is **Picuris Lookout**, with exceptional mountain views. **Capulin/La Sombra**, about 5 miles east of Taos off US 64, is a flat, 1.5-mile trail that's great for skating.

Popular routes in the **Tres Piedras Ranger District** (575-758-8678) include Maquinita Canyon, Biscara Trail, Burned

FALL IN ALL ITS GLORY BECKONS ASPEN VISTA TRAIL HIKERS

Mountain, and Forest Road 795. In the **Questa Ranger District** (575-586-0520), try East Fork, Ditch Cabin, Long Canyon, or Goose Creek.

Detailed guides for many of the trails listed are available at Carson National Forest offices. Remember that some trails are designated for skiers or snowmobilers only, and some are shared. Restrictions are posted, but be sure to check with the forest service for detailed information. Also get hold of the forest service's *Winter Recreation Safety Guide*, which lists winter hazards and how to prepare for them.

TOURS AND PRIVATE TOURING CENTERS For instruction, tours, and overnight ski-touring packages in the Santa Fe area, **Santa Fe Detours** (505-983-6565) will arrange half- or full-day trips.

For cross-country ski instruction and tours in the Taos area, your best bet is to call **Millers Crossing** (575-754-2374; 417 W. Main St., Red River, NM 87558). The place to go touring near Taos is the **Enchanted Forest XC Ski & Snowshoe Area** (575-754-6112; enchantedforestxc.com; 29 Sangre de Cristo Dr., Red River, NM 87558). Just east of Red River atop Bobcat Pass, it offers 30 km of groomed and ungroomed trails amid 600 forested acres. Here, you'll find 5 km of dog-friendly trails and prime ski terrain for classical, freestyle, and telemark. There's also miles of backcountry, instructors, patrols, warming huts, rentals, snowshoeing, and special events like moonlight ski tours. Summer yurt rentals as well.

There's an exhilarating network of trails for snowmobilers through both the Santa Fe and Carson National Forests. Many of these regularly groomed mini-highways twist and turn through thick forests to high-alpine meadows where speedsters can zoom across wide-open spaces to their hearts' content. Be sure to check with district forest service offices (listed under "Public Ski Touring," above) before you choose a trail. Remember to slow down and stay clear of skiers and snowshoers. For maximum safety and fun, choose a trail that's designated for snowmobiles only. Three of the best are Fourth of July Canyon, Old Red River Pass, and Greenie Peak in the **Questa Ranger District** (575-758-6200) near Red River. A number of businesses in Red River also provide safe, guided snowmobile tours, complete with mountaintop hot dog cookouts. **Angel Fire Excursions** (575-377-2799) provides guided snowmobile tours of the forest area for riders 16 and older. Just north of Angel Fire on NM 38 is **Bobcat Pass Wilderness Adventures** (575-754-2769), which also has snowmobiling during the winter months in the Carson National Forest.

SPAS AND HOT SPRINGS Still bubbling and steaming in the aftermath of its relatively recent volcanic activity, northern New Mexico is dotted with natural hot springs. Private bathhouses have been built over two such spots, at Ojo Caliente and Jemez Springs (outside the area), and numerous other gurgling hot spots can be found in the open air. Just outside Santa Fe there's even a Japanese bathhouse offering everything you could want in a natural spring and more.

NEAR SANTA FE

Ten Thousand Waves (505-982-9304; www.tenthousandwaves.com; 3451 Hyde Park Rd., Santa Fe, NM 87501; open daily; reservations strongly recommended). Only 10 minutes' drive from the Santa Fe Plaza, Ten Thousand Waves is the premier spa in the Santa Fe–Taos area. Disengagement from everyday cares begins when you park in the lot and walk up a winding path illuminated at night by ground-level Japanese lanterns. Up top, gurgling water and giant goldfish slip by as you cross a bridge and ascend to the lobby. Here, you may sign in for any of a host of pleasures, including public or private hot tubs, with special men's and women's tub hours scheduled.

Some of the mountainside tubs, though discreetly screened, have lovely views through the pines. The public tubs (including coed and women's tubs) are convivial places where idle conversation and subdued jollity prevail, while private tubs have the allure of romance or the challenge of solitary meditation. Locker rooms are handsome, with extras ranging from kimonos and thongs to soap, shampoo, and cedar lotion. Massage therapy runs the gamut from Swedish to shiatsu and every sort of body work and skin treatment you can imagine.

There are salt rubs, herbal wraps, and more. A well-stocked health food snack bar in the lobby and a cozy fireplace make lingering an added pleasure. Services are not cheap (in 2016 private tubs ran $35–$57 per person per hour; communal and women's tubs were around $25 for unlimited time; massages $115 and up an hour, and facials $135 on up). Warning: While the Waves is a popular destination—some say a Santa Fe must-do—I find the water here extremely hot.

NEAR TAOS

Ojo Caliente Mineral Springs Resort & Spa (505-583-2233; www.ojospa.com; 50 Los Banos Dr., Ojo Caliente, NM 87549, southwest of Taos or north of Española on US 285; closed Christmas; reservations required for private tubs). A delightful getaway for all. This is the most popular mineral springs spa in northern New Mexico, featuring natural hot waters with therapeutic iron, arsenic, and lithium. Attendants in separate men's and women's locker areas pamper and guide you either to individual cubicles with fresh water for 15-minute arsenic soaks (great for arthritis and rheumatism) or to a large, enclosed outdoor grotto area with hot iron water. There's also a coed bathhouse with individual rooms for couples. After your soak, an attendant will put you on a table and cover you head to toe with steaming hot cotton blankets (aka the mummy wrap) for further relaxation or in preparation for a full-body massage. Separate charges for towel rentals.

Before returning to the world, you're invited to take a shower, a swim in the heated outdoor pool, or a peaceful walk beside giant cottonwoods—hike up to see the petroglyphs or to fill canisters with any of the three mineral waters. You can even go riding if you want.

As of 2016, prices were $20 for an all-day pass Mon.–Thurs.; $32 for the same on weekends and holidays; $16 sunset rate (after 6 PM) on Mon.–Thurs. and $28 weekends. Expect to pay $89 and up for body work. The inn also offers overnight packages for couples, including breakfast and two mineral baths apiece. Reduced rates are available for New Mexicans and frequent users.

SWIMMING Opportunities for swimming abound in the Santa Fe–Taos area, from lakes and rivers to numerous fine municipal and private pools. Please see numbers listed below for windsurfing. Swimming in the Rio Grande is discouraged due to the rocky bottom and strong undertow, but you can spend time near the river at the **BLM Wild Rivers Recreation Area** (575-758-8851) north of Taos and the **Orilla Verde Recreation Area** (575-758-8851) on the south end of Taos. Beware of rattlesnakes in all rocky areas near the river, and guard your pets. **Heron Lake** (575-588-7470) north of Abiquiu in Heron Lake State Park is the favorite swimming area.

SANTA FE

In Santa Fe, you'll find four indoor public pools and one outdoor pool available for a small fee for adults and free for children 7 and younger. For details on times, classes, and activities, call the city recreation division: 505-955-2602. For numbers and addresses of private pools, see "Fitness Centers" and individual entries in "Lodging." Municipal pools include:

Bicentennial Pool: 505-955-4779; 1121 Alto St. Open only in summer.
Fort Marcy Pool: 505-955-2511; 490 Bishop's Lodge Rd.
Salvador Perez Pool: 505-955-2604; 601 Alta Vista St.

TAOS

For swimming opportunities in Taos, the **Taos Youth and Family Center** has a municipal pool at the **Taos Aquatic Center** (575-737-2583, 407 Paseo del Canon E.) and charges $3 per session for adults, $2 per session for children. The **Taos Spa & Tennis Club** (575-758-1980; 111 Dona Ana Dr.) also has a pool, available to nonmembers for $12 a day.

TENNIS With clean air and clear skies most of the year, courts in the Santa Fe–Taos area are usually popping with tennis balls—except when they're snow covered during winter. Even then, both towns have numerous private indoor courts that can be rented any time of year.

SANTA FE

The city of Santa Fe offers some 27 public tennis courts and four major private tennis facilities, including indoor, outdoor, and lighted courts. Some public parks with tennis courts include Fort Marcy Complex, Genoveva Chavez Community Center Ortiz, and Salvador Perez Recreation Center. For specifics and other locations, call the **City Recreation Department** (505-955-4480 for tennis lesson information).

Santa Fe–area clubs with tennis courts include:
El Gancho: 505-988-5000; 104 Old Las Vegas Hwy.
Sangre de Cristo Racquet Club: 505-983-7978; 1755 Camino Corrales.
Santa Fe Country Club: 505-471-2626; 4360-A Country Club Rd.

TAOS

The **Taos Parks and Recreation Department** (575-737-3860) maintains tennis courts at Kit Carson Park and Fred Baca Park. There are more outdoor courts at the **Taos Spa & Tennis Club** (575-758-1980; 111 Dona Ana Dr.) for $12 an hour per person.

WATER SPORTS See also "Hunting and Fishing" on page 55.

Surprisingly, New Mexico boasts more small boats per capita than almost any other state in the Union. Some say it's because of the yearning for water in a state so high and dry. Others say it's because of the spirit of a land once covered by inland seas. But those who really know say it's simply because New Mexico has a lot of good boating. Canoeing, waterskiing, fishing, and boating can be found at the following lakes.

NEAR SANTA FE

Cochiti Lake (505-465-0307; Army Corps of Engineers, 82 Dam Crest Rd., Peña Blanca). About half an hour southwest of Santa Fe off I-25, Cochiti is a no-wake lake with free public boat ramps and rentals of canoes, rowboats, and fishing boats. There's also a recreation center about half a mile from the lake, with pool and table tennis, a swimming pool, and a basketball court. And people do swim in the lake.

Nambé Reservoir (about 20 miles north of Santa Fe via US 285 and NM 503; take turnoff to Nambe Falls). For boating information, contact Nambé Pueblo (505-455-2036; 61 Np 102 E., Santa Fe, NM 87501).

Santa Cruz Lake Recreation Area (505-927-3314; Bureau of Land Management, 226 Cruz Alto Rd., Taos, NM 87571). This small no-wake lake and recreation area near Española has a small-boat ramp and a 5 mph speed limit. Swimming is allowed only in the northeast picnic area.

NEAR TAOS

At **Eagle Nest Lake State Park** (575-377-1594; 42 Marina Ln., east of Taos on the edge of the Enchanted Circle), **Eagle Nest Marina** (575-377-6941; 28386 US 64, Eagle Nest, NM 87718) can give you information on boat rentals and activities.

OUTSIDE THE AREA

Abiquiu Lake (505-685-4371; about 65 miles northwest of Santa Fe on US 84; managed by U.S. Army Corps of Engineers). This large, scenic reservoir behind Abiquiu Dam offers a little of everything, from canoeing and windsurfing to fishing and waterskiing. No boat rentals are available. Camping at Riana Campground.

Heron and El Vado Lakes (near the town of Chama). These lakes are administered by the New Mexico State Parks Division (505-588-7247; State Road 112, Tierra Amarilla, NM 87575). Both have boat ramps and camping facilities. Heron is a no-wake lake, especially popular for small sailboats and Hobies. Frequent regattas. Waterskiing is allowed at El Vado. A 5.5-mile trail connects the lakes. For further information, contact the **Stone House Lodge** (575-588-7274; HC 75 Box 1022, Los Ojos, NM 87551). Stone

EAGLE NEST LAKE, A POPULAR FISHING AND BOATING ATTRACTION, IS STUNNING ALL YEAR ROUND

House rentals, available Apr.–Nov., include 24-foot pontoon boats with awnings and outboard engines. Fishing guide services available. Open year-round.

Storrie Lake (505-425-7278; 6 miles north of Las Vegas, NM, via NM 518, Mile Marker 3.5). When it has sufficient water, this lake is one of the most popular windsurfing spots in the state. It includes a boat ramp and courtesy dock but no boat rentals. Fishing, swimming, campsites.

For more information on ramps, rentals, and activities, contact the **New Mexico Parks and Recreation Division** (505-476-3200; www.emnrd.state.nm.us/nmparks). For new and used boats, motors, parts, accessories, and a full-service shop, contact **High Country Marine** (505-471-4077; 27736 W. Frontage Rd., Santa Fe, NM 87505).

WINDSURFING Clear weather and strong breezes wafting across easily accessible lakes combine to make for some fine windsurfing. The most popular nearby lakes are **Cochiti** (505-465-0307) near Santa Fe, **Eagle Nest Lake State Park** (575-377-1594) near Taos, and **Storrie Lake State Park** (505-425-7278) and **Abiquiu** (505-685-4371) outside the area. Lakes may be affected by prolonged drought, however, so be sure to check on conditions before you go. At most lakes the strongest winds tend to come up in the afternoon, whipping up whitecaps and whisking surfers across the water at dizzying speeds. Watch out for thunderstorms, though; they sometimes blow in with the afternoon winds.

For more information on these and other windsurfing lakes, see "Water Sports" on page 68–70.

YOGA See also "Fitness Centers" on page 48–49.

SANTA FE

Body Studio (505-986-0362; 332 W. Cordova Rd.). Daily yoga classes, workshops, child care, café, massage, and body treatments. Signature Vinyasa classes for the serious practitioner, plus hatha, ashtanga, kundalini, yoga to Indian music—what a menu! Vegan restaurant on the premises.

Santa Fe Community Yoga Center (505-820-9363; 826 Camino de Monte Rey, Ste. B1). A complete nonprofit yoga network with bargain prices with instructors of various lineages; prenatal, men's, and children's classes; and meditation. Flow, restorative, qigong. The emphasis is on defining the correct level for the practitioner.

Yogasource Santa Fe (505-982-0990; 902 W. San Mateo, Ste. Y). Very popular, small classes, respected instructors.

Studio NIA (505-989-1299; 851 W. San Mateo #6). Wildly popular no-impact dance-movement classes. Pilates, yoga, and more.

Yoga Moves (505-989-1072; 825 Early St.). Yoga plus swing dance; kids' acting classes, too.

INFORMATION

✳ Practical Matters

Here is a modest encyclopedia of useful information about the Santa Fe and Taos area. Our aim is to ease everyday life for locals and help ensure that vacation time goes smoothly for visitors. This chapter covers the following topics:

✳ Ambulance, Fire, Police, and Hospitals

EMERGENCY NUMBERS The general emergency number (fire, police, ambulance) for Santa Fe and Taos is 911. Other emergency numbers are as follows:

SANTA FE

Crisis Intervention: 505-820-6333
Esperanza Support Center: 505-474-5536
Esperanza Shelter: 505-473-5200
Landlord-Tenant Hotline: 505-930-5666
New Mexico Suicide Intervention Project: 505-473-6191
Poison Control: 800-222-1222
Rape Crisis Center: 505-986-9111

TAOS

Ambulance: 575-737-6430
Fire: 575-758-3386
Poison Control: 800-222-1222
Police: 575-758-2217
Sheriff: 575-737-6485

STATE POLICE **Española:** 505-753-2277
Santa Fe: 505-827-9300
Taos: 575-758-8878

HOSPITALS

ESPAÑOLA

Española Hospital: 505-753-7111; 1010 Spruce St.

LOS ALAMOS

Los Alamos Medical Center: 505-662-4201; 3917 West Rd.

SANTA FE

Christus St. Vincent Hospital: 505-913-3934; 455 Saint Michaels Dr.

TAOS

Holy Cross Hospital: 575-758-8883; 1397 Weimar Rd.

✳ Banks

Most banks in Santa Fe and Taos are linked electronically to nationwide automatic teller systems. Here is a list of telephone numbers and addresses of some of these banks' main offices.

SANTA FE

Bank of America (505-955-9500, 101 Paseo de Peralta; and 505-473-8211, 1234 Saint Michaels Dr.) Linked to PLUS, MasterCard, Maestro, Lynx, PULSE, Visa, and BankMate systems.
First National Bank of Santa Fe (505-992-2000; main office at 62 Lincoln Ave. on the Plaza). Linked to Lynx, PLUS, PULSE, and BankMate systems.
Wells Fargo (505-984-0500; 241 Washington Ave.).

TAOS

Centinel Bank of Taos (575-758-6790; 707 Paseo del Pueblo Norte). Linked to Cirrus, Lynx, and Pulse systems.
Peoples Bank (575-758-8331; main office at 1356 Paseo del Pueblo Sur). Linked to Cirrus, Lynx, Pulse, and Money systems.

✳ Chambers of Commerce

Local chambers of commerce and visitors bureaus are usually a quick and convenient way of getting information about the specific area you want to visit.

SANTA FE

Santa Fe Community Convention Center (505-955-6200; santafe.org; 201 W. Marcy St., Santa Fe, NM 87501, in the Santa Fe Convention Center).

Santa Fe County Chamber of Commerce (505-988-3279; 1644 St. Michael's Dr., Santa Fe, NM 87505).

TAOS

Taos Visitor Center (575-758-3873; 800-732-8267; taos.org; 1139 Paseo del Pueblo Sur, Taos, NM 87571).

Taos County Chamber of Commerce (575-751-8800; 1139 Paseo del Pueblo Sur, Taos, NM 87571).

TAOS AREA

Angel Fire Chamber of Commerce (575-377-6353; www.angelfirechamber.org; 3407 Mountain View Blvd., Angel Fire, NM 87710).

Eagle Nest Chamber of Commerce (575-377-2420; www.eaglenestchamber.org; 100 W. Therma Dr., Eagle Nest, NM 87118).

Red River Chamber of Commerce (575-754-2366; www.redriver.org; 100 E. Main St., Red River, NM 87558).

❄ Climate and Weather Reports

Santa Fe and Taos are blessed with a healthful, dynamic, high-desert climate. The air is dry all year, and at 7,000 feet (the approximate elevation of both cities), nights are always cool. There are 300 days of sunshine a year.

Sound wonderful? It is. But you'll enjoy it more if you take a few precautions. Bring and use sunscreen (with a protection level of at least 30), lip balm, and skin lotion. Be sure to take it easy when you arrive to give your body a chance to adjust to the altitude. To keep your energy up, eat foods high in carbohydrates. Go easy on alcohol, tranquilizers, and sleeping pills. And drink lots of water.

You can get information on road conditions by calling the state police at 505-827-9300, New Mexico Road Conditions at 505-827-5100, or the 511 hotline. Your best bet is to go to www.nmroads.com, which is updated frequently and gives information on road closures as well as driving conditions. You can reach the National Weather Service in Albuquerque at 505-243-0702.

❄ Disability Services

To obtain a copy of a booklet that identifies handicapped-accessible facilities, contact the Governor's Committee on Disability at 505-476-2200; Fourth Floor, New Mexico State Capitol, Santa Fe, NM 87501. For further information, contact City of Santa Fe, Community Services Division at 505-955-6568; 500 Market Station, Ste. 200, Santa Fe, NM 87501.

Out-of-state handicapped visitors can obtain a temporary placard for handicapped parking by calling the New Mexico Motor Vehicle Division at 888-683-4636. Capital City Cab Co. (505-438-0000) offers disabled people a discount on fares with a coupon available from City Hall. You must have proof of American Disabilities Act qualification to receive a 21-day visitor's pass. Your best bet for information on accessibility and parking in Taos is the Taos County Chamber of Commerce (575-751-8800; www.taoschamber.com; 1139 Paseo del Pueblo Sur, Taos, NM 87571).

✳ Guided Tours

There are a number of delightful and informative sight-seeing tours in the Santa Fe–Taos area. Local cabdrivers can usually be persuaded to drive you around, adding colorful histories that only a cabbie might know. For more organized, detailed tours, consider the following.

SANTA FE

For a complete list of tour operators, please visit Tourism Santa Fe at http://santafe.org/Visiting_Santa_Fe/Things_to_Do/Tours/

Afoot in Santa Fe (505-983-3701). Tours, conducted by longtime guide Charles Porter, gather at 207 and 211 Old Santa Fe Trail.

Custom Tours by Clarice (505-438-7116). Offers luxury transportation, charters, and special events as well as tours of Santa Fe for $20 per person.

Loretto Line Open Air Trolley Tram City Tours (505-982-0092). Departure times are 10 AM, 11 AM, noon, 1 PM, 2 PM, and 3 PM. Meet in the Loretto Chapel area, 207 Old Santa Fe Trail. Arrive at least 15 minutes before departure time to purchase your tickets for $15 from the bus driver. The tour lasts approximately 1¼ hours. $15 per person.

Recursos de Santa Fe (505-982-9301). This nonprofit organization specializes in educational tours, including excursions to archaeological sites, lectures in Georgia O'Keeffe country, and visits to the homes and studios of local artists.

Santa Fe Detours (505-983-6565). First-rate walking tours of the downtown area with guides who are longtime residents and know local history and anthropology. Motorized tours will pick you up at your hotel at 9 AM. For walking tours, meet under the T-shirt tree at 107 Washington Ave. Reservations required. Stop by the Santa Fe Detours office (54½ E. San Francisco St. above Häagen-Dazs on the Plaza) for a discount. They also offer a hotline for unique area B&Bs and lodging.

Santa Fe Ghost and History Tours (505-986-5002). Tours that visit Santa Fe's many haunted places.

TAOS

Ghosts of Taos: Walking Tours from Taos Plaza (575-613-5330). $20, discounts available.

Historic Taos Trolley Tours (505-550-5612; $43 adults, $14 children (7-12), free for children 6 and younger). Includes one-hour stop at Taos Pueblo and tour of Taos Plaza; another History & Culture Tour visits museums and cultural sites. Fares include entry fees. May–Oct.

✳ Late-Night Food and Fuel

If the munchies hit or your fuel gauge drops perilously low in the wee hours, there are places you can go. Santa Fe has convenience stores, restaurants, and gas stations that stay open 24 hours a day.

CONVENIENCE STORES, GAS STATIONS, AND RESTAURANTS **Allsup's:** 505-988-3862; 305 N. Guadalupe St., Santa Fe (open 24/7) and 505-758-0037; 507 Paseo del Pueblo Norte, Taos (open 24/7).
> **Denny's:** 505-471-2152; 3004 Cerrillos Rd., Santa Fe (open 24/7).
> **Dunkin' Donuts:** 505-983-2090; 1085 S. St. Francis Dr., Santa Fe (open 24/7)
> **Giant Service Station:** 505-473-9744; 2691 Sawmill Rd., Santa Fe (open 24/7).
> **The Kettle:** 505-473-5840; 4250 Cerrillos Rd. at Villa Linda Mall, Santa Fe.

PHARMACIES **Walgreen's:** 505-474-3507; 3298 Cerrillos Rd., Santa Fe (open 24/7).

✳ Local Government: City Halls and Zip Codes

Santa Fe, New Mexico's capital, is the seat of Santa Fe County, which is headed by a five-member county commission. Taos is the seat of Taos County, which is headed by a three-member county commission. The two other major cities in the region with sizable local governments are Española and Los Alamos. In addition, there are 11 Indian pueblos in the area located on reservations. Politically and legally, each pueblo is a sovereign nation led by a tribal governor and a tribal ruling council. Each also has its own police force. For general information, call the following numbers or write to the city or county clerk, in care of the city or county in question, or to the tourist information centers at the pueblos.

Town or Pueblo	Telephone	ZIP Code
Cochiti Pueblo	505-465-2244	87072
Española	505-747-6100	87532
Los Alamos County	505-663-1750	87544
Nambé Pueblo	505-455-2036	87506
Ohkay Owingeh Pueblo	505-852-4400	87566
Picuris Pueblo	575-587-2519	87553
Pojoaque Pueblo	505-455-4050	87506
Rio Arriba County	575-588-7254	87575
San Felipe Pueblo	505-867-3381	87001
San Ildefonso Pueblo	505-455-2273	87506
Santa Clara Pueblo	505-753-7326	87532
Santa Fe	505-955-4400	87501
Santa Fe County	505-986-6200	87501
Santo Domingo Pueblo	505-465-2214	87052
Taos	575-758-3873	87571
Taos County	575-751-8800	87571
Taos Pueblo	575-758-1028	87571
Taos Ski Valley	800-992-7669	87525
Tesuque Pueblo	505-983-2667	87506

✳ Media

For current information about events in Santa Fe (music, arts and culture, business, nightlife, family activities, and more), go to www.santafe.com.

MAGAZINES AND NEWSPAPERS *Journal North* (505-988-8881; www.abqjournal.com; 328 Galisteo St., Santa Fe, NM 87501). A branch of the statewide *Albuquerque Journal.*

The Magazine (505-424-7641; 320 Aztec St., Ste. A, Santa Fe, NM 87507). A monthly magazine of the arts with regional, national, and international perspectives.

New Mexico Magazine (505-827-7447; www.nmmagazine.com; Lew Wallace Building, 150 Old Santa Fe Trail, Santa Fe, NM 87501). A general-interest monthly published by state government, covering New Mexico culture, history, and travel.

Santa Fe New Mexican (505-983-3303; www.santafenewmexican.com; 202 E. Marcy St., Santa Fe, NM 87501). A general-interest daily distributed in northern New Mexico. Morning paper.

Santa Fe Reporter (505-988-5541; 132 E. Marcy St., Santa Fe, NM 87501). A general-interest weekly published each Wed. and distributed free of charge throughout Santa Fe and vicinity. Read for entertainment and film listings.

Taos News (575-758-2241; www.taosnews.com; 226 Albright St., Taos, NM 87571). A weekly newspaper covering local news and human interest. Comes out every Thurs.

RADIO STATIONS
KSFR-FM 90.7 (505-428-1527). Santa Fe; community radio, arts, culture, jazz, classical, local talk, and weather.
KTAO-FM 101.9 (575-758-5826). Taos; adult rock and local news.

TELEVISION STATIONS The major television stations are located in Albuquerque.
KASA FOX TV Channel 2 (505-246-2285). Albuquerque; reruns.
KNME TV Channel 5 (505-277-2121). Albuquerque; public television station.
KOAT TV Channel 7 (505-884-7777). Albuquerque; ABC affiliate.
KOB TV Channel 4 (505-243-4411). Albuquerque; NBC affiliate.
KRQE TV Channel 13 (505-243-2285). Albuquerque; CBS affiliate.

✳ Pueblos

The ancestors of Indians living today on New Mexico's 19 Indian pueblos dwelled in the Southwest for many centuries; literally thousands of ruins dot the landscape. Their prehistoric period was marked by frequent migration and resettlement, but the 16th century opened a different era. During that time, Spanish conquistadors and settlers arrived. Concurrently, nomadic tribes of Athapaskan Indians began making periodic raids on the pueblos for slaves, food, and goods. Americans who came from the East in the 19th century brought more cultural, political, and economic pressures.

Today's Pueblo Indians are justly proud not only of their cultural and artistic traditions but also of their growing economic self-sufficiency. The pueblo villages are self-governing, sovereign entities with their own schools, clinics, and police forces. The Pueblo people operate numerous thriving businesses, in particular resorts and casinos. Many offer bargain buffets as well.

Many Pueblo Indians speak English and Spanish in addition to their native tongues. Their artwork is in great demand by collectors all over the world, and their powerful legacy enriches this part of the world in untold ways.

PUEBLO ETIQUETTE Here are some things to keep in mind when visiting a pueblo:

- Inquire ahead of time about visitors hours. Remember that some pueblos are closed to outsiders on certain days for religious activities.
- Drive slowly.
- Never bring drugs or alcoholic beverages to a pueblo.
- Stop at the visitor center or tribal office when you arrive. This is a requirement at all the pueblos. Some charge fees; others ask visitors to register.
- Do not walk into or on a kiva (circular ceremonial structures).
- Homes, kivas, and cemeteries are not open to non-pueblo visitors. However, if you are invited to come into someone's home to eat, it is considered impolite to refuse. (It's also considered polite to eat and leave promptly so that others can come in and eat.) Most pueblos have food concessions on feast days, when visitors can sample pueblo cooking.
- Remember that dances are religious ceremonies, not performances. Conduct yourself as if you were in a church. Revealing clothing, such as shorts and halter tops, is not acceptable. Don't talk or obstruct the view of others during the dances, don't applaud afterward, and don't approach the dancers or ask about the meaning of dances. The Pueblo people prefer not to discuss their beliefs with outsiders.
- Do not cut across the plaza or area where the dances are being performed. Always walk along the perimeter.
- For your comfort, bring along folding chairs to watch the dances from.
- Observe each pueblo's regulations on use of cameras, tape recorders, and drawing. Most pueblos forbid these activities during dances. (See pueblo listings below for particulars.) If you want to photograph a pueblo resident, ask permission first and give a donation to the family.

One of the best times to visit is on a feast day, the major public celebration at each pueblo. Ostensibly, feast days are named for particular saints; however, the tradition predates the arrival of the Spanish priests, who applied the names of saints to what were already holy days for the Pueblo people.

Feast days usually start with a Mass at the Catholic church. A priest may lead a procession of dancers to the church, and the dances begin sometime after Mass. In spring, summer, and early autumn, such dances as the Blue Corn Dance, Butterfly Dance, and Harvest Dance may be performed in observance of the planting and harvest. In winter, the hunting cycle is celebrated with Deer, Elk, and Buffalo dances. (See pueblo listings below for dates of feast days.)

On Christmas Eve and Christmas Day, you may see the Matachines dance at the Taos, Picuris, San Juan, Santa Clara, and San Ildefonso Pueblos. Dancers clothed in beaded headdresses with scarves over their mouths move to 16th-century Spanish folk tunes played on guitars and violins. The origins of the Matachines dance are obscure, but it is probably rooted in Moorish customs brought from Spain. Similar dances are performed in neighboring Spanish villages and throughout the hemisphere.

KEY NUMBERS **New Mexico Indian Affairs Department:** 505-476-1600; www.iad. state.nm.us; Wendell Chino Building, Second Floor, 1220 S. St. Francis Dr., Santa Fe, NM 87505.

Indian Pueblo Cultural Center: 505-843-7270; 866-855-7902; www.indianpueblo. org; 2401 12th St. N.W., Albuquerque, NM 87104. The best source for information on feast days and events, open to the public.

NEAR SANTA FE

Cochiti Pueblo (505-465-2244; www.pueblodecochiti.org; tribal office: P.O. Box 70, Cochiti Pueblo, NM 87072, Exit 264 from I-25, about 25 miles south of Santa Fe; Keresan language; feast day: July 14, San Buenaventura; no admission fee; cameras not allowed). Cochiti Pueblo remains firmly rooted in its past while building a strong future. The church, built in 1628 to honor San Buenaventura, still stands. Not far away is Cochiti Lake, a recreational community built on land leased from the pueblo, which also operates Cochiti Lake services such as fishing. Cochiti Lake has an 18-hole golf course. (See also "Swimming" on page 67–68 and "Water Sports" on page 68–70.)

Cochiti Pueblo is best known for its drums and evocative clay storyteller figurines. The popular storyteller figure was created in 1964 by Cochiti potter Helen Cordero, who says she was inspired by her grandfather telling stories to children. Now many pueblo potters make these popular storytellers in human and animal forms, but Cochiti storytellers are still the most highly prized. Cochiti drums, essential to the pueblo's ceremonies, are also widely coveted by collectors. Individual pueblo artists sell crafts out of their home studios.

Nambé Pueblo (505-455-2036; www.nambepueblo.org; Rt 1, Box 117-bb Santa Fe, NM 87506, drive 15 miles north of Santa Fe on US 285, 3 miles east on NM 503 to sign for Nambé Falls, then 2 miles to pueblo entrance; Tewa language; feast day: Oct. 4, St. Francisco de Asis; fees: sketching $15, still cameras $5, movie/video cameras $10; fees subject to change). A small pueblo set near the Sangre de Cristo Mountains in a piñon and juniper valley, Nambé (nam-BAY) retains a few original buildings, including mission ruins. Many tribal members work at nearby Los Alamos National Laboratory, in Española, or in Santa Fe. Beautiful Nambé Falls, one of the state's few waterfalls, is the setting for the annual Fourth of July Ceremonials. Nambé Falls Recreational Site (505-455-2304) offers fishing, picnicking, camping, boating, and sightseeing Apr.–Oct. Fees are charged for each activity. Many artists offer their pottery and wares for sale. For tours led by Native American guides, call **Buffalo Tours** (505-455-0526).

Pojoaque Pueblo (505-455-2278; www.pojoaque.org; 39 Camino del Rincon, Santa Fe, NM 87506; Tewa language; feast day: Dec. 12, Our Lady of Guadalupe; contact tribal governor's office at 505-455-3334 before sketching or filming). The 20 businesses that line the east side of US 285 at Pojoaque (po-WAH-kee) speak of an enterprising spirit and prosperity; you would not guess that Pojoaque is a pueblo that has pulled itself back from near extinction. Only mounds of earth remain of the original pueblo, and in the late 1800s the people themselves were almost wiped out by a smallpox epidemic.

In the 1930s, a new Pojoaque was founded, and a milestone was reached in 1983 when tribal members danced for the first time in more than 100 years. Now they celebrate Our Lady of Guadalupe Day and Reyes Day on Dec. 12.

Next to the Pojoaque Pueblo Tourist Information Center on US 285 is the **Poeh Center** (pronounced POE), a museum that hosts artist exhibits, weekend dance performances, and workshops (505-455-3334 www.poehcenter.org; 78 Cities of Gold Rd., Santa Fe, NM 87506; Mon.–Fri. 10 AM–4 PM, Sat. 10 AM–2 PM). The museum also serves as a training complex for Tewa artists, with archives and Tewa art collections. Also on Cities of Gold Road is **Cities of Gold Casino & Hotel** (800-455-3313; www.citiesofgold. com; 10-A Cities of Gold Rd.).

San Ildefonso Pueblo (505-455-2273; www.sanipueblo.org; 36 Tunyo Place, Santa Fe, NM 87501, drive 15 miles north of Santa Fe on US 285, turn left at NM 502, then 6 miles to entrance on right; Tewa language; feast day: Jan. 23, San Ildefonso; fees: $5 per carload, sketching and painting $25, videotaping $20, still cameras $10; fees subject to change; no photography allowed on feast day). San Ildefonso is world famous for its black-on-black pottery, a technique developed by Maria Martinez and her husband, Julian, in the 1920s. Maria was also among the first Pueblo potters to sign her work. Her pots are prized by private collectors and museums nationwide, and her descendants still make pottery, both innovative and traditional. Other artisans sell wares out of their homes. Inquire at the visitors and information center.

San Ildefonso also operates the **Maria Martinez Museum** (505-455-3549, Mon.–Fri. 8 AM–4 PM) with displays of local arts, embroidery, photography, pottery-making techniques, and Pueblo history. A stocked fishing lake is open Mar.–Oct.; permits can be obtained at the lake.

Ohkay Owingeh Pueblo (505-852-4400; www.indianpueblo.org/19-pueblos/pueblos; P.O. Box 1099, San Juan, NM 87566, drive 1 mile north of Española on NM 68, turn left onto US 74 at San Juan Pueblo sign, entrance is 1 mile farther; Tewa language; feast day: June 24, San Juan; cameras not allowed; contact tribal governor's office at 505-852-4400 to see whether pueblo is open).

In 1598 conquistador Don Juan de Oñate declared this prosperous and friendly pueblo the first capital of New Mexico. When Spanish demands for gold and slaves became too insistent, the people asked Oñate to take his capital somewhere else. (It ended up in Santa Fe.) A native named Popé (Po-PAY) organized the Pueblo Revolt in 1680 (see page 25).

The largest and northernmost of the Tewa-speaking pueblos, Ohkay Owingeh has two central plazas, with its Catholic Church and ceremonial kivas side by side. It also runs the **Ohkay Owingeh Arts & Crafts Cooperative**, a multipurpose complex where visitors can view and buy the pueblo's distinctive red incised pottery, a ware whose luster and geometric designs are coveted by collectors worldwide. San Juan artisans also excel at jewelry making, carving, weaving, and other arts.

The **Ohkay Casino and Restaurant** is a popular stop with a hotel and RV park. Fishing at the tribal lakes is open winter and summer; contact the tribal office for regulations. The powerful Turtle Dance is performed each Dec. 26.

Santa Clara Pueblo (505-753-7326; www.indianpueblo.org/19-pueblos/pueblos; P.O. Box 580, Española, NM 87532, 1.3 miles from Española on NM 30; Tewa language; feast day: Aug. 12, Santa Clara; fees: $5 adults, $4 seniors and children, adult fee includes still-camera permit, no sketching or video cameras allowed). The **Santa Claran Hotel** (877-505-4949; www.santaclaran.com) offers rooms with adobe fireplaces and espouses the values of the pueblo itself.

Set in the wide Rio Grande Valley with vistas of mountains on either side, Santa Clara is home to 2,600 enterprising tribal members who farm, work at jobs outside the pueblo, and create stunning red and black polished pottery, sculpture, and paintings. They are the descendants of the ancient Puye cliff dwellers, and their name for their pueblo, Kha P'o, means "singing water."

Santa Clara potters are noted for their intricately carved pottery (sgraffito), particularly the etched miniatures. Look for POTTERY FOR SALE signs on houses; you'll be invited to come in and meet the artist. Santa Clara also offers guided tours of the pueblo and its historical church. On the tours, you'll be allowed to photograph, see pottery demonstrations, buy native foods, and perhaps see a dance. Tours are offered weekdays only, with five days' advance notice. Inquire at the tourism office or phone the number for the pueblo above.

Santa Clara Canyon Recreational Area, a rugged natural spot, is open to visitors Apr.–Oct. for camping, picnicking, and fishing. Inquire about fees at the tourism office.

The Conchas Fire of 2011 badly burned and damaged the pueblo and its watershed. Restoration is in process.

Santo Domingo Pueblo (505-465-2214; www.santodomingotribe.org; P.O. Box 99, Santo Domingo Pueblo, NM 87052, about 34 miles south of Santa Fe on I-25; Keresan language; feast day: Aug. 4, Santo Domingo; no cameras, sketching, or recording allowed; donations accepted). For information on the Santo Domingo Pueblo Arts & Crafts Market, held Labor Day weekend and featuring 300 booths of jewelry, pottery, artwork, and Indian food, call 505-465-0406. Santo Domingo is home to an amazing number of creative and enterprising artists. Many have transformed the traditional *heishi* and turquoise jewelry-making techniques into beautiful contemporary designs. Others have revived the ancient Santo Domingo pottery tradition and are producing superb blends of old and new. Santo Domingo jewelry is available from artists selling under the portal of the Palace of the Governors in Santa Fe and at shops at the pueblo. The Aug. 4 Feast Day Corn Dance is an unforgettable scene, with hundreds of dancers, singers, and clowns participating in all-day ceremonies.

Tesuque Pueblo (505-955-0139; www.indianpueblo.org/19-pueblos/pueblos; 503 Riverview Lane, Box, Pack and Mail, Española, NM 87532, 9 miles north of Santa Fe on US 285, main village is 1 mile west of highway; Tewa language; feast day: Nov. 12, San Diego; no photography or video). Though close to Santa Fe and operating several successful businesses, Tesuque (te-SOO-kay) is one of the most conservative of the pueblos. The site was occupied as far back as 1250; however, the original pueblo was at another location that was abandoned after the Pueblo Revolt of 1680.

The present pueblo was established in 1694. Listed on the National Register of Historic Places, Tesuque has a large central plaza with a Catholic Church. The tribe operates **Camel Rock Casino** (800-462-2635; www.camelrockcasino.com) on US 84/285, along with a store (505-983-2667) and the **Tesuque Natural Farm** (505-983-2667), where certified organic blue corn, chile, and other vegetables are grown. Several artists' studios are open to the public, selling mostly traditional Tesuque clay figurines, pottery, beadwork, drums, weavings, and carvings. Inquire at the tribal office.

NEAR TAOS

Picuris Pueblo (505-587-2519; www.indianpueblo.org/19-pueblos/pueblos; P.O. Box 127, Peñasco, NM 87553, drive 17 miles north from Española to junction with NM 75, turn right and continue 13 miles to Picuris; Tewa language; feast day: Aug. 10, San Lorenzo; fees: sketching $20, still cameras $5, movie/video cameras $15, self-guided ruin tours $3, call in advance about tours; fees also for fishing and camping, inquire at Picuris Pueblo Fish & Game and Parks & Wildlife, 505-587-1601).

In 1519, Picuris (pee-ku-REES) was the last pueblo to be discovered by the Spaniards; it is nearly hidden in the Sangre de Cristo Mountains. It was settled in the 1200s and about 200 years later had grown into a multistoried adobe complex. Picuris was abandoned after the 1680 Pueblo Revolt and reestablished in the 1700s. It has never made a treaty with another government and retains its status as a sovereign nation and tribe.

The smallest of the pueblos, Picuris operates several facilities for visitors. The Hidden Valley Shop and Restaurant includes a small convenience store and smoke shop, fishing equipment, and arts and crafts. Inquire at the tribal office about hours. Pu-Na and Tu-Tah Lakes are stocked ponds with a picnic area. The Picuris Pueblo Museum displays authentic Indian arts, crafts, and pottery.

✳ Real Estate

If owning a home in the Land of Enchantment sounds like a dream come true, then you might be interested in a little housing information.

If you're shopping for real estate in the Santa Fe or Taos areas, you can get information in a variety of ways. For a list of realtors, consult the Yellow Pages or contact the chambers of commerce. The **Santa Fe County Chamber of Commerce** (505-988-3279) is located at 1644 St. Michael's Dr., Santa Fe, NM 87507. The mailing address for the **Taos Visitor Center** (575-758-3873) is 1139 Paseo del Pueblo Sur, Taos, NM 87571. Both organizations will send lists of their realtor members.

If you're thinking about buying property here, it's a good idea to study local zoning laws, building permits, restrictive covenants, and so forth. Also see "Local Government: City Halls and ZIP Codes" on page 75–76.

✳ Road Services

Here is a list of some 24-hour emergency road services in the Santa Fe–Taos region.

SANTA FE

A-1 Towing: 505-983-1616
A-Jack Towing: 505-438-6042
Flores Wrecker Service: 505-471-5271

TAOS

AA-1 Wrecker Service: 575-758-8984
AC Towing & Transport Service: 575-758-1111

ESPAÑOLA

Holmes Wrecker Service: 505-753-3460

LOS ALAMOS

Knecht Automotive: 505-662-2868
RPM Automotive Towing: 505-662-7721

GLOSSARY

For the most part, Spanish pronunciation is phonetic. That is, it sounds the way it looks—with a few exceptions: *ll* sounds like "yuh"; *j* sounds like "h"; *qu* sounds like "k"; and *ñ* sounds like "ny." There are also a few tricky rules—for example, double *r*'s are trilled, and *d* is often pronounced "th"—but we'll leave these details for Spanish classes. Following, then, are reasonable pronunciations and short definitions for Spanish words (and a few other terms) that are commonly used in the Santa Fe–Taos area.

acequia (ah-SEH-kee-ya)—irrigation ditch.

Anasazi (an-a-SAH-zee)—Navajo word meaning "ancient strangers," used to refer to the peoples who inhabited such places as Chaco Canyon, Mesa Verde, and Bandelier National Monument A.D. 900–1300.

arroyo (a-ROY-oh)—dry gully or streambed.

arroz (a-ROSS)—rice.

banco (BONK-oh)—adobe bench, usually an extension of an adobe wall.

bizcochitos (biz-koh-CHEE-tose)—cookies.

bulto (BOOL-toh)—traditional Hispanic three-dimensional carving of a saint.

burrito (boo-REE-toh)—flour tortilla usually wrapped around a filling of beans, meat, cheese, and sauce.

canales (ka-NAL-ess)—gutters, rainspouts.

cantina (kan-TEE-na)—saloon or barroom.

capirotada (ka-pi-ro-TA-da)—bread pudding.

carne (KAR-ne)—meat.

carne adovada (KAR-ne ah-do-VA-da)—meat chunks (usually pork) marinated in red chile sauce.

carne asada (KAR-ne ah-SA-da)—roast beef.

carnitas (kar-NEE-tas)—strips of beef or pork marinated in green chile.

carreta (ka-RET-ah)—wagon.

casita (ka-SEE-ta)—cottage; one-room guesthouse.

chicharrones (chick-a-ROH-nees)—crispy fried pork rinds.

chile (CHEE-leh)—sauce made from either red or green chile peppers, used for seasoning most foods in northern New Mexico.

chile relleno (CHEE-leh re-YEH-no)—crisp, batter-fried green chile pepper stuffed with chicken and/or cheese.

chimenea (chee-me-NEH-ya)—chimney.

chorizo (cho-REE-so)—spicy Mexican sausage.

concha (KON-cha)—belt of inscribed silver plates originally made by the Navajo Indians.

con queso (cone KEH-so)—with cheese.

corbel (kor-BELL)—wooden beam support, usually ornately carved.

curandera (coor-an-DEH-ra)—female Hispanic healer who uses a combination of herbal and other folk remedies.

empanada (em-pa-NAH-da)—fried pie stuffed with seasoned, chopped meat and vegetables or fruit, then sealed and deep-fried; in northern New Mexico, often filled with piñon nuts, currants, spices, and wine.

enchilada (en-chi-LA-da)—flour tortilla filled with cheese, chicken, or meat and covered with red or green chile.

fajitas (fa-HEE-tas)—small strips of highly seasoned, charbroiled meat eaten in a rolled tortilla with guacamole and sour cream.

farolito (far-oh-LEE-toh)—paper bag containing a glowing candle, often displayed in rows around Christmastime to symbolize the arrival of the Christ Child.

flan—caramel custard covered with burned-sugar syrup, a traditional northern New Mexican dessert.

fry bread (not "fried bread")—*sopaipillas* made by the Pueblo Indians.

guacamole (gwok-a-MOLE-eh)—a thick sauce or paste made with a mix of mashed avocados and salsa.

hacienda (AH-see-EN-da)—a large estate, dwelling, or plantation.

heishi (HEE-she)—jewelry made of tiny, hand-carved shell beads.

horno (OR-no)—beehive-shaped outdoor oven for the making of bread, originally brought from Spain.

huevos (WEH-vose)—eggs.

huevos rancheros (WEH-vose ran-CHEH-ros)—fried eggs with red chile sauce, cheese, and lettuce.

jalapeño (HALL-a-PEN-yoh)—small hot pepper.

kachina doll (ka-CHEE-na)—a small wooden doll representing a Hopi spirit, usually carved from cottonwood.

kiva (KEE-va)—circular underground chamber used by the Pueblo Indians for ceremonial and other purposes.

kiva fireplace—traditional adobe fireplace, usually small, beehive shaped, and placed in a corner.

latillas (la-TEE-ahs)—network of thin wooden strips placed over beams or vigas just beneath the roof.

luminaria (loo-mi-NA-ree-ah)—hot, smoky bonfire made of pitchy piñon pine to celebrate the Christmas season.

nachos (NA-chos)—tortilla chips covered with a mix of beans, cheese, and chile, baked and served as hors d'oeuvres.

natillas (na-TEE-ahs)—vanilla custard, a traditional northern New Mexican dessert.

nicho (NEE-cho)—recessed niche in an adobe wall for holding a statue or other ornament.

panocha (pan-OH-cha)—wheat flour pudding.

placita (pla-SEE-ta)—patio.

pollo (PO-yo)—chicken.

portal (por-TALL)—covered patio or sidewalk with supports and fixed roof.

posada (po-SA-da)—resting place or inn.

posole (po-SOLE-eh)—a hominy-like corn stew.

pueblo (PWEB-loh)—a Native American communal village of the Southwest consisting of multitiered adobe structures with flat roofs around a central plaza.

quesadillas (KEH-sa-DEE-yas)—lightly grilled tortillas stuffed with chicken, beef, or beans.

reredos (reh-REH-dose)—carved altar screen for church.

retablo (reh-TAB-loh)—traditional Hispanic painting of a saint on a wooden plaque.

ristra (REES-tra)—string of dried red chiles, often hung on front porches.

salsa (SAL-sa)—traditional northern New Mexican hot sauce composed of tomatoes, onions, peppers, and spices.

santero (san-TEH-roh)—artist who depicts saints.

santo (SAN-toh)—a painted or carved representation of a saint.

sopaipilla (so-pie-PEE-ya)—Spanish popover. These "little pillows" puff up when fried, providing convenient hollows to fill with honey or butter.

taco (TA-koh)—folded corn tortilla usually filled with beans, meat, cheese, tomato, and lettuce.

tamale (ta-MAL-eh)—cornmeal stuffed with chicken or pork and red chile, wrapped in corn husks and steamed.

tapas (TAP-ahs)—appetizers.

tortilla (tor-TEE-ya)—thin pancake made of cornmeal or wheat flour.

tostados (tos-TA-dos)—corn tortillas quartered and fried until crisp, usually eaten as hors d'oeuvres.

trastero (tras-TER-oh)—wooden, freestanding closet or chest of drawers dating from the 17th century; usually ornately carved.

vigas (VEE-gas)—heavy ceiling beams usually made of rough-hewn tree trunks, traditional in Southwest architecture.

zaguan (zag-WAN)—long, covered porch.

SANTA FE

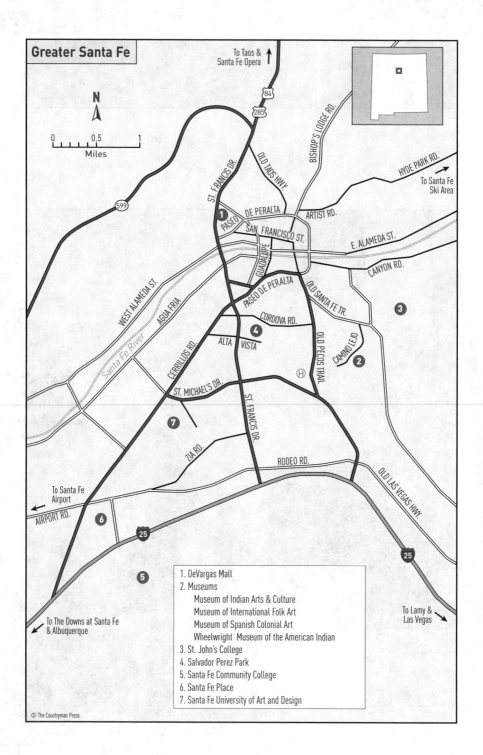

Greater Santa Fe

To Taos &
Santa Fe Opera

To Santa Fe
Ski Area

N

0   0.5   1
Miles

84
285

BISHOP'S LODGE RD.
HYDE PARK RD.

ST. FRANCIS DR.
OLD TAOS HWY

599

PASEO DE PERALTA
ARTIST RD.

① SAN FRANCISCO ST.
E. ALAMEDA ST.

GUADALUPE
CANYON RD.

WEST ALAMEDA ST.
AGUA FRIA
Santa Fe River
PASEO DE PERALTA
OLD SANTA FE TR.

③

CORDOVA RD.

CERRILLOS RD.
ALTA VISTA
④
CAMINO LEJO
②

OLD PECOS TRAIL

Ⓗ

ST. MICHAEL'S DR.

ST. FRANCIS DR.

⑦

ZIA RD.
RODEO RD.

OLD LAS VEGAS HWY

To Santa Fe
Airport

AIRPORT RD.
⑥

㉕

⑤

To The Downs at Santa Fe
& Albuquerque

㉕

To Lamy &
Las Vegas

1. DeVargas Mall
2. Museums
    Museum of Indian Arts & Culture
    Museum of International Folk Art
    Museum of Spanish Colonial Art
    Wheelwright Museum of the American Indian
3. St. John's College
4. Salvador Perez Park
5. Santa Fe Community College
6. Santa Fe Place
7. Santa Fe University of Art and Design

© The Countryman Press

SANTA FE

The Santa Fe–Taos area offers hundreds of restaurants serving everything from New Mexican, American, and Continental to French, Chinese, Japanese, and East Indian cuisine. In addition, scores of food purveyors offer unique drinks, pastries, baked goods, candies, and delicacies. The combination is enough to satisfy the most far-ranging or curious appetite.

We searched for a variety of places and price ranges—everything from Santa Fe's internationally acclaimed gourmet dining spots to corner taco stands. We looked for unique local dining experiences and so avoided fast-food and chain restaurants. Fortunately, we were free to write honest reviews, because we were in no way beholden to these establishments. The results, we are confident, will steer you to the best dining the area has to offer. We have attempted to provide a range of dining opportunities, from the casual pizza or sandwich to the world-famous new southwestern cuisine that has its origins here. The combination of fresh local ingredients—inspired by growers' markets—and some of the most creative and well-traveled chefs in the world make this an exciting dining scene. Exploring the cuisine is one of the most memorable aspects of a visit here.

A note to smokers: Smoking is not allowed in Santa Fe or Taos restaurants. Some places permit smoking on the patio, and certainly some establishments that qualify more as bars than restaurants permit smoking. A few have separate smoking rooms.

One thing you'll find on your gastronomic travels in Santa Fe and Taos is a plethora of New Mexican restaurants. Remember: New Mexican cooking—particularly northern New Mexican cooking—is not Mexican or Tex-Mex; it's a unique mix of Spanish, Mexican, Pueblo Indian, and local cuisine that includes many familiar foods like burritos, enchiladas, and tacos, as well as less familiar foods such as *flautas, sopaipillas,* and *chicharrones.* This cuisine has its roots in the native foods of corn, chile, beans, and squash.

The most important single ingredient in northern New Mexican cuisine is chile, which should not be confused with chili, the tomato-sauce-based concoctions found in Texas, Ohio, and other parts of the country. New Mexican chile sauces have little or no tomato. They're flavorful, spicy, sometimes hot sauces made with a mix of chile peppers, garlic, oregano, and

LOVE A GOOD FRY BREAD? FIND FABULOUS JUST-MADE INDIAN TACOS AT LOCAL ARTS FESTIVALS LIKE THE ANNUAL DIXON STUDIO TOUR

I THINK I LIKE THIS ONE BEST!

cumin, and they're served with almost every meal. Chile can be red or green, hot or mild, and there's no telling by color which is which. So when your waiter says, "Red or green?"—a query that happens to be the official state question—don't be afraid to ask which is hotter. If you say Christmas, you'll get some of both.

While the best-known Santa Fe restaurants may carry a well-earned reputation for being expensive, if you know where to go and follow our suggestions as well as your own traveler's instincts, you should be able to dine surprisingly well, even on a budget. We'll point you to the locals' favorites where both excellent food and fine service can be had for a modest price.

The restaurants listed in this book are given a price code based on the average cost of a single meal, including appetizer, entrée, dessert, tax, and tip, but not including alcoholic beverages..

For the sake of convenience and interest, this book divides Santa Fe into several neighborhoods so that each one may be explored in depth. Each one has its own distinct sense of place. Due to the difficulty of parking, and understanding the limits of time, we hope this organization makes the most efficient and effective way to explore. However, nothing is that far away, so you can feel free to devise your itinerary as you go. The districts, or neighborhoods, are: The Plaza, Canyon Road, Guadalupe/Railyard/Baca St. District, Museum Hill, Cerrillos Road/Southside, and North Side. Within each district are listed Lodging, Dining, Museums, Sites, Shopping, and Outdoors, as well as particular attractions each area is noted for.

Nightlife, music, annual calendar events, and fiestas are grouped together toward the end of the Santa Fe section.

✳ Santa Fe—stroll

For a 30- to 45-minute walking tour of Santa Fe, we suggest starting on the Plaza, perhaps at the monument that stands in the middle of the old square. Take time to look at the blend of the old and new, the Spanish and Territorial architecture that coexists with gleaming art galleries and boutiques. Then head east for a block, stopping in at Sena Plaza on Palace Avenue, a hidden courtyard filled with shops. Turn south onto Cathedral Place past tree-filled Cathedral Park, and pay a visit to the magnificent Cathedral Basilica of St. Francis of Assisi. Then go west on San Francisco Street back toward the Plaza and peek in at the historic La Fonda

CAFÉ PASQUAL'S IS THE PLACE FOR A LEGENDARY BREAKFAST IN SANTA FE OR A MESO-AMERICAN-INSPIRED DINNER

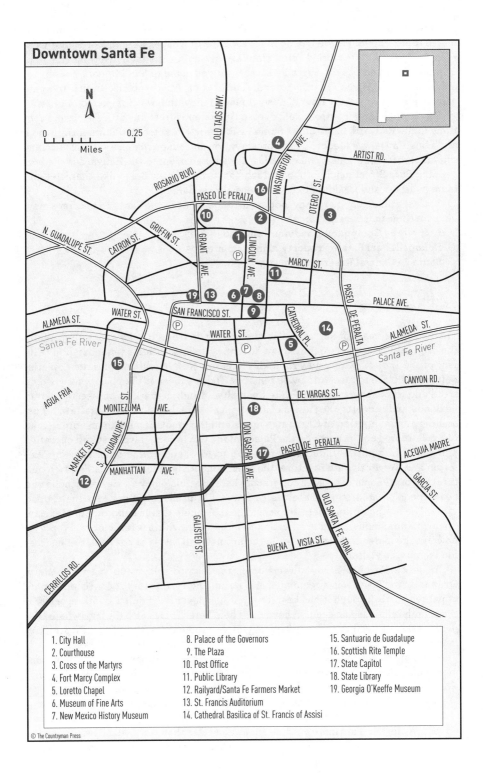

Downtown Santa Fe

N

0   0.25
Miles

OLD TAOS HWY.

ARTIST RD.

WASHINGTON AVE.

ROSARIO BLVD.

PASEO DE PERALTA

OTERO ST.

N. GUADALUPE ST.

CATRON ST.

GRIFFIN ST.

GRANT AVE.

LINCOLN AVE.

MARCY ST.

PASEO DE PERALTA

PALACE AVE.

WATER ST.

SAN FRANCISCO ST.

CATHEDRAL PL.

ALAMEDA ST.

WATER ST.

Santa Fe River

ALAMEDA ST.

Santa Fe River

CANYON RD.

AGUA FRIA

MONTEZUMA AVE.

ST.

DE VARGAS ST.

MARKET ST.

S. GUADALUPE ST.

MANHATTAN AVE.

DON GASPAR AVE.

PASEO DE PERALTA

ACEQUIA MADRE

GARCIA ST.

GALISTEO ST.

OLD SANTA FE TRAIL

BUENA VISTA ST.

CERRILLOS RD.

1. City Hall
2. Courthouse
3. Cross of the Martyrs
4. Fort Marcy Complex
5. Loretto Chapel
6. Museum of Fine Arts
7. New Mexico History Museum
8. Palace of the Governors
9. The Plaza
10. Post Office
11. Public Library
12. Railyard/Santa Fe Farmers Market
13. St. Francis Auditorium
14. Cathedral Basilica of St. Francis of Assisi
15. Santuario de Guadalupe
16. Scottish Rite Temple
17. State Capitol
18. State Library
19. Georgia O'Keeffe Museum

Hotel, located at the end of the Old Santa Fe Trail. Stroll south along this famous commerce route, and you'll soon come to lovely Loretto Chapel, a replica of Sainte-Chapelle in Paris, with its storied spiral staircase giving it a distinctly New Mexico flair. Continue south across the Santa Fe River until you come to San Miguel Mission, the oldest church in America, dating from the early 1600s. Another block south is the state capitol, also known as the Roundhouse. A major renovation was completed in 1992.

For another Santa Fe stroll, walk over to Guadalupe Street, then take a left and continue to the Railyard, home of the Santa Fe Farmers Market, a Rail Runner train stop, and a bustling new center of historic preservation and adaptive reuse with restaurants, nightlife, cafés, boutiques, and galleries. Directly adjacent to the Railyard is the burgeoning Baca Street neighborhood, which has its own funky SoHo-like character and more galleries, and is adding to its offerings almost daily.

For last-minute or emergency lodging arrangements in the Santa Fe and Taos area, here are some numbers to phone.

Fort Marcy Compound Condominiums: 505-988-2800
Kokopelli Real Estate Property Management: 505-988-7244
Santa Fe Central Reservations: 505-983-8200

✳ The Plaza

The Plaza, the heart of Santa Fe, has changed little from the city's founding. While the original Plaza was larger, laid out according to specifications mandated in "The Law of the Indies," which governed all of Spain's New World colonies, its essential nature as a place to meet and trade remains. Today's plaza is the place where people stroll and where special events—like Spanish and Indian markets and fiestas, Santa Fe Bandstand concerts, the Fourth of July pancake breakfast, arts and crafts exhibits, and the annual lighting of Christmas lights and the giant Hanukkah menorah—take place. Bordered on the north by the Palace of the Governors, the oldest still operative public building in the United States, dating to 1610, and on the other sides by Victorian and Territorial architecture, the Plaza embodies much of Santa Fe's rich cultural history. People of all ages congregate here to stroll, enjoy an ice cream cone or a snack, people watch, sun themselves, grab a rest from shopping, and take in the good vibes. The dining options here are sensational. Cuisine that is a mixture of Mexican, Spanish, indigenous, Mediterranean, and more is all within a few blocks. World-renowned chefs give it their best, while the aromas and tastes of cozy cafés and street food tempt the visitor.

At the center of town and always open, the Plaza displays 400 years of history. Originally the Plaza was a rectangle, and for much of its history it consisted mainly of packed earth. Though it has been dusty, it has never been dull. Countless celebrations, both religious and secular, have been held here. This is also the spot where Hispanic residents used to conduct Saturday-night promenades, complete with strolling musicians.

Today strollers and teenage plaza rats still keep the Plaza hopping on pleasant summer evenings. Hardly anyone would think of holding a demonstration or vigil anywhere but the Plaza, and it's still one of the best people-watching spots in the city.

Strolling the streets that radiate out of the Plaza—Don Gaspar, Lincoln, Washington, over to Palace and Marcy—yields a knowledge of the city that can only be obtained on foot. While there are more alluring shops and cafés than time will allow, it's good to make note of them for another day or another trip. Here are just a few of my tried-and-true places to dine, stay, shop, and learn.

✳ Dining

Santa Fe is loaded with fine dining options, and many world-famous chefs ply their trade here. As expected, the price tag for a dinner at several of these establishments can run well over $200 per person. While places like Geronimo, Santacafé, The Old House, and the Coyote Café used to reign supreme when it came to a splurge, the diner may now choose among many high-end restaurants: Eloisa, in the Drury Inn, is headed up by Chef Jon Sedlar; Martin's is captained by James Beard Award–winning chef Martin Rios; longtime Santa Fe restaurateur Fernando Olea now runs Sazon; and there are many more, including Joseph's, Georgia, and the Four Seasons Terra in Tesuque. Other notable, newer high-end dining spots are Bouche and Radish and Rye. Each is outstanding in its own way, and there is neither enough time nor pages to do each justice. Instead, this book will concentrate on sharing many lesser-known and out-of-the-way places to get a good, affordable meal.

The Shed (505-982-9030; 113½ E. Palace Ave., Santa Fe, NM 87501; closed Sun., Thanksgiving, Christmas, New Year's; inexpensive–moderate; Mexican, American; L, D; partial handicapped access; reservations recommended; special features: fireplaces, patio, enclosed in winter). Located in an adobe dating from 1692, this long-established restaurant is a landmark. The winding rooms and narrow hallways add to the historic atmosphere. Wear casual or go stylish. Located off the street, tucked back into an enclosed patio, it appeals to Mexican food lovers. Aside from the many blue corn entrées, what sets this restaurant apart is the chile. Straight from the farm, the chiles are ground on the premises; for more subtle palates, the freshness is indeed noticeable. Selections of fish and beef dishes help widen the choice for those a little timid about Mexican food. Wine is served by the glass or the bottle; beer is on draft. In

MOJITOS, ANYONE? IT'S COYOTE CAFE'S ROOFTOP CANTINA FOR CHIPS AND SALSA OR A FULL MENU OF MEXICAN FARE DURING THE WARM SEASON

summer, the patio makes for perfect dining, and a table by one of the corner fireplaces can take the winter chill off and add to the romance of a good meal. You'll know you can't be anywhere on earth but Santa Fe. Usually crowded, so plan accordingly.

Santa Fe Bite (505-982-0544; 311 Old Santa Fe Trail, Santa Fe, NM 87501; Tues.-Thurs. 11 AM–8 PM, Fri. 11 AM–9 PM, Sat. 8 AM–9 PM, Sun. 8 AM–8 PM [breakfast served 8 AM–2 PM]; closed Mon.; inexpensive–moderate; American, Mexican; B, L, D). Located in Garrett's Desert Inn, Santa Fe Bite is a relocation of the legendary Bobcat Bite on Las Vegas Highway. This place couldn't be more different—it's convenient, light and bright, and there's rarely a wait. Fine for a burger, but what it gained in accessibility it lost in character. If you've never been to the original, you wouldn't notice.

Plaza Café Downtown (505-982-1664; 54 Lincoln on West Side of Santa Fe Plaza, Santa Fe, NM 87501; open daily 7 AM–9 PM; inexpensive–moderate; American, Greek, New Mexican; B, L, D; partial handicapped access). A shout of glee went up from the citizenry when the Plaza Café, a downtown fixture since 1905, reopened mid-2012 after a devastating kitchen fire. And it really does look the same—a trip back in time. As close as Santa Fe gets to a diner serving everything from cashew mole enchiladas to Greek salad, a mighty fine burger, gyros, club sandwiches, and excellent green chile stew, the comfy Plaza Café is where folks love to meet up. Towering coconut cream pie and moist carrot cake will tempt you. You can't beat the breakfast of blue corn piñon pancakes or huevos rancheros.

La Plazuela Restaurant (505-982-5511; La Fonda Hotel, 100 E. San Francisco St., Santa Fe, NM 87501; open daily; moderate–expensive; Spanish, Mexican, New Mexican, Continental; B, L, D; full handicapped access; reservations recommended for dinner; special features: covered patio, hand-painted windows, hand-carved wood furniture, stone floor). The central courtyard of the landmark La Fonda Hotel was once a patio open to the sky. Now enclosed, the restaurant retains the charm of outdoor dining as diners sit beneath huge potted trees basking in filtered sun through the skylight. Color and light are everywhere—brightly painted panes of glass run from floor to ceiling, gaily covered with designs of birds and flowers by local artist Ernesto Martinez, who also created the hotel's hallway decorations, murals, and painted ballroom. The menu is known for its traditional northern New Mexico specialties, including a combination plate with tamales, cheese enchilada, and green *chile relleno*. The *rellenos* de La Fonda are homemade, served with *posole* and fluffy *sopaipillas*. Lamb, cedar-planked salmon, and steak are on the menu as well.

Chef Lane Warner's signature dishes include chipotle-glazed filet mignon and chicken breasts marinated in tequila and lime. Desserts, made on the premises, include Mexican chocolate streusel, the perennial favorite, or a brownie served with homemade banana ice cream. Ice cream flavors change daily and may include everything from vanilla to prickly pear. The black bean soup is almost too beautiful to eat. Almost but not quite. Order the guacamole made tableside and you may never go home. A great spot for a working breakfast, too.

Il Piatto Italian Farmhouse Kitchen (505-984-1091; 95 W. Marcy St., Santa Fe, NM 87501; open daily; moderate; innovative Italian; L, D; full handicapped access; reservations recommended; special features: patio dining, take-out). Reinventing itself as an Italian farmhouse hasn't hurt Il Piatto a bit. Come here for the green-lipped mussels baked in garlic aioli, or the creamy wild mushroom risotto. The antipasto makes an excellent start to a meal. Small, unpretentious, with superb food, Il Piatto features fresh soups and crisp salads, a variety of tasty antipasti and pastas, traditional Italian specials such as chicken cacciatore, and grilled selections, all with homemade pasta. But the pasta dishes with delectable sauces are the real treat. The chef shops for seasonal local produce at the farmers' market and isn't shy about making seasonal menu changes. Homemade desserts include such delectables as tiramisu (sponge cake soaked in coffee liqueur) and baked chocolate mousse with blackberries. There's also a moderately priced wine list and a selection of dessert wines and port. On warm days you can dine on the little streetside patio, and in the evening, Il Piatto creates a romantic mood with music and candlelight. Chef Matt Yohalem goes all out for his customers. The three-course prix fixe menu allows all kinds of flexibility in ordering. Special late afternoon bar menu with wine bargains and later night hours add to the appeal.

Rio Chama Steakhouse (505-955-0765; 414 Old Santa Fe Trail, Santa Fe, NM 87501; closed Christmas; expensive; American; L, D; partial handicapped access; reservations recommended; special features: full bar, patio dining). Here's a good place to get back to the basics: prime dry-aged beef in the form of thick, tender, succulent rib eyes, filets, and luscious Black Angus prime rib; fabulous house-made onion rings, beefsteak tomato salad, rich creamed spinach, and shrimp cocktail. So you're going light or your sister-in-law is a vegetarian? Rio Chama serves grilled chicken, lamb, tuna, and a veggie plate. This informally elegant eatery is enough to transform a vegetarian into an omnivore. An ooey-gooey fondue, served to be shared in the lively bar, especially popular during the January legislative session, warms up a chilly night. And don't forget that Rio Chama serves a mean blue cheese green chile burger that will help keep you within budget without sacrificing a thing.

French Pastry Shop (505-983-6697; La Fonda Hotel, 100 E. San Francisco St., Santa Fe, NM 87501; closed Christmas; inexpensive; French; B, L; partial handicapped access [enter from La Fonda Hotel]; no reservations; no credit cards). Chocolate éclairs, croissants, palmiers, napoleons, café au lait, espresso, fresh fruit tarts, chocolate mousse, dessert crêpes, fresh strawberries with crème Chantilly . . . are you drooling yet? This little shop of gastronomic delights has provided the Santa Fe community with authentic French cuisine since 1974, both for café au lait with pastry and for light lunch. A sign says ALL PASTRIES ARE MADE WITH PURE BUTTER AND ARE MADE FRESH DAILY. Famous, too, for breads baked in whimsical animal designs—you can order your own. The reasonably priced menu includes ratatouille, torte Milanaise, and French onion soup as well as quiche Lorraine. The perfect spot for a cozy cup of cocoa on a wintry afternoon. Bon appétit! The restaurant's iconic Santa Fe style was created by Mary Elizabeth Jane Colter, designer for the Fred Harvey Company.

Tia Sophia's (505-983-9880; 210 W. San Francisco St., Santa Fe, NM 87501; closed Sun., major holidays; inexpensive; New Mexican; B, L; handicapped access; no reservations). Located in the heart of San Francisco Street, Tia Sophia's is an unassuming little restaurant that serves consistently good New Mexican meals in a family atmosphere. Daily breakfast and lunch specials are popular and affordable, and it's still patronized by loyal old-timers and politicos. This is the place for a classic Santa Fe breakfast. The breakfast burritos and huevos rancheros are worth ordering for those with a hearty morning appetite. For lunch, order one of the homemade stuffed *sopaipillas*. Please note that Tia Sophia's closes promptly at 2 pm. Eat, then shop.

India Palace (505-986-5859; 227 Don Gaspar Ave., Santa Fe, NM 87501; open daily; inexpensive–moderate; East Indian; L, D; partial handicapped access; no smoking; reservations recommended for dinner; special features: patio dining, take-out, lunch buffet, Indian art). The India Palace offers the exquisite and complex tastes of the Indian subcontinent in an intimate and luxurious setting with pink linen. A fountain plays and statues of gods smile serenely as diners sample delicacies from all regions of India. Appetizers include the crisp fried patties called samosas and many Indian breads, from leavened naan to paratha stuffed with spinach, all baked fresh to order. Tandoori specialties include several kinds of chicken and lamb. Curries abound and can be prepared mild enough for any taste. There are also the vegetarian dishes for which India is famous, from creamed lentil dal to bhindi masala or spiced okra. Lunch is the best time to go, when you can sample their reasonably priced buffet to your heart's content. The buffet provides a cross section of the menu—beautifully presented and a great bargain feast. You'll want a siesta afterward.

Cafe Pasqual's (505-629-0283; 121 Don Gaspar Ave., Santa Fe, NM 87501; closed Thanksgiving, Christmas; moderate–expensive; New Mexican, new southwestern cuisine; B, L, D; partial handicapped access; reservations strongly recommended for dinner; special features: community table, T-shirts, cookbooks). There's good reason for the lines down Water Street waiting to get into this legendary Santa Fe eatery, much as there's ample reason why Cafe Pasqual's consistently makes lists of "best places to have breakfast in the U.S." That famous huge, delicious, Mexican-flavored breakfast is served all day, and no visit to Santa Fe is complete without it. Carefully prepared food; consistency; friendly service (once you get in); a bustling atmosphere with colorful murals, chile *ristras*, and bright Mexican banners make this cozy café memorable. To avoid the crowd, arrive in the off-hours or sit at the congenial community table.

For breakfast, you'll ooh and aah over the Genovese omelet with sun-dried tomatoes and pine nuts. For lunch, savor the tangy taste of a zesty shrimp cocktail, a heavenly grilled salmon burrito, or a healthful Yucatán free-range chicken breast salad. You can slice dinner costs with half orders and still come away satisfied. And you'll drool over the rich assortment of desserts and pastries. (Hint: Try the toasted piñon ice cream with caramel sauce.) Owner Kathy Kagel is almost as well known for organizing to feed the hungry in northern New Mexico as she is for her abilities as a chef!

One of the best and most popular places in Santa Fe is the **The Burrito Company** (505-982-4453; 111 Washington Ave.), less than a block from the Plaza. Breakfast and lunch menus feature such favorites as fast burritos, Mexican plates, hot dogs, hamburgers, and New Mexico–style chile dogs. Here you can get a good blue corn chicken enchilada for a song. They also sell their own salsa and chile by the quart. It's a convenient local hangout, highly recommended for families and folks in a hurry.

While on the Plaza, you can get a delicious lunch as well as the quintessential Santa Fe experience for about $6 at **Roque's Carnitas**. Just follow the tantalizing aroma to the Roque's cart on the corner of Washington and Palace Avenue, then claim a bench on the Plaza for some people-watching.

At **Del Charro** (505-954-0320; 101 W. Alameda St; open daily; inexpensive), where you can get a yummy lunch for less than $8, including homemade fries, creamy green chile chicken soup, burgers, and enchiladas that taste far more costly, you can also sip a margarita or Guinness on tap. Dine at the bar or on the heated patio with a large outdoor fireplace.

Coyote Café (505-983-1615; 132 W. Water St.; open daily; very expensive; new southwestern; L [summer weekends], D; full handicapped access; reservations strongly recommended; special features: patio dining). Santa Fe's Coyote Café is restaurateuring on a grand scale. Virtuoso chef Mark Miller practically invented Santa Fe–style cooking. Each dish is an inspired blend of flavorful ingredients, usually with a spicy edge, and the results are some of the most creative food around.

In warm weather, the lighthearted rooftop patio serves delicious lower-priced fare, fabulous salsas to go with your mojitos, satisfying enchiladas, and an ample, savory Cuban sandwich; service is also available at the Coyote's main bar. While you're there, be sure to try a Chimayó cocktail, a concoction made with apple juice, tequila, and Cointreau. A favorite place for the author to meet with friends.

Upper Crust Pizza (505-982-0000; 329 Old Santa Fe Trail; closed Thanksgiving; inexpensive; pizza, sandwiches; L, D; partial handicapped access; no reservations;

special features: free delivery, patio and front-porch dining, live music, parking in rear). Location, location, location. Consistently one of the best, most convenient to sight-seeing bargain lunches in town. This clean, casual eatery is nestled in an old adobe structure with vigas, skylights, and saltillo tile floors. Weekday lunches, you'll encounter a line out the door and down the street. Locals know that between 11 AM and 1 PM they can get a huge piece of pizza, salad, and a drink for a few bucks, made to order with fresh ingredients, and the service is prompt. Pizzas such as the Grecian gourmet are made with either traditional Italian or whole-wheat crusts. Sandwiches and house specials come with side salad and chips. Try the house special whole-wheat calzone filled with a blend of three cheeses, spinach, pesto, and tomatoes. Be sure to order a side of mouthwatering garlic bread made with fresh diced garlic and herbs sautéed with butter.

The Pink Adobe (505-983-7712; 406 Old Santa Fe Trail; closed major holidays; moderate–expensive; Continental, New Mexican with Cajun twist; Tues.–Sun. D, brunch Sun.; partial handicapped access; reservations required for dinner; special features: fireplaces, patio dining). The Pink, as it is affectionately known, is located in Santa Fe's historic neighborhood, the Barrio de Analco, across the street from San Miguel Mission, the oldest church in the United States. The restaurant is set in a 300-year-old house, painted the distinctive hue for which it is named. Finding a more romantic spot on a chilly night when the fireplaces are alight is not easy. At the adjacent Dragon Room bar, politicians, cowboys, and artists mingle in a setting hospitable to locals and visitors alike, munching on popcorn and sipping margaritas. Happy Hour 4–6 PM. Rosalea Murphy, a great Santa Fe personality, founded The Pink in 1944. Continental dishes are subtly altered for The Pink's special style. Steak Dunigan, my reliable favorite dish, adds green chile, and the spaghetti Bolognese is from an old family recipe. New Mexican dishes of blue corn enchiladas and tamales boast a particularly hot and spicy chile. The favorite dessert at The Pink Adobe is French apple pie.

✳ Lodging

Eldorado Hotel & Spa (505-988-4455; 800-955-4455; rez@eldoradohotel.com; www. eldoradohotel.com; 309 W. San Francisco St., Santa Fe, NM 87501, 3 blocks west of the Plaza; very expensive; rooms with full handicapped access). If any hotel in Santa Fe has an air of big-city luxury, it's the Eldorado. Spacious and imposing, this AAA Four Diamond winner has its own underground parking lot, valet service, two restaurants, several retail shops, live music every night in the Agave Lounge, butler service, and the largest banquet halls in the city. This is a place intended for grown-ups and those accustomed to sophisticated travel. Built in the 1980s, the five-story, 291-room hotel has a monolithic appearance that initially seemed out of scale for Santa Fe, but it is actually about the same height as the much older La Fonda Hotel. The Eldorado also has a couple of oddities for a hotel its size: a tiny swimming pool and no lobby. Guests rave about the service, which sets the Eldorado apart from many other lodgings; the Nidah Spa is a ticket to relaxation. The views from the top floor are magnificent; they will run $400 a night.

Inn and Spa at Loretto (505-988-5531; 800-727-5531; reservations@innatloretto. com; www.innatloretto.com; 211 Old Santa Fe Trail, Santa Fe, NM 87501, 2 blocks south of the Plaza; very expensive; 2 rooms with full handicapped access). Built in 1975 on the site of Loretto Academy, a reputedly haunted girls' school founded in the 19th century, this inn's terraced architecture is modeled after Taos Pueblo. The building, with 135 guest rooms, is an impressive sight, especially at Christmastime, when it's decked

THE LORETTO CHAPEL'S MIRACULOUS STAIRCASE CONTAINS NO NAILS

out with hundreds of electric *farolitos*. It includes a swimming pool, a bar with live entertainment, a restaurant, and a number of retail businesses. The Loretto Chapel with its Miraculous Staircase is next door. The hallways are adorned with Indian-style murals, and the rooms, while of standard design, are attractive. Some of the southwestern furnishings are made by local craftspeople. There is an insanely deluxe spa on the premises.

El Farolito B&B Inn (505-988-1631; innkeeper@farolito.com; www.farolito.com; 514 Galisteo St., Santa Fe, NM 87501, 5 blocks south of the Plaza; expensive; no handicapped access). This B&B offers seven renovated adobe casitas, some with private courtyard, each with a kiva fireplace, plus one suite. The establishment has a few unusual touches such as cedar ceilings and varnished plaster walls for an antique, rough-hewn look. The rooms also include some of the more typical features of southwestern style: flagstone floors, Mexican hide chairs, *trasteros*, Spanish-style beds, exposed vigas, and skylights. Nice but pricey.

Dancing Ground of the Sun (505-986-9797; 800-745-9910; dgsfrontdesk@santafe-hotels.com; www.dancingground.com; 711 Paseo de Peralta, Santa Fe, NM 87501, 3 blocks east of the Plaza; expensive; 1 room with full handicapped access). From the outside, this B&B, named for the original Indian pueblo that stood in Santa Fe, looks like a tiny apartment or condominium complex. But walk into any of the five 1930s-era bungalows, now spacious casitas, each with an evocative name such as Buffalo Dancer or Spirit Dancer, and you'll enter a delightfully different world. They're all distinctive and offer a great sense of privacy. Authenticity prevails in the décor. *Nichos*, vigas, Indian drums, locally made furniture, hand-painted tiling, alcoves, and archways abound. Most units have a fireplace, a couple have their own washer and dryer, and all have their own kitchen. There is a delightful courtyard with a fountain. This place sings of being lovingly cared for, as is evident from the surroundings and the exceptional welcoming friendliness of the innkeeper.

El Paradero (505-988-1177; info@elparadero.com; www.elparadero.com; 220 W. Manhattan Ave., Santa Fe, NM 87501, 5 blocks south of the Plaza; moderate–expensive; limited handicapped access). This family-owned and -operated B&B, one of the oldest in town, has an informal air to it. The front part of the building was a Spanish farmhouse in the early 1800s. Later additions, both Territorial and Victorian, give the inn a rambling character. It's full of nooks, crannies, private alcoves, and hideaways to curl up in with a book, talk, or unwind. The 15 rooms are charming, sunlit, and accented with handwoven textiles and folk art. The mood here is delightfully unpretentious, and it is apparent the owners take pride in the hospitality they offer. The location, just off the Guadalupe Street shopping area and 10 minutes' walking distance from the Plaza, is most convenient. A major plus is the substantial delicious breakfast prepared daily that will set you up for a day of sight-seeing.

La Fonda Hotel (505-982-5511; 800-523-5002; stay@lafondasantafe.com; www.lafondasantafe.com; 100 E. San Francisco St., Santa Fe, NM 87501, on the Plaza; very expensive; 2 rooms with full handicapped access). For almost all of Santa Fe's nearly 400-year history, there has been an inn of some sort on the southeast corner of the Plaza. Throughout much of the 19th century, the U.S. Hotel stood there, and its location at the end of the Santa Fe Trail made it a major destination for trappers, traders, merchants, soldiers, gamblers, politicians, and others. Kit Carson and a brigade of Confederate soldiers stayed here, and Billy the Kid did a stint as a dishwasher. By the 1920s, the old hotel, which had become a boardinghouse, was torn down. Within a few years, a new hotel, La Fonda (*fonda* means "inn") rose in its place. Today, this grand dame hotel remains locally owned, and the days when it was the hotel in Santa Fe are long gone. But it is still the only hotel on the Plaza, and no other can match its storied past. The La Fonda still embodies the essence of Santa Fe romance, though with a recent remodel of the bar and lobby, many locals and longtime visitors feel that past has been taken from them. Visit the rooftop lounge for a marvelous view of the city, or sip a margarita in the updated, comfortable bar and enjoy live music nightly. The rooms are small; however, the bedding is the best. There's also a restaurant (see "La Plazuela," page 92), plus the delightful French Pastry Shop, a swimming pool, hot tubs, and a spa. La Fonda features 14 totally nontoxic deluxe suites for environmentally sensitive guests at the privately accessed, concierge-level Terrace, and *bizcochitos* (cookies) and milk for kids at night. A word to the wise: Prices have gone up phenomenally since the renovation, and they may continue to rise.

Garrett Desert Inn (505-982-1851; 311 Old Santa Fe Trail, Santa Fe 87501). A moderately priced motel, which is probably why the 83 rooms are perennial favorites with those who do business in Santa Fe. If you want to be less than two blocks from the Plaza and avoid the hassle of driving and parking, it's nothing fancy, but this is as good a bargain as it gets. And how much time do you spend in your room anyway? Cerrillos Road motels provide similar accommodations at more reasonable rates, but it's nice to be downtown. Note: Daily parking fee.

Drury Plaza Hotel (1-800-DRURYINN; 228 E. Palace Ave., Santa Fe, NM 87501; inexpensive–moderate). The rooms are small but the service divine, as are the extras, like hot breakfast and "Kickback Hour" with hot food and three (yes, three!) drinks per guest, rooftop hot tub, year-round heated pool, and bar. This renovated hospital is just steps from the Plaza and reasonably priced. Best book early, as it's Santa Fe's newest property and has already been discovered. Pet friendly, too.

Inn of the Governors (505-982-4333; 101 W. Alameda St., Santa Fe, NM 87501, 2 blocks south of the Plaza; expensive; 1 room full handicapped access). Enclosed patios, carved vigas, and deep red doors set this inn apart from standard motels. Many of the 100 rooms, located in three buildings, have a wood-burning kiva fireplace, most have a stocked mini refrigerator, and there's complimentary coffee, newspapers, and a restaurant on the premises. There's also a year-round heated outdoor pool in this efficiently run lodging. The site is considered one of the best examples of Territorial architecture in downtown Santa Fe. You are invited to ask about discounts. This is the home of Del Charro, one of the liveliest bars and most reasonable eating places in downtown.

Inn of the Five Graces (866-992-0957; 150 E. DeVargas St., 4 blocks south of the Plaza; very expensive; partial handicapped access). Secluded in the city's oldest neighborhoods, a five-minute stroll to the Plaza, this ultra-luxurious inn offers 26 suites in a complex of six restored historic buildings, two interior courtyards, and elegant touches of antiques, tapestries, hand-carved furnishings, richly colored carpets, and featherbed mattresses. The style is "Oriental meets Old West." Most suites have a wood-burning fireplace. A full buffet breakfast is served, and the inn provides parking. Suites start at $500 per night, but it is possible to get three nights for the price of two at certain times. The inn distinguishes itself by its high level of personal service to guests. "Well-trained and quiet" pets are welcome, but expect to put up a hefty security deposit, refundable provided your pet behaves. This lodging receives top ratings on TripAdvisor despite the price tag.

Inn on the Alameda (877-785-2401; 303 E. Alameda St., Santa Fe, NM 87501, 3 blocks east of the Plaza; expensive; 1 room with full and 3 with partial handicapped access). I am partial to this boutique inn. Maybe it's the slightly out-of-the-hustle-and-bustle location; maybe it's the divine breakfast buffet with vegan and gluten-free selections included; maybe it's the complimentary afternoon wine and cheese by the fire. Within easy walking distance of the Plaza and Canyon Road, this 72-room inn across the street from the Santa Fe River has hot tubs, an exercise room, a full-service bar, a comfortable sitting room, and a conference room. The décor is a tasteful mix of southwestern style and modern convenience. With private patios and a daily breakfast feast, this inn makes a good choice for the guest who prefers the casual elegance and custom service of a smaller inn. And pets are welcome!

Adobe Abode (505-983-3133; fax 505-983-3132; www.adobeabode.com; 202 Chapelle St., Santa Fe, NM 87501, 4 blocks west of the Plaza; moderate; 1 room with full handicapped access). Tucked away in a turn-of-the-20th-century neighborhood, this small, unpretentious B&B is a wonderful jumble of architectural styles, works of art, and knickknacks. There are 10 units. The rooms combine New Mexican, Victorian, and art deco furnishings. Some rooms are quite spacious, with 12-foot ceilings, vigas, brick floors, patios, and fireplaces. This inn specializes in hearty breakfasts. It's located in a quiet residential area a short, lovely walk from downtown and has received raves from many national publications. It is especially convenient to the Santa Fe Community Convention Center and the Georgia O'Keeffe Museum.

La Posada de Santa Fe (505-982-6950; www.laposadadesantafe.com; 330 E. Palace Ave., Santa Fe, NM 87501, 5 blocks east of the Plaza; expensive; 7 rooms with full handicapped access). La Posada is the place for a pampering, with its full-service spa with eight treatment rooms. It has changed ownership frequently. A 19th-century mansion, a complex of pueblo-style casitas, and six acres covered with huge cottonwoods and fruit trees are some of the hallmarks of this unusual inn. The central building is known as the Staab House, for 19th-century German immigrant, merchant, and prominent citizen Abraham Staab. The three-story brick residence was a classic of its time, and the original interior remains intact. On its main level is a restaurant and lounge that offers live music. Upstairs are four turn-of-the-20th-century rooms, including Room 100, where the ghost of Julia Staab, Abraham's wife, is alleged to reside. The majority of guests stay in the casitas, where the décor is classic New Mexican: adobe fireplaces, flagstone floors, archways, hand-painted tiles, stained-glass windows, Indian rugs, exposed vigas, and skylights. La Posada has a good-sized swimming pool and a lovely courtyard for drinking and dining in nice weather.

Rosewood Inn of the Anasazi (505-988-3030; 113 Washington Ave., Santa Fe, NM 87501, half a block north of the Plaza; very expensive; 1 room with full handicapped access). An impeccable address. A place to impress and be impressed. This striking and surprisingly intimate 57-room hotel is about as close to the Plaza as you can get without being on it. It is decorated in classic Pueblo Revival style, with viga-and-*latilla* ceilings throughout, stone floors and walls, and a beautiful flagstone waterfall on the second floor. The local artwork reflects New Mexico's three major ethnic groups. The austerely elegant hotel also maintains a small library. An underground wine cellar with a capacity of 12 guests is available for dinner. Offering the best sense of peace and privacy money can buy, this small luxury hotel reigns among Santa Fe's most chic addresses for visitors. Convenient on-site services are available for business travelers.

❋ Museums

Note: The New Mexico CulturePass, $30, invites you to visit each of the 15 state museums and historic sites once during a 12-month period and may be purchased at any museum or historic site or online at www.newmexicoculture.org. In addition, the FamilyPass may be borrowed for a week at the Santa Fe Public Library and offers free admission to museums and historic sites for up to six people. While Sundays have traditionally been free for New Mexico residents, new regulations specify that only the first Sunday of each month is free to New Mexicans. Different museums have different policies and free and reduced rates for seniors, veterans, youth, and groups. Be sure to ask.

Georgia O'Keeffe Museum (505-946-1000; www.okeeffemuseum.org; 217 Johnson St., Santa Fe, NM 87501, 4 blocks west of the Plaza; open daily 9 AM–5 PM, until 7 PM Fri., closed Thanksgiving, Christmas, New Year's Day, Easter; $12 per day, $8 New Mexico residents). A variety of tours available: docent-led, group tours, and before hours tours. Said to be the most visited museum in Santa Fe. This is the opportunity of a lifetime to view the iconic artist's work in a historic and artistic context. The discerning iconoclast O'Keeffe herself would probably have approved of this classically simple, adobe-colored, elegantly lit museum that houses her inspired work. Visitors can take in the span of the pioneering modernist's work—from early figurative watercolors, to her paintings of New York in the first decades of the 20th century, to her celebrations of New Mexico in enormous flowers, crosses, clouds, and studies of rocks, sky, and bone. To tour the O'Keeffe home in Abiquiu, call 505-685-4539 for information and reservations, which customarily must be made well in advance.

IAIA Museum of Contemporary Native Arts (505-988-6211; 108 Cathedral Place, Santa Fe, NM 87501), across from Cathedral Basilica of St. Francis Assisi, open summer, Mon.–Sat. 9 AM–5 PM, Sun. 10 AM–5 PM; winter Mon.–Sat. 10 AM–5 PM, Sun. noon–5 PM; $10 adults, $5 seniors, students with ID, and New Mexico residents; free for children under 16, Native people, veterans and their families; free to New Mexico residents on Sun.; gift shop). The work of many of the best-known names in Indian art—Allan Houser, Fritz Scholder, T. C. Cannon—are displayed here. The museum houses the nation's largest collection of contemporary Indian art. Fascinating and provocative. Don't miss the Performance Gallery and the Allan Houser Sculpture Park.

New Mexico Museum of Art (505-476-5068; 107 W. Palace Ave., Santa Fe, NM 87501, on northwest corner of the Plaza; open daily 10 AM–5 PM May–Oct., closed Mon. Nov.–Apr.; $7 New Mexico residents, $12 nonresidents, $30 for Culture Pass multiple museum admission, free on Fri. 5–8 PM May–Oct. and free on first Fri. of the month, Nov.–Apr., free to New Mexico residents with ID on first Sun. of month; gift shop). The Isaac Hamilton Rapp–designed 1917 Spanish Pueblo Revival structure houses more than 8,000 works of art, including paintings, prints, drawings, photographs, and sculptures. The collection emphasizes 20th-century American art, particularly southwestern.

On permanent exhibition are works by early 20th-century New Mexico artists such as Jozef Bakos, Gustave Baumann, and William Penhallow Henderson. Also look for changing exhibitions of traditional and contemporary art assembled from the permanent collection or loaned by other institutions. The Alcove Show, which changes several times a year, features exciting contemporary work by area artists.

Art walking tours of Santa Fe are offered by the museum Apr.–Nov., Mon. at 10 AM. Tours are $10; children under 18 free.

New Mexico History Museum/Palace of the Governors (505-476-5200; 113 Lincoln Ave.; open daily 10 AM–5 PM May–Oct., closed Mon. Nov.–Apr.; closed New Year's Day, Easter, Thanksgiving, and Christmas; $7 New Mexico residents, $12 general admission, free on Fri. 5–8 PM May–Oct. and free on first Fri. of the month, Nov.–Apr., free to New Mexico residents with ID on first Sun. of month). The state's newest museum; the jewel in the crown. Newest permanent exhibit celebrates the Fred Harvey Company. Next door, the previous history museum, the Palace of the Governors, is located in the oldest public building in the country still in use. Built in 1610, it offers permanent exhibits largely related to Spanish colonial history. Historical downtown walking tours offered for $10, children free, 10:15 AM Mon.–Sat. Apr.–Oct. at 113 Lincoln Ave.

✳ Sites

Cross of the Martyrs Walkway (on Paseo de Peralta between Otero St. and Hillside Ave; always open). Only a five-minute walk from the Plaza, this historic spot boasts the best view of downtown. A brick walkway winds up a small hill, and plaques posted along the way summarize highlights of Santa Fe's prehistory and history. The cross at the summit is a memorial to 21 Franciscan monks killed in the Pueblo Revolt of 1680 (see page 25).

The Plaza (center of town; always open). Four hundred years of history speak from the Santa Fe Plaza. Originally the Plaza was a rectangle, laid out according to plans specified by Spain's King Philip II in 1610. For much of its history, it consisted mainly of packed earth. Though it has been dusty, it has never been dull. Countless celebrations, both religious and secular, have been held here. This is also the spot where Hispanic residents used to conduct Saturday-night promenades, complete with strolling musicians.

Today strollers and teenage plaza rats still keep the Plaza hopping on pleasant summer evenings. Hardly anyone would think of holding a demonstration or vigil anywhere but the Plaza, and it's still one of the best people-watching spots in the city.

The **Cathedral Basilica of St. Francis of Assisi** (505-982-5619; 131 Cathedral Pl., Santa Fe, NM 87501), east end of San Francisco St.; open Mon.–Sat. 6 AM–6 PM, Sun. 7 AM–7 PM; donations accepted). This is one of Santa Fe's most spectacular structures—and also one of its most incongruous. Built in French-Romanesque style, it was the inspiration of Frenchman Jean Baptiste Lamy, Santa Fe's first archbishop. The cornerstone was laid in 1868, and construction proceeded with stone quarried in an area south of Santa Fe.

The Cathedral Basilica was dedicated in 1886 but was never fully completed. Its stained-glass windows, including the rose window in front and the lateral nave windows, were brought from France and installed in 1884. The bronze doors of the cathedral, installed for its rededication in 1986, contain 16 panels depicting scenes in the history of the Catholic Church in Santa Fe. Also worth viewing is the *reredos* (altar screen) carved for the 100th anniversary celebration in 1986.

La Conquistadora Chapel, an adobe structure on the northeast side of the cathedral, was built in the 1600s to honor a statue of the Virgin Mary brought to Santa Fe in 1626. Originally called the *Lady of the Rosary*, the statue was renamed *Our Lady of the Conquest* in 1692, when the Spaniards reentered the city 12 years after the Pueblo Revolt. It is probably the oldest representation of the Virgin Mary in the United States. *Note:*

Visitors not attending Mass may slip into the cathedral quietly at other times, using the side doors and taking care not to disturb those at prayer.

Loretto Chapel Museum (505-922-0092; 207 Old Santa Fe Trail, Santa Fe, NM 87501); open summer, Mon.–Sat. 9 AM–4:30 PM, Sun. 10:30 AM–4:30 PM; call for winter hours; closed Christmas; $3 admission, $2 seniors; gift shop). Loretto Chapel was built at the same time as the Cathedral Basilica of St. Francis of Assisi for the Sisters of Loretto, the first nuns to come to New Mexico. The Chapel of Our Lady of Light, as it was called then, was begun in 1873 and intended to replicate Sainte-Chappelle in Paris, France. Stones for the chapel came from the same quarry as that for the Cathedral Basilica, and the same French architects and French and Italian stonemasons worked on the two structures.

The architects were a father and son named Mouly. The son was killed before the chapel was completed, and he left no plans for a stairway to the choir loft. Indeed, there wasn't enough space left for a conventional staircase. The story goes that the sisters prayed for help to St. Joseph, patron saint of carpenters. In due time an unknown carpenter arrived and proceeded to build an amazing circular staircase—a structure lacking both nails and visible means of support. He departed without leaving his name or asking for pay.

Sena Plaza (125–137 E. Palace Ave., Santa Fe, NM 87501; enter on Palace Ave., just east of the Plaza; always open). A separate world that resonates with the flavor of colonial Santa Fe, Sena Plaza is reached by an adobe passage from busy Palace Avenue. In the 19th century, the most gracious homes were built as compounds, with rooms surrounding a central *placita* (courtyard). In the 1860s, Major José D. Sena built just such a home a block from the downtown Plaza—and kept adding rooms as more children were born. Now Sena Plaza houses private shops and a restaurant where you can enjoy a margarita in the patio garden.

ARCHBISHOP LAMY MADE HIS MARK ON TERRITORIAL NEW MEXICO WITH THE CATHEDRAL BASILICA OF ST. FRANCIS OF ASSISI, REMINISCENT OF HIS CHILDHOOD IN FRANCE

The **Santa Fe Public Library** (505-955-6780; 145 Washington Ave.) is notable for its Santa Fe–style Territorial architecture, southwestern furnishings, excellent collections, art exhibits, and public events. The Southwest Room contains a fine collection of noncirculating Southwest literature

The **Museum of New Mexico** (www.museumofnewmexico.org) research libraries, open to researchers, are part of each of the Santa Fe museums. (Be sure to call ahead.) The **Fray Angélico Chavez History Library** (505-576-5090) at the Palace of the Governors houses more than 12,000 volumes on regional history, as well as a vast repository of original documents and maps. Its photo archives section (505-476-5026) contains more than 340,000 historical images; prints are available for purchase or rental. The **Museum of Fine Arts Library** (505-476-5061) contains about 5,000 volumes emphasizing New Mexican and southwestern art.

The state of New Mexico operates five museum facilities in Santa Fe under the aegis of the Museum of New Mexico. The museums include the **Palace of the Governors** and the **Museum of Fine Arts**, the **New Mexico History Museum** on the Plaza, and the **Museum of Indian Arts and Culture** and the **Museum of International Folk Art**, both on Camino Lejo, about a 15-minute drive southeast of downtown. Starting at 7:15 AM, at the Sheridan Street Station, seven days a week, is the M bus to Museum Hill. Fees: $1 each way, $2 all-day pass; seniors 50 cents each way, $1 all-day pass; under 17 free. For information on specific museums, please visit the websites below.

Museum of Indian Arts and Culture
www.indianartsandculture.org
Museum of International Folk Art
www.internationalfolkart.org
New Mexico Museum of Art
www.nmartmuseum.org
New Mexico Historic Sites
www.nmhistoricsites.org
Office of Archaeological Studies
www.nmarchaeology.org
New Mexico History Museum
www.nmhistorymuseum.org

✳ Shopping

Santa Fe Boot Company (505-989-1168; 60 E. San Francisco St.). The right boots are certainly necessary to a cowboy, and they are also the basis for a Santa Fe–style outfit. Luckily, Santa Fe Boot Company offers both working boots and boots that work well with your wardrobe. A large selection includes trusted brand names.

Origins (505-988-2323; 209 Galisteo St.). One of the best wearable-art boutiques in the country, Origins is an Aladdin's cave of treasures. Fabrics from around the world mingle with designer clothing and one-of-a-kind art creations. Explore the store to discover tribal arts, antique jewelry, fantasy hats, embroidered shawls, and the new gold-and-antiques room. Find the perfect outfit for the opera or your class reunion. The owner's motto is: "We feature forever dressing," and that is true. I am still wearing (and getting compliments on) a handmade antique Pendleton jacket I "invested" in more than 20 years ago. However, bring big bucks if you intend to shop there now.

Sign of the Pampered Maiden (505-982-5948; 123 W. Water St.). The Maiden is my first choice Santa Fe shop to put together the perfect outfit, be it a spring dress with a little jacket or the most fashionable sweater and skirt for fall. A bit on the pricey side, but not forbiddingly so, at least not for that one perfect outfit. Shop here and you are guaranteed to look like a class act, and not only in Santa Fe.

Zephyr Clothing (505-988-5635; 125 E. Palace Ave.). Sophisticated pieces of women's clothing in velvet, silk, wool, and rayon. The coats are specially designed for sale in the store. The place to find that one-of-a-kind piece.

Doodlet's (505-983-3771; 120 Don Gaspar Ave.). Whimsical shop packed with toys for all ages as well as sweets, cards, everything you had no idea you needed.

Fourth World Cottage Industries (505-983-0483; 102 W. San Francisco St., upstairs). Imports from Central and South America in a range of prices. Casual cotton and wool garments for men and women add a bit of ethnic chic to any wardrobe. The store also has art hangings, pottery, masks, and Guatemalan handwoven fabric.

Glorianna's Beads (505-982-0353; 55 W. Marcy St.). Exotic beads tell tales of trade and travel, and there are strands and strands of everything from amber to crystal to glass at Glorianna's. Also bead books and other craft information.

Guadalupe's Fun Rubber Stamps (505-982-9862; 114 Don Gaspar Ave.). "Our store reflects the quirky times we live in," is the motto. Stamp your own creative mark on the world by choosing from hundreds of imaginative and outrageous rubber stamps. Also pads, inks, and handmade icons to stir the soul of the crafter. Workshops, too: make an artist's journal or multimedia postcards. The place to come do what you've always wanted to do.

Keishi (505-989-8728; 227 Don Gaspar Ave.). Founded by a teacher at Zuni Pueblo and now run by her daughter, this is the shop of authentic Zuni needlepoint and pettipoint jewelry you will never regret. Plenty of beautifully curated Pueblo pottery, Santo Domingo inlay earrings by top artists, fetishes galore, and so much more. Reasonable prices in this jam-packed little house of wonders and extremely knowledgeable and trustworthy staff make shopping here a pleasure.

Collected Works Bookstore & Coffeehouse (505-988-4226; 202 Galisteo St., Ste. A). This is the place to go if you are in the mood to read something—but don't yet know what. A fine selection of current fiction and memoirs greets you at the entrance. Also extensive southwestern books—from local guidebooks to the history and literature of the region. This "new" location is more spacious than the old San Francisco Street shop with the pluses of a central fireplace, coffee bar, and pastries from Harry's Roadhouse. Longtime owner Dorothy Massey is a great supporter of local writers, and there's usually a signing or event going on. Wonderful place to cuddle up by the fireplace with excellent coffee and pastry.

Montecristi Custom Hat Works (505-983-9598; 122 McKenzie St.). You don't have to have money to look like you do, but having it will come in handy here. A custom hat from Monecristi is the last word in fine dressing. Finish off the look with one of their rare and unusual hat bands.

Passementrie: Textiles, Clothing, Accessories (505-989-1262; 115 Old Santa Fe Trail). Whether you fancy a gypsy scarf, an elegant jacket, or a casual throw, this is the place to find a Santa Fe purchase they will envy back home. Reasonable prices, a great selection of flattering woven and knit garments you can travel the world in or wear to work, in colors and styles from basic to wild. Be stylish, whatever your style. Full disclosure: I shop here.

Sun Country Traders (505-982-0467; 123 E. Water St.). Huge selection of authentic Native American folk art, beadwork, woodcarving, and jewelry, too. This remains an affordable place to shop and to find the most unique items in town. In business since 1979.

Mira (505-988-3585; 101 W. Marcy St.). Stylin' clothing, T-shirts, jewelry (including the inimitable Goldie Garcia), and other accessories for the young and young-at-heart.

Delightful and inspiring shopping experience. Plenty of Frida Kahlo and Dia de los Muertos accessories to wear and decorate with.

Street Feet (505-984-2828; La Fonda Hotel, 100 E. San Francisco St.). Street Feet has shoes galore from Italy and South America, as well as Canadian boots. You'll also find stylish clothing, with an emphasis on soft fabrics, tunics, jackets, and sweaters, including leggings, bags, scarves, and belts.

Andrew Smith Gallery, Inc., Masterpieces of Photography (505-984-1234; 122 Grant Ave.). Acclaimed as the world's leading gallery selling 19th- and 20th-century masterworks, both European and American, this "house of photography" is always worth a look. Ansel Adams, Edward Curtis, Laura Gilpin, and contemporary photographers of the western landscape.

Monroe Gallery of Photography (505-992-0800; 112 Don Gaspar Ave.). Following 9/11, Sidney Monroe moved his fine photography gallery from lower Manhattan to Santa Fe. Excellent shows of historical 20th-century photography and the photographers who made that history. Always exciting exhibits.

Verve Gallery of Photography (505-982.-5009; 219 E. Marcy St.). A must-do for anyone who loves contemporary photography. No limit to the technique of these big format artworks. Mouth-wateringly gorgeous and stimulating.

James Reid, Ltd. (800-545-2056; 114 E. Palace Ave.). This shop offers breathtaking concha belts and belt buckles in silver and gold, in both traditional and contemporary designs. High end and awesome.

Andrea Fisher Fine Pottery (505-985-1234; 100 W. San Francisco St.). Where do you draw the line between a gallery and a museum? Just stroll past this impeccable gallery and ogle the display of Maria Martinez black pottery in the window. You'll find the best of the best here. It will make you want to become a collector if you aren't one already.

Ortega's on the Plaza (505-988-1866; 101 W. San Francisco St.). This venerable trader has a first-class selection of Indian jewelry, emphasizing traditional designs in turquoise and silver. Also pottery, kachina dolls, and some elegant velvet clothing.

Palace of the Governors Portal (Palace Ave., entire north block of the Plaza). One of the best places to shop for traditional Indian jewelry is beneath the portal of the historic Palace of the Governors. Artists and artisans assemble from the surrounding pueblos and as far away as the Navajo Reservation to sell traditional silver and turquoise jewelry, small pots, and other items. Prices are reasonable, and there is a special pleasure in buying from the jeweler or a family representative. Earrings, necklaces, bolo ties, and rings are in particular abundance, and a tiny bracelet makes a special baby present. The work is juried and certified authentic. Vendors are assigned slots daily by lottery, so if you find something you love, buy it—it might be difficult to trace later.

Susan's Christmas Shop (505-983-2127; 115 E. Palace Ave.). Santa couldn't do better than this dazzling array of handmade Christmas ornaments from New Mexico, Mexico, and beyond. Incredibly fanciful and ornate ornaments for all. Look for seasonal changes: hearts on Valentine's Day and collector-quality decorated eggs for Easter.

Things Finer (505-983-5552; La Fonda Hotel, 100 E. San Francisco St.). Nestled in the classic Pueblo Deco lobby of the La Fonda Hotel, Things Finer is a treasure trove of jewelry, antiques, silver, miniatures, and rare icons from Russia. The staff will also do appraisals on items you bring in.

Back at the Ranch Cowboy Boots (505-989-8110; 209 E. Marcy St.). Don't be surprised if your jaw actually drops here at the fabulous selection of wild and fanciful cowboy boots in designs from peacock to retro. You'll be forgiven if this is where you bust the budget.

HANDS-ON CLASSES TEACH LOVERS OF SOUTHWEST CUISINE THE BEST WAYS TO MAKE TRADITIONAL NEW MEXICAN FARE

Boots & Boogie (505-983-0777; 102 E. Water St.). Choose from among 350 pairs of handmade boots on display or create your own custom footwear: your choice of design, heel, and leather (they have dozens), hand tooled in Texas. Prices start from $600 and go all the way to five figures; average cost is $1,200 to guarantee you'll be kicking it and taking names for a long time to come. Formerly located in Santa Fe Village.

Goler Fine Imported Shoes (505-982-0924; 125 E. Palace Ave.). If shoes have personalities, these range from the saucy to the chic to the downright elegant, in materials from leather to brocade. Upscale shoes from everywhere on the fashion map.

Davis Mather Folk Art Gallery (505-983-1660; 141 Lincoln Ave., a block north of the Plaza). One of the best collections of New Mexico animal woodcarvings and Mexican folk art. Owner Davis Mather delights in recounting how he discovered the work of Felipe Archuleta, the New Mexico artisan who popularized the whimsical animal carvings in the 1960s.

Santa Fe School of Cooking (505-983-4511; www.santafeschoolofcooking.com; 125 N. Guadalupe St.). In addition to classes on the traditional chile-flavored cuisine of New Mexico, this venerable cooking school also can show you how to prepare Spanish, vegetarian, Mexican, and contemporary southwestern dishes. Culinary tours, kitchen skills, too. You'll wow your family and dinner guests. You can find an in-depth assortment of southwestern cookbooks, kitchenware, and everything you need to dress up your table in fine Southwest style.

ADORE CHILE RELLENOS? TAKE A CLASS AT SANTA FE SCHOOL OF COOKING AND LEARN HOW TO MAKE THEM AT HOME

FARMERS' MARKETS

At harvest time, the Santa Fe–Taos area is rich with roadside stands strung with red chile *ristras* and offering a variety of fresh-picked, home-grown fruits, vegetables, preserves, and piñon nuts. In-season, the most abundant cluster of such spots can be found on NM 68 between Velarde and Dixon. From time to time, families even gather to cook and sell their freshly harvested green chile in shopping centers. Keep in mind that not all the produce is locally grown. When in doubt, ask the vendor.

Between June and October, there are a number of excellent farmers' markets in the Santa Fe–Taos area. The largest is the **Santa Fe Area Farmers' Market** (505-983-4098; 1607 Paseo de Peralta), held Tues. and Sat. 7–11:30 AM in the Santa Fe Railyard, a hot collection of specialty retail shops, galleries, and restaurants. Here you can get ultrafresh, locally grown produce (much of it organic), specialty vegetables like baby squash, as well as prepared foods such as salsas, jams, and jellies—even fresh-squeezed apple cider and honey. Grab a pastry or a breakfast burrito to go with your fresh coffee, and you'll be a happy camper.

Saturday mornings are an event, with live music, tastings, and cooking demonstrations. Beware, however, as there is no guarantee the produce is either local or organic. The market is so popular that parking can be a real hassle. Don't say we didn't warn you. The market also has winter hours on weekends.

Three other regional markets offer similarly fresh local produce and specialty items July–Oct. These are the **Taos Farmers' Market** (575-751-7575), which meets Sat. around 7 AM on the Plaza; the **Española Farmers' Market** (505-753-5340), which meets 10 AM–5 PM Mon. at 1005 N. Railroad Ave.; and the **Los Alamos Farmers' Market** (505-581-4651), held 7 AM–noon Thurs. at the Mesa Public Library parking lot, 20th and Central, and 8 AM–12:30 PM on the second Thurs. of each month at Fuller Lodge. Call for specific information.

Cheesemongers (505-795-7878; 130 E. Marcy St.; closed Mon.). Deliriously fabulous selection of cheese and cured meats. Famous for stunning and unusual cheese plates. Special opera tailgate picnics packed here. Knowledgeable staff to advise. Best if price is no object. How did Santa Fe ever get along without them? Local delivery available.

The Hive Market (505-780-5084; 101 W. Marcy St.). Shelves packed with local, domestic, and imported honey plus all manner of locally produced jam, baking mixes, lavender sachets, exotic herbal products and so much more for gifts or gifts to self. Greg, the owner, will happily give you a honey tasting.

Ecco Espresso & Gelato (505-986-9778 128 E. Marcy St.). Open daily. Cool little spot to rest up with an authentic Italian gelato or Italian soda, or even grab a quick sandwich. Good assortment of gelato flavors like Oreo and caramel sea salt, strawberry and peach.

Todos Santos Chocolates & Confections (505-982-3855; 125 E. Palace, #31). You've never seen chocolate like this. The extensive domestic and imported artisan chocolates in this tiny out-of-the-way shop in Sena Plaza fascinate and stun. Many locally made designer chocolates as well. All displayed in an imaginative, wildly colorful, New Orleans–influenced, magical setting.

Kaune's Neighborhood Market (505-982-2629; 511 Old Santa Fe Trail). One of the oldest groceries around, Kaune's offers a wide variety of meats, including natural beef and poultry, Colorado lamb, and game meats from venison and buffalo to rabbit and pheasant. The only place in Santa Fe you can purchase prime beef and specialty cuts. Their new soup and salad bar is a fine place to pick up a quick picnic lunch.

Señor Murphy Candymaker (505-982-0461; La Fonda Hotel, 200 San Francisco St.;

closed Sun., major holidays). The specialty here is anything with piñon nuts—for example, piñon toffee and piñon fudge—as well as spicy chile concoctions with peanut brittle and chocolate cream. They also make chile jellies and outstanding condiments for meats and hors d'oeuvres. Great gifts for yourself, those back home, or friends abroad. Another location is at Santa Fe Place mall at the south end of town.

CANYON ROAD

One of Santa Fe's oldest and most colorful streets, storied Canyon Road was originally an Indian trail through the mountains to Pecos Pueblo. It is wide enough for burro carts to carry wood down from the mountains. In the 1920s, it was adopted by artists from the East Coast. The narrow, winding street, only a mile long, has since become an internationally acclaimed art district.

A stroll along Canyon Road is a must for visitors. Enter off Paseo de Peralta, just south of East Alameda about six blocks southeast of the Plaza. Take time to view the old adobe buildings, constructed in typical Spanish Colonial style, with walls that begin at the edge of the street. A compound may surround a lovely patio or garden. The street is the location of several of the country's best known and most exclusive restaurants, and the shopping is divine.

Best navigated on foot.

✳ Dining

The Compound (505-982-4353; 653 Canyon Rd.; closed major holidays; very expensive; Continental, New American; no handicapped access; reservations strongly recommended; special features: full bar, patio). Chef-owner Mark Kiffin has racked up awards aplenty, including James Beard honors. The Alexander Girard–designed white interior is the epitome of chic yet minimal Santa Fe style—although gentlemen are no longer required to wear ties as in days of yore. The Compound has perfected the art of welcoming, professional service. Here we have the concept of food as entertainment on a grand scale: Santa Fe's beautiful people, dressed to the nines, plus fresh ingredients from all over the world shipped overnight to be shaped by the chef's imagination. The menu changes seasonally. You can order sweetbreads and foie gras, blue-corn-dusted softshell crabs, slow-baked salmon, or grilled lamb rib eye, and be sure to leave room for the molten chocolate cake. The Compound makes an unforgettable dining experience and ought to be on any visitor's "special splurge" list. A good place to propose.

Geronimo (505-982-1500; 724 Canyon Rd.; closed Mon. lunch; very expensive; contemporary Southwest; L, D, SB; partial handicapped access; reservations recommended; special features: fireplace, courtyard). Geronimo has been drawing raves since it opened in 1991. Housed in one of the city's finest old adobes, it's airy and elegant in drop-dead-gorgeous minimalist Santa Fe style, and the food is over-the-top spectacular. The menu consists of American staples updated with southwestern and other ethnic ingredients. Start with roast lobster bisque with red pepper crab cake, sautéed quail breast with Iroquois corn polenta cakes, or seared French foie gras, and go on from there to mesquite-grilled salmon with Meyer lemon and spinach ravioli or peppery elk tenderloin with applewood-smoked bacon. The cuisine is touched by all of today's trends, including Asian fusion, French, and New American.

To enjoy Geronimo without breaking your budget, try lunch. Desserts vary daily, and the entire menu changes at least once a season. For cool evenings, try the intimate bar with kiva fireplace and brass-topped tables.

SYNONOMOUS WITH ELEGANT DINING, GERONIMO SERVES SOME OF THE MOST HIGHLY-ACCLAIMED, HIGH-END CUISINE IN TOWN

El Farol Restaurant and Lounge (505-983-9912; 808 Canyon Rd.; closed major holidays; expensive; Spanish tapas; L, D; no handicapped access; reservations recommended; special features: patio dining, live music). This Santa Fe landmark bills itself as the city's oldest restaurant and cantina, and indeed, it dates from 1835, when canyon residents stopped by for a haircut and refreshments. El Farol taught Santa Fe to eat tapas and not a little about flamenco. The menu includes tapas *frias* (marinated white Spanish anchovies and chilled mussels in sherry vinaigrette) and tapas *calientes* (calamari, grilled baby chorizo with mashed potatoes, and pork tenderloin with figs and port). Or start with a soup like *posole* clam chowder and go on to an entrée such as herb-crusted halibut with Pernod saffron cream, the house special of paella Valencia, or grilled beef tenderloin fillet with portobello mushroom and asparagus. End with Spanish cheeses of Manchego and Cabrales. The flan is laced with lemon, rosemary, and caramel, and the steamed chocolate pudding is deliciously not-too-sweet. The wine list features one of the most extensive inventories of Spanish wines in New Mexico. Enjoy the Alfred Morang murals and the thick adobe walls that have welcomed prophets, poets, and punks. Parking can be challenging—try the city lot across the street. With tango, salsa, and Latin music, there's plenty of live song and dance here, drawing in the city's top performers, many with international reputations. Performances are held almost

WINE, BEER, AND SPIRITS

Cliff's Packaged Liquor Store: 505-988-1790; 903 Old Pecos Trail.
Kaune's Grocery Co.: 505-982-2629; 511 Old Santa Fe Trail.
Lamplighter Liquor Store: 505-438-9132; 2411 Cerrillos Rd.
Owl Liquors: 505-982-1751; 913 Hickox St.
Rodeo Plaza Liquors: 505-473-2867; 2801 Rodeo Rd.
Susan's Fine Wines & Spirits: 505-984-1582; 1001 Pen Rd. With a wine bar!

nightly, plus special flamenco-dinner shows. Especially notable are Latin music diva Nacha Mendez's Sunday night performances, a must-do.

Downtown Subscription (505-983-3085; 376 Garcia St.; inexpensive). In the Canyon Road neighborhood, the grandma of them all, is a spacious, cheerful bar and patio with rack upon rack of newspapers and magazines to browse, plus strong coffees and fresh-baked pastries. In good weather, the patio is a delightful place to browse the Sunday *New York Times*—but be sure to reserve your copy.

Kakawa Chocolate House (505-982-0388; 1050 Paseo de Peralta; inexpensive). Historic and artisan drinking chocolates, sinfully yummy truffles and baked goods; gluten-free products. A must-do for chocoholics.

Caffe Greco (505-820-7996; 233 Can-

NACHA MENDEZ, SANTA FE'S DIVA OF INTERNATIONAL LATIN SONG, PERFORMS AT VENUES ALL OVER TOWN

yon Rd.; inexpensive). Warm, unpretentious, relaxing, and reasonable breakfast and lunch spot. The red chile is earthy and the Frito pie is satisfying.

The Teahouse (505-992-0972; 821 Canyon Rd.; expensive). Starting out as a true teahouse serving a mind-bending selection of fine teas from throughout the world, including those designed to de-stress, plus coffees, inventive meals and snacks, as well as adult beverages. Cozy in winter, and lovely on the patio in fair weather.

DOWNTOWN SUBSCRIPTION, NO LONGER DOWNTOWN, IS ONE OF SANTA FE'S LONGEST-RUNNING COFFEEHOUSES AND STILL FEATURES A DIVERSE SELECTION OF MAGAZINES ALONG WITH FINE COFFEE

THE MOST DELECTABLE ARTISANAL CHOCOLATES AND EXOTIC SIPPING CHOCOLATES ARE FOUND AT KAKAWA CHOCOLATE HOUSE

Dulce Bakery (505-989-9966; 1100 Don Diego Ave.; inexpensive). No sugar-shaming here in this minimalist café. Or butter. Masterful baking and cases loaded with turnovers and Danishes fresh from the oven. Resistance is futile. Cinnamon rolls with all the icing you can stand.

✳ Lodging

Alexander's Inn (505-986-1431; info@alexanders-inn.com; www.alexanders-inn.com; 529 E. Palace Ave., Santa Fe, NM 87501, 5 blocks east of the Plaza; moderate–expensive; no handicapped access). Alexander's Inn is actually one of three neighborhood sister inns that can accommodate just about any size group, plus a luxury spa. Located in a wooded residential area, this lovely Victorian B&B, done up with Southwest charm, is within walking distance of the Plaza and Canyon Road. Originally built in 1903, windows and skylights have been added to make it sunnier, but it retains a delightful charm. Breakfast and social hour goodies are included only in certain rooms, so be sure to inquire. The outdoor hot tub is available for guests, as are mountain bikes and guest privileges at a nearby spa. Luxurious bedding, meticulous attention, and a romantic Santa Fe feel make this a good bet.

Dunshee's Bed and Breakfast and Casita (505-982-0988; sdunshee.santafe@gmail.com; www.dunshees.com; 986 Acequia Madre, Santa Fe, NM 87501, 10 blocks southeast of the Plaza; moderate; no handicapped access). Absolutely precious! Tucked into Santa Fe's historic and picturesque east side, this romantic B&B is located on the town's most beautiful, winding old street. It features two units: one, a spacious suite done up tastefully with all the usual New Mexico touches (kiva fireplace, viga ceilings, folk art, Mexican tile bath); the other, a two-bedroom adobe casita. In warm weather, there's a sheltered, flower-filled patio for relaxing. Best of all, perhaps, is the hostess, a gracious artist who can clue you in on the local arts scene and serve as your personal concierge. This B&B is only a short hop away from the gallery district of Canyon Road and Camino del Monte Sol. Be sure to get specific directions before you arrive, because this place is really tucked away! You get a scrumptious gourmet breakfast if you stay in the suite; the casita is furnished with fresh fruit and granola.

✳ Sites, Parks, and Museums

Cristo Rey Church (505-983-8258; www.cristoreyparish.org; 1120 Canyon Rd., Santa Fe, NM 87501, intersection of Canyon Rd. and Camino Cabra; open weekdays 8 AM–5 PM; call 1 month ahead to arrange tours; donations appreciated). An outstanding example of Spanish Colonial Mission architecture, Cristo Rey Church was designed by Santa Fe architect John Gaw Meem and built to commemorate the 400th anniversary of Coronado's arrival in the Southwest. This is one of the largest modern adobe structures in existence. The church is famous for the stone *reredos* (altar screen) carved by craftsmen from Mexico in 1760.

El Zaguan (545 Canyon Rd., Santa Fe, NM 87501). Now a private apartment complex and the site of Historic Santa Fe Foundation. The Victorian garden supports giant chestnut trees, so the story goes, planted by anthropologist Adolph Bandelier, who once lived here. You may enter the garden through the building and enjoy a picnic or quiet respite. One of Santa Fe's loveliest spots, hidden in plain sight.

Santa Fe Children's Museum (505-989-8359; 1050 Old Pecos Trail, Santa Fe, NM 87505). Named one of the country's 10 best museums by *USA Today*, the Children's Museum offers both indoor and outdoor activities for children age 0–9. Specializing in hands-on interactive exhibits that promote play and imagination, SFCM also offers a diverse range of weekly programs along with frequent special events. The extensive outdoor gardens provide a lush enclosed landscape to explore.

Upaya Zen Center (505-986-8518; www.upaya.org; 1404 Cerro Gordo Rd., Santa Fe, NM 87501). A Buddhist retreat and learning center, Upaya offers weekday Zen meditation throughout the day beginning at 6 AM Wed.–Fri. and 7 AM every other day, with the last meditation beginning at 5:30 PM daily. On Wednesday, dharma talks by Joan Halifax Roshi, founder and head teacher, as well as other practitioners are included. Please call for a tour of the zendo or information on personal retreats. Please write for a schedule of Upaya courses on subjects such as healing, dreams, the neuroscience of meditation, and death and dying.

THE LOVELY HISTORIC GARDEN AT EL ZAGUAN INVITES A RESPITE FROM A DAY OF STROLLING AND SHOPPING

BRILLIANT COLOR AND VINTAGE ADOBE INVITE PASSERSBY TO ENTER AND EXPLORE THE GALLERIES OF CANYON ROAD

✴ Shopping

Act 2 (505-983-8585; 839 Paseo de Peralta). "Affordable retail therapy" is the way this boutique advertises itself. Good stock of fashionable bargains and treasures, often designer labels marked way down. Truly a place to enhance or build a wardrobe. If it's your lucky day, you'll feel blessed indeed. Look for the colored tag specials.

Desert Son (505-982-9499; 725 Canyon Rd.). Custom leatherwork for men and women, including boots, moccasins, and a particularly good selection of belts. The store also features bags and hats in western and other styles

Garcia Street Books (505-986-0151; 376 Garcia St., Ste. B). A good display of new titles by regional authors, as well as general interest titles plus quality literature; books on art, architecture, and style; and an excellent collection of affordable paperback classics. Specializes in fast special orders. A small bookshop with a good eye.

CANYON ROAD PROVIDES UNLIMITED SHOPPING OPPORTUNITIES FOR FINDING THE PERFECT HOME DÉCOR ACCESSORIES

photo-eye Books & Prints (505-988-5152; 370 Garcia St.). Calling itself the "world's foremost online photography bookstore," the sampling on display here is a knockout.

Silver Sun (505-983-8743; 656 Canyon Rd.). With jewelry arranged according to the pueblo of origin, this is an eye-dazzling array of turquoise and silver finery. Some of the city's most knowledgeable salespeople will assist you in finding the piece that speaks to your heart. Buy here with confidence. The store was founded decades ago by two schoolteachers who were in love with turquoise.

Clairborne Gallery (505-982-8019; 608 Canyon Rd.). Owner Omer Clairborne, a respected expert on Spanish colonial antiques, travels the world in search of items for his shop. Antiques from Mexico, Spain, Guatemala, the Philippines, and South America are featured

Pachamama (505-983-4020; 223 Canyon Rd.). More of a gallery than a shop, this is a bazaar of Latin American folk art, with *milagros, santos, retablos,* and antiques you will find nowhere else. Silver jewelry, books, and toys galore.

Jacqueline's Place (505-820-6542; 233 Canyon Rd.). Ladies' boutique with clothing and accessories both colorful and tasteful. Get your Santa Fe style on here, and it's guaranteed you'll stand out in any crowd.

✳ Galleries

Turner Carroll Gallery (505-986-9800; 725 Canyon Rd.). A fresh, distinct aesthetic characterizes the well-selected, sometimes startling work displayed here, much from Eastern Europe. International contemporary art by daring, museum-bound artists. In business 25 years.

ADOBE GALLERY IS ONE OF CANYON ROAD'S BEST-ESTABLISHED AND RESPECTED GALLERIES OF NATIVE AMERICAN POTTERY AND ART

Waxlander Art Gallery and Sculpture Garden (505-984-2202; 622 Canyon Rd.). A strong sense of color characterizes the largely sculptural work of the 10 or so New Mexico contemporary artists featured in a 150-year-old adobe. Absolutely delightful.

Morning Star Gallery (505-982-8187; 513 Canyon Rd.). One of Santa Fe's most reputable dealers in antique Indian art: pottery, weavings, clothing, basketry, blankets, kachina dolls, and more. Collectors come hither.

Nuart Gallery (505-988-3888; 670 Canyon Rd.). Contemporary abstract and figurative work, including the exquisite, dreamy magical realism of Alexandra Eldridge. The best of the best from around the world.

Gerald Peters Gallery (505-954-5700; 1011 Paseo de Peralta). This international gallery features classic western and Taos Society of Artists as well as contemporary paintings, sculpture, and photography. Peters is known for his O'Keeffes. Think of a fine museum where everything is for sale. Worth a visit in any event.

Adobe Gallery (505-955-0550; 221 Canyon Rd.). Art of the Southwest Indian. Classic pottery, painting, and more by the very best. Quintessence of Canyon Road charm and quality.

✳ Outdoors

Randall Davey Audubon Center and Sanctuary (505-983-4609; nm.audubon.org; 1800 Upper Canyon Rd., Santa Fe, NM 87504; trails open Mon.–Sat. 8 AM–4 PM; nature store/visitors center open Mon.–Sat. 10 AM–4 PM; $5 house tours 2 PM every Fri., free bird walks at 8 AM Sat.; $2 trails, $1 children under 12; gift shop and Nature Center bookstore open 1–4 PM). One of the few historic homes in Santa Fe open to the public, the Randall Davey Center is a state office, an environmental education center, and a National Audubon Society wildlife refuge. Set on 135 acres at the mouth of the Santa Fe River Canyon, the home of musician and artist Randall Davey is listed in national, state, and city registers of historical and cultural buildings. What is now the house was the original mill; the *acequia* behind it served both as irrigation ditch and mill-race. The house features massive beamed ceilings and 16-inch-thick stone walls covered by plaster.

Randall Davey moved to Santa Fe in 1920. His innovative works are exhibited throughout the house and his adjacent studio. The center is also a good introduction to local flora and fauna. Trails wind through natural vegetation of piñon, juniper, and ponderosa pine, and there is a large meadow. The area is rich in bird life and home to black bears, mountain lions, bobcats, coyotes, raccoons, and mule deer. The center offers an extensive schedule of bird walks, natural history workshops, home tours, and children's programs. There's also a fine picnic area.

Trailheads for the **Dale Ball and Dorothy Stuart Trail Systems**, managed by Santa Fe Conservation Trust (505-989-7019; www.sfct.org), are barely a 5-minute drive from downtown. These extensive urban trails through the Santa Fe foothills are perfect for when I need a quick, easy hike, especially around sunset. With beautiful city and mountain views at an elevation of 7,000 to 7,500 feet, enjoy these trails for biking as well as hiking. City access on the East Side. The trail system links to numerous others. Contact the Conservation Trust at the number above for details.

GUADALUPE STREET, RAILYARD DISTRICT, BACA STREET ARTS DISTRICT

These three contiguous areas may be explored by foot. Here you will discover an energy of a changing Santa Fe, one that embodies contemporary sensibilities within the city's historic context. This is the part of town with an urban edge, even as it remains a work in progress. The anchors, the Rail Runner commuter train within the old Railyard and the burgeoning Santa Fe Farmers' Market and Railyard Artisan Market, make this an especially enjoyable area to explore. Weekends experience the newly-installed Santa Fe Artists Market stroll with the entrance adjacent to Site Santa Fe. Several of Santa Fe's leading contemporary galleries are located here, including James Kelly Contemporary at 1611 Paseo de Peralta, Charlotte Jackson Fine Art at 554 S. Guadalupe St., and LewAllen Galleries at 1613 Paseo de Peralta. William Siegal Galleries, with ancient and contemporary art and textiles, is at 540 S. Guadalupe St.

For a complete list, visit www.therailyardsantafe.com or call 505-982-3373.

Baca Street Arts District: The SoHo of Santa Fe (926 Baca St., just west of Cerrillos Rd.). A cluster of studios on Baca Street, stroll around the back for the expanded district, featuring modern art and design. Not exactly a mall, this area is the up-and-coming, hip new neighborhood of Santa Fe, with artists at work in their studios and galleries and an energy that begs exploration. Check out **Liquid Light Glass**, the studio of Elodie Holmes (505-820-2222; 926 Baca St.) and grab a light, creative lunch on the patio at **Counter Culture Café** (930 Baca St.). Imaginative pottery, furniture, jewelry, and cutting-edge design.

SITE SANTA FE HAS SUCCESSFULLY ESTABLISHED THE PRESENCE OF A MODERN ART SENSIBILITY IN A TOWN LONG KNOWN FOR TRADITIONAL ART

✳ Dining

Second Street Brewery at the Railyard (505-989-3278, 1607 Paseo de Peralta; closed Christmas, Easter, Thanksgiving). A strong entry in the microbrewery scene, this one consistently wins major awards for its custom suds. The brewery is a success with locals, who enjoy the relaxed pub—its fish-and-chips, soups, and salads after work or on the weekends. There's often live music.

Counter Culture (505-995-1105; 930 Baca St., adjacent to the Railyard neighborhood). A cool lunch and breakfast stop with grilled sandwiches, Asian noodles, and notable soups. Serves well-prepared, tasty, healthful, and reasonably priced dinners make this a family-friendly stop. Enjoy the patio in nice weather.

Caveman Coffee Café (505-992-2577; 1221 Flagman Way). If you like your caffeine cutting edge, this is the place. They go where no other café in town ventures. Nitro, MCT oil, butter coffee. Adjacent to a gym.

Andiamo! (505-995-9595; 322 Garfield St.). An intimate neighborhood trattoria serving handcrafted lunches and dinners, reasonably priced and always just right. Scrumptious pastas, chicken marsala to win your heart, and championship pizzas.

Cowgirl Bar & Grill Cowgirl Hall of Fame Bar-B-Q (505-982-2565; 319 S. Guadalupe St.; closed Thanksgiving,

GLASS ARTIST ELODIE HOLMES RECEIVED THE GOVERNOR'S AWARD FOR THE ARTS IN 2016. WATCH HER WORK IN HER BACA STREET STUDIO

DON'T OVERLOOK THE BACA STREET DISTRICT OF THE SANTA FE RAILYARD IN YOUR EXPLORATION OF THE CITY

Christmas; moderate; barbecue, western; partial handicapped access; reservations recommended for dinner; special features: patio, fireplaces, take-out). The Cowgirl is known as a watering hole and place to meet as much as a restaurant. Beginnings include appetizers such as nachos, quesadillas, soups, and chile. Their forte is the mesquite-smoked barbecue, but you'll find burgers and fish platters; smoked chicken, black bean, and blue corn enchiladas; and good old T-bone steaks. Sprinkled through-out are choice vegetarian dishes such as the vegetarian chile and butternut squash casserole. An unusual item on any menu is collard greens, and this dish is worth order-ing at the Cowgirl. If you're particular about spicy food, ask. Finish up with chocolate espresso mud pie or peach cobbler, or, for laughs, order the Baked Potato, actually a chocolate sundae disguised as a spud, which kids of all ages adore. The place is usually jumping, frequented by a casual crowd, and live music plays in the full bar on week-end nights. The spurs, saddles, and photographs of Prairie Rose, Faye Blessing, and other rodeo cowgirls on their rearing horses make a fine memorabilia collection. The comfortable bar is a magnet for an interesting group, and there are plenty of no-cover entertainment events.

Tomasita's (505-983-5721; 500 S. Guadalupe St.; closed Sun., major holidays; inex-pensive; northern New Mexican; L, D; handicapped access; no reservations; special features: take-out, adjoining lounge, children's portions). Tomasita's is housed within the red brick Guadalupe station of the Chile Line railroad, which connected northern New Mexico pueblos and towns from 1880 to 1941. Handed down from generations, Tomasita's recipes produce a distinctly northern New Mexico cuisine that melds the corn, chile, beans, and fruit of the area. Specials include tamales, *chile rellenos*, blue corn chicken enchiladas, *carnitas* Antonio, and stuffed *sopaipillas*. The dining atmo-sphere is exuberant, the chile is hot, and the chips and salsa are bound to whet the appetite. A seat at the bar gets you new friends almost instantly. The delicious frozen margaritas are a signature item and rated highly by Santa Feans. Mexican, Spanish, or Irish coffee will warm you up if you've been out skiing all day. After-dinner treats include *natillas*, a delicious custard pudding, and ice cream–filled *sopaipillas* served with strawberries—Tomasita's version of a New Mexico strawberry shortcake. Ample seating easily accommodates large families. But be prepared to wait a little while for dinner; Tomasita's is very popular and a good value. Sit at the bar if you're looking for conversation. Live mariachis Tuesday evening add to the conviviality.

Dinner for Two (505-820-2075; 106 N. Guadalupe St.; expensive). One of the best little hidden gems in town—especially the Sunday dinner prix fixe menu, featuring scrumptious fried chicken. Billing itself as a French restaurant, the intimate bistro puts on a great show of the tableside Caesar salad. The mushroom soup, natural tenderloin, and so much more are the best around. Service is impeccable, but this place is not at all stuffy. Highest recommendation. You can pay more elsewhere for a big name, but it's hard to find a more delightful place to dine.

Sage Bakehouse (505-820-7243; 535-C Cerrillos Rd.; closed major holidays). When Sage Bakehouse first opened its doors, it changed Santa Feans' concepts of the staff of life to the finest crunchy-crusted artisan delight. From their special ovens come loaves of Kalamata olive and pecan breads, all made of the purest, most basic ingredients. Try a sandwich of Black Forest ham and Gruyère cheese for lunch, and by all means taste their hearth breads.

✳ Lodging

Pueblo Bonito Inn (800-461-4599; pueblo@pueblobonitoinn.com; www.pueblo bonitoinn.com; 138 W. Manhattan Ave., Santa Fe, NM 87501, 3 blocks south of the Plaza; inexpensive–moderate; 1 room with full handicapped access). Of all the B&Bs that popped up in Santa Fe in the 1980s, this one has some of the most charming and distinctive guest rooms, with each of the 20 rooms and suites named for an area Indian tribe. The look is rustic and colorful southwestern, with wood floors, 3-foot-thick adobe walls, small corner fireplaces, Indian rugs, Mexican pottery, and Spanish carvings of saints, called *bultos*. Enjoy a healthy, serve-yourself breakfast. Grounds are graced by private courtyards, narrow brick paths, adobe archways, and huge shade trees. Although near a busy street, this inn is secluded while still convenient to shopping, restaurants, and cultural activities. The owners pride themselves on providing a good value.

✳ Sites

Santuario de Nuestra Senora de Guadalupe (505-988-2027; 100 S. Guadalupe St., Santa Fe, NM 87501; open Mon.–Fri. 9 AM–4 PM, Sat. 10 AM–4 PM; closed Sun. in summer; donations accepted; gift shop). The Santuario is a longtime Santa Fe landmark and a performing arts center. It was built by Franciscan missionaries between 1776 and 1796 with adobe walls 3 to 5 feet thick. It is the oldest shrine in the United States dedicated to the Queen of the Americas, Our Lady of Guadalupe, who revealed herself in a vision to Indian convert Juan Diego in Mexico in 1531. Across the altar hangs a spellbinding painting of Our Lady of Guadalupe, the work of José de Alzibar, one of Mexico's finest colonial painters. A striking shrine in front of the building commemorates this site as the oldest shrine to the Virgin of Guadalupe in North America.

✱ Museums

El Museo Cultural de Santa Fe (505-992-0591; 555 Camino de la Familia, Santa Fe, NM 87501; open Tues.–Sat. 1–5 PM; free to exhibits; variable for performances). This Hispanic museum showcases living contemporary and traditional artists of northern New Mexico. Exhibits of photography, weaving, tinwork, painting, and sculpture live alongside environmental and cultural issue–oriented exhibits. Check the website for live performances and classes.

SITE Santa Fe (505-989-1119; 1606 Paseo de Peralta, Santa Fe, NM 87501; open year-round, Thurs. and Sat. 10 AM–5 PM, Fri. 10 AM–7 PM, Sun. noon–5 PM [closed Mon.–Wed.]; $10 general admission, $5 seniors and students, free Fri. and 10 AM–noon Sat.). No Southwest style here. Rather, you will find international

OUR LADY OF GUADALUPE SHRINE IN SANTA FE IS THE OLDEST SUCH SHRINE IN THE UNITED STATES

art exhibitions and a serious entrant on the biennial circuit. This is a seriously avant-garde, contemporary art space with an international biennial. Expect to see non-narrative video, huge images on bare walls, and art designed more to shake you up than comfort you.

Warehouse 21 (505-988-4423; 1614 Paseo de Peralta, Santa Fe, NM 87501). Arts events and workshops that involve youth participation and audience.

✱ Shopping

Santa Fe Flea Market (505-982-2671; El Museo Cultural in the Railyard, 555 Camino de la Familia). Sat. 8 AM–3 PM, Sun. 10 AM–4 PM. Also visit the Artisan Market Sun. in the Farmers' Market Pavilion.

Design Center (no phone; 418 Cerrillos Rd.). A rich collection of cafés, furniture stores, import shops, galleries, and home design studios, as well as ethnic eateries. Great browsing turf.

El Paso Import Company (505-982-5698; 419 Sandoval St.). For the home decorator looking to add a touch of the warmth of old Mexico, this is the place to shop. El Paso Import sells rustic chairs, tables, sideboards, and a wide variety of painted wooden furniture. The store also features pots, pot stands, ceramic candleholders, trunks, ironwork lamps, hardware for doors, and old spurs. Vintage, contemporary, distressed, and chic.

Santa Fe Farmers' Market (505-983-4098; www.santafefarmersmarket.com; 1607 Paseo de Peralta). An assembly of growers, crafters, and food vendors bring their wares to market here on Sat. and Tues., Apr.–early Nov. The indoor market is open year-round. Displays of seasonal fruits and vegetables are dazzling. This is Santa Fe's most happening event! Also, the Santa Fe Farmers' Market Shops feature wine, gifts, garden ornaments, and more, as well as fine coffee and tea.

APPLE TASTINGS AT THE SANTA FE FARMERS' MARKET PROVIDE CUSTOMERS WITH ALL THE INFORMATION THEY NEED TO SELECT FROM THE FALL CROP

Santa Fe Artists Market (505-414-8544; the Railyard) Sat., Mar.–Dec. Woodworking, painting, textiles, pottery—every conceivable craft is displayed here on Sun. The work is authentic, and the setting is perfect to meet and converse with the artists. This is an authentic marketplace.

The Raven (505-988-4775; theravensantafe.com; 1225 Cerrillos Rd.). More than 30,000 feet of awesome objets d'art displayed with originality. Jaw-dropping browsing. All things you had no idea you needed, but as soon as you see them, you require them to enhance your décor. Very hard to tear yourself away.

Marc Howard Custom Jewelry Design (505-820-1080; www.marc-howard.com; 328 S. Guadalupe St., Ste. E) Master Santa Fe goldsmith Marc Howard creates one-of-a-kind fine jewelry in high-karat golds and platinum set with diamonds and colored gemstones, with an emphasis on exquisite design, exceptional quality craftsmanship, and superior customer service. The shop also has a well-curated selection of vintage turquoise and silver handmade jewelry.

Molecule Design (505-989-9806; 1226 Flagman Way). Modern furniture and design. If your sensibility is modern, you'll love this place. As they describe themselves, "Molecule is the place where the newest, most innovative ideas in

THE NEW SANTA FE ARTISTS MARKET SHOWCASES THE TOWN'S MANY LOCAL CREATORS OF FINE ART AND CRAFT

contemporary and new modern design are housed, showcased, and discovered." Could your new sofa be waiting for you here?

Liquid Light Glass/Elodie Holmes (505-820-2222; 926 Baca St., Ste. 3). Fine sculptured glass made on-site and hand-blown. Stop by the studio and watch this artist at work. Classes available.

Antique Warehouse (505-984-1159; 530 S. Guadalupe St., Ste. B, at the Railyard). Spanish colonial antiques, including hard-to-find architectural elements, doors, unusual tables, and gracious benches.

Double Take (505-989-8886; 321 S. Guadalupe St.). Santa Fe's premier resale shop, this store has an extensive, well-chosen stock, from wardrobe basics to more exotic items. Also an excellent selection of children's clothing, much of it in mint condition. Hit it first and often!

Double Take at the Ranch (505-820-7775; 321 S. Guadalupe St.). Delightful array of classic cowboy and cowgirl wear as well as western kitsch and memorabilia. This place is a palace packed with pawn jewelry, knockoffs of vintage cowboy shirts, fiesta skirts, fringed leather jackets, and anything else you need to indulge your western whim and rodeo queen fantasy. You'll also find items of décor to add western flair to your surroundings. This shop is incredible!

Kowboyz (505-984-1256; 345 W. Manhattan Ave.). Died and gone to cowboy heaven. Vintage and secondhand. Thousands of bargain cowboy shirts, used boots, fringed buckskin jackets and vests, hats, home of the $99 boot. Get the look at a better price here than anywhere else. Parking lot, too.

Ark Books (505-988-3709; 133 Romero St., off Agua Fria, west of downtown). This New Age bookstore is a complete environment for browsing, with comfortable chairs, pleasant atmosphere, statues, and crystals galore. Six rooms of books specialize in healing, world religions, relationships, mythology, and magic. You can also buy music and shop an extensive collection of Tarot cards, jewelry, incense, and accoutrements useful on the path to enlightenment. A splendid spot for a relaxing idyll in the New Age.

✳ Entertainment

Jean Cocteau Cinema (505-466-5528; 418 Montezuma Ave.). In 2013 *Game of Thrones* author and Santa Fe resident George R. R. Martin purchased and re-opened the art cinema theater that now showcases eclectic independent cinema, director and author presentations, festivals, music events, midnight madness, and "the best popcorn in town." Full liquor license.

Violet Crown Theater (505-216-5678; 1606 Alcadesa St.). Dozens of craft beers on tap, a stone hearth pizza oven, housemade ice cream, and a full menu of seasonal and locally sourced snacks and entrées makes the Railyard's luxury movie palace a place to seek a full evening of entertainment in a comfortable and stylish environment. First-run movies. Reservations taken.

MUSEUM HILL

A cluster of museums, a botanical garden, and a café surround a lively plaza. Wheels or public transportation are necessary to get up here—and it's well worth the expedition. For bus information, call Santa Fe Trails at 505-955-2001 or visit www.santafenm.gov. The site of Santa Fe International Folk Art Market, second weekend in July.

✳ Museums

Museum of Indian Arts and Culture (505-476-1250; www.indianartsandculture.org; 710 Camino Lejo, Santa Fe, NM 87501; open Tues.–Sun. 10 AM–5 PM Nov.–Apr., 10 AM–5 PM daily May–Oct.; closed Thanksgiving, Christmas, New Year's, Easter; $12, $7 New Mexico residents, children 16 and younger free, first Sun. free to New Mexico residents, Wed. free to New Mexico seniors with ID; gift shop). This state museum brings together the past and present of Southwest Indian culture. It houses an extraordinary collection of more than 50,000 Native American art and craft objects. Included in the collection are basketry, pottery, textiles, jewelry, clothing, and other items. Artifacts are rotated on exhibit, emphasizing the Navajo, Apache, and Pueblo peoples.

The continuing exhibit "From This Earth: Pottery of the Southwest" covers archaeological, historic, and contemporary southwestern Indian pottery. "Natural Belongings: Classic Art Traditions from the Southwest" includes baskets, textiles, and jewelry. Artist demonstrations, from pottery making to basket weaving, are offered in summer.

Museum of International Folk Art (505-476-1200; www.internationalfolkart.org; 706 Camino Lejo, Santa Fe, NM 87501; open 10 AM–5 PM daily May–Oct., closed Mon. Nov.–Apr.; closed Thanksgiving, Christmas, Easter, New Year's; $12, $7 New Mexico adults, under 16 free, first Sun. free to New Mexico residents, Wed. free to New Mexico seniors over 60 with ID). You'll never see a collection like this unless you travel to six continents and 100 countries. Founded in 1953 by Florence Dibell Bartlett, who believed that the art produced by craftspeople, not highbrow artists, would unite the different cultures of the world. Judge for yourself as you wander among traditional clothing and textiles, masks, folk toys, miniatures, and items of everyday use. The collection numbers more than 125,000 pieces, including 106,000 from the Girard Foundation Collection, which the museum received in 1976.

The Hispanic Heritage Wing, opened in 1989, must also be described in superlatives. With about 5,000 artifacts dating from the late 1600s to the present, it's the largest collection of Spanish colonial and Hispanic folk art in the United States. It emphasizes northern New Mexico but includes folk art from the Spanish colonial empire around the world—including religious folk art, textiles, tinwork, utilitarian implements, gold and silver jewelry, and furniture. Truly a must see.

Museum of Spanish Colonial Art (505-982-2226; www.spanishcolonial.org; 750 Camino Lejo, Santa Fe, NM 87502; open 10 AM–5 PM daily May–Sept., closed Mon. Oct.–Apr.; $8, free for children under 16, free for New Mexico residents on Sun.; gift shop). Opened in 2002, the museum is housed in an intimate adobe structure designed by renowned architect John Gaw Meem in 1930. It was donated to the Spanish Colonial Arts Society in 1998.

The museum was created to house the society's 3,000-piece collection, which contains five centuries of art spanning four continents. Aside from the extensive art collection, the museum has a library with a 1,000-volume collection of books pertaining to Spanish colonial art and culture. A visit here makes a wonderful, yet not overwhelming, introduction to a more meaningful tour of Santa Fe. All exhibits are given a rich, clear historical context. Offers exploratory trips and hands-on workshops in traditional New Mexican Spanish arts.

Wheelwright Museum of the American Indian (505-982-4636; www.wheelwright. org; 704 Camino Lejo, Santa Fe, NM 87502; open Mon.–Sun. 10 AM–5 PM, closed Thanksgiving, Christmas, New Year's; $8; gift shop). Mary Cabot Wheelwright, a wealthy New England heiress, scholar, and world traveler, went by horseback to the Navajo

Reservation in 1921 at age 40. There she met Hosteen Klah, a powerful Navajo singer and healer. He spoke no English and she spoke no Navajo, but somehow they developed a rapport. She wanted to know more about his religion, and he revealed that he was ready to pass on some of his knowledge to people who could write it down. Both feared that the traditional Navajo way of life was about to be lost.

The two spent years researching on the Navajo Reservation. In 1927 they founded the Museum of Navajo Ceremonial Art in Santa Fe to house all their sacred artifacts.

As it turned out, Navajo culture proved much more resilient than the two had predicted. Even today the Navajo ceremonial system remains very much alive. In acknowledgment of this fact, the museum returned much of the sacred material to the Navajo Nation in the 1970s, and its name was changed to the Wheelwright Museum of the American Indian to express the institution's interest in all Native American cultures.

The Wheelwright's collection is strong in Navajo weavings, including tapestries of sand-painting designs made by Hosteen Klah himself; southwestern jewelry, basketry, and pottery; cradleboards from throughout the United States; and contemporary Indian art. The museum is dedicated to celebrating both traditional and contemporary Native American art; notable is the new jewelry exhibit.

Don't miss the **Case Trading Post**. Modeled after southwestern trading posts of the early 1900s, the Case is stuffed with top-quality Indian artwork in a range of prices, from Navajo weavings and Hopi baskets to old pawn jewelry and Pueblo pottery. You'll also find contemporary sculpture, books on Indians, and many tapes of Indian music. Discount to museum members. A reliable place to begin or add to a collection.

The **Bartlett Library and Archives in the Museum of International Folk Art** (505-476-1200; www.moifa.org) has more than 10,000 volumes on folk art topics, much available online. The **Laboratory of Anthropology Library** (505-476-1264; www.miaclab.org), next to the Museum of Indian Arts and Culture on Museum Hill contains volumes on the Southwest, anthropology, and archaeology.

MUSEUM HILL CELEBRATES NEW MEXICO'S INDIGENOUS CULTURES IN MEMORABLE FASHION

Cinematheque (505-982-1338; www.ccasantafe.org; Center for Contemporary Arts, 1050 Old Pecos Trail, Santa Fe, NM 87505). Besides producing a full range of arts programs, the Center for Contemporary Arts offers foreign and American art films, including classics. Ethnographic and video presentations by independent artists are stimulating events.

The Screen (505-473-6494; thescreensf.com; 1600 St. Michael's Dr., Santa Fe, NM 87505). When you find The Screen by following the signs on the campus of Santa Fe University of Art and Design, you will discover an intimate setting for independent film. Founded at the university, The Screen showcases the finest in world, art, and independent cinema. Featuring a 16-speaker Dolby Digital 6.1 surround sound system, a high definition curved screen, and luxurious stadium seating, The Screen is a good place to catch actors' and directors' live presentations.

WITH ITS DIVERSITY OF MUSEUMS AND EVENTS, FROM NATIVE AMERICAN TO SPANISH COLONIAL TO FOLK ART, MUSEUM HILL MAKES THE IDEAL FAMILY OUTING

✲ Cafés

Museum Hill Café (505-984-8900; 710 Camino Lejo; 11 AM–5 PM Tues.–Sun. only. closed Mon.; moderate; L). Piquant and stylish southwestern flair permeates salads, soups, and sandwiches. Or just stop in for a cool beverage, coffee, beer, or wine between museum-hopping. "Simple food done well" is the motto. Hundred-mile views.

✲ Outdoors

Santa Fe Botanical Garden (505-471-9103; 715 Camino Lejo). $7 general admission. The most recent addition to Museum Hill, this rather formal outdoor space offers warm weather picnicking and expansive views. First Thurs. of the summer months offer After Hours in the Garden at sunset. The garden encompasses off-site wetlands and trails.

Milner Plaza. A large, open, plaza-like public space on Museum Hill where crowds gather and celebrations are held. To one side is the Museum of International Folk Art; across the circle sits the Museum of Indian Arts and Culture. It's jammed during the International Folk Art Market.

NORTHSIDE/TESUQUE

As St. Francis and Guadalupe wind northward and climb the hill past the National Cemetery on the way up to Taos and points north, Santa Fe continues to offer rich opportunities for dining, shopping, entertainment, and outdoor exploration. It's a more settled, less flashy, less "Fanta Se" part of town that exists primarily to serve locals. Hang out here, and you'll soon feel right at home.

✳ Restaurants and Cafés

Bumble Bee's Baja Grill (505-820-2862; 301 Jefferson St.; closed Thanksgiving, Christmas; inexpensive; Baja style; L, D; partial handicapped access; no reservations). Best fish tacos! The fresh salads, salsas, and homemade chips, Baja-style grilled fish and shrimp, and soft corn tacos—all prepared for maximum flavor and health consciousness, dished up at bargain prices—have made Bumble Bee's popular with Santa Fe diners and families. One burrito is big enough to share. Savory marinated roast chicken, served with black beans and cilantro-lime rice, is delectable. Phone in your order and drive through for zero wait time.

Jinja Bar & Bistro (505-982-4321; 510 N. Guadalupe St., North DeVargas Center; open daily; moderate; Asian; L, D; partial handicapped access; no reservations). With an emphasis on wraps, noodles, and pot stickers, Jinja creatively blends the flavors Pacific Island and Asian cuisine and serves them up in dark wood surroundings with a luxurious feel and prices that won't devastate your wallet. Go for a full meal or an appetizer at the exotic bar. When the need for a noodle dish spiced with ginger or lemongrass strikes, this is the place. Inventive cocktails.

Gabriel's (505-570-4487; 4 Banana Ln.; closed Christmas, Thanksgiving; moderate; New Mexican, Mexican; L, D; full handicapped access; reservations recommended). Overlooking the Pojoaque Valley lies a restaurant offering delicious local fare. Expect generous portions of flavorful New Mexican– and Mexican-style dishes. Mesquite-smoked pork ribs, sizzling fajitas, chile stew, and frozen margaritas are just some of the superb concoctions available at this local favorite. Don't leave without partaking of the mouthwatering guacamole prepared tableside: It's their signature dish and also the floor show on the lovely patio. The restaurant is just 15 miles north of Santa Fe, so it's a bit off the beaten path. This fact makes them work harder to please you. Stop in for lunch or dinner.

Tesuque Village Market (505-988-8848; 138 Tesuque Village Rd., junction of NM 591 and Bishop's Lodge Rd.; open daily; inexpensive; New Mexican, American; B, L, D; partial handicapped access; no reservations; special features: patio dining, take-out). When you walk into Tesuque Village Market, you'll find an upscale grocery store with shelves and coolers stocked with beer, cookies, ice cream, candies, canned goods, and elaborate selections of mustards and salsas. There's an entire room full of California and local wines. The deli bar offers an inviting assortment of gourmet cheeses, meats, cakes, and breads for take-out. The menu includes a varied selection of New Mexican and American offerings, from huevos rancheros and bean burritos to sandwiches. Sunday morning brunch with the *New York Times* is a tradition for many locals—go with the blue corn pancakes. Popular lunches include a huge green chile burger with spicy fries and a tasty green chile stew. Desserts, made fresh daily, include Glurpy Cakes, pies, cobblers, éclairs, cheesecakes, and more. Indoors or outside on the front porch, you'll find a sympatico place to hang out with a coffee and read. Known for pizza.

Masa Sushi (505-982-3334; 927 W. Alameda St.). Infallible sushi and sake served in classic Japanese serenity. Reasonable. Local favorite.

Santa Fe Bar & Grill (505-982-3033; 187 Paseo de Peralta; moderate). The midrange, comfortable place is a go-to among locals. Consistent salads, fish, burgers, soups, and drinks, plus decent parking. Located in DeVargas Mall, so you can eat here and do your errands, too.

Clafouti (505-988-1809; 402 N. Guadalupe St.; inexpensive). The pastries, quiche, and bread here are all native speakers. You can run in and grab yummy pastries. Exquisite tiny French café serving breakfast and lunch. Parking challenged—the only drawback.

Terra Four Seasons (505-946-5700; 198 State Road 592, Santa Fe, NM 87506; expensive–very expensive). Here in the former Rancho Encantado location, this premier dining establishment caters to the sophisticated palates of world travelers with elegant, New American, locally sourced fare. The bar offers less pricey noshes and unremittingly gorgeous sunset views.

✳ Lodging

Casa Cuma Bed & Breakfast (505-216-7516; info@casacuma.com; www.casacuma.com; 105 Paseo de la Cuma, Santa Fe, NM 87501, 4 blocks north of the Plaza; moderate; no handicapped access). Informal and unpretentious, this B&B features three attractive southwestern-style rooms, an outdoor hot tub, and a common patio. Continental breakfasts feature strong coffee, fresh fruit, and homemade breads. If you walk up the road, you'll find a hill leading to a large cross, a Santa Fe landmark known as the Cross of the Martyrs. The climb will give you a superlative view of Santa Fe. Cozy with warm, attentive hospitality. Breakfast is served alfresco in the warmer months and is a memorable, delightful experience.

✳ Galleries

Shidoni Foundry and Galleries (505-988-8001; 1508 Bishops Lodge Rd., Tesuque, 5 miles north of Santa Fe). A must-visit. This 8-acre sculpture garden in the lush Tesuque River Valley is internationally known. Bronze pourings are on Saturday afternoons; call for times. Open year-round.

✳ Shopping

DeVargas Center (505-982-2655; www.devargascenter.com; 564 N. Guadalupe St.). The oldest mall in Santa Fe is a shopping center for residents in the northern half of town. It has been recently refurbished, and it's just the right size. It has about 50 stores, including Ross Dress for Less, CVS, Office Depot, Starbucks, Five Star Burger, Albertson, and Sprouts groceries. The mall also has jewelry stores, a spa and gym, movie theaters, pizza, ice cream, and now, Café Roha Ethiopian food.

WINTER OR SUMMER, THE SCULPTURE GARDEN AT SHIDONI MAKES A FINE ADVENTURE FOR THE FOOTLOOSE

op.cit. books (505-428-0321; DeVargas Mall). op.cit. is a general bookstore that carries new and used books, including first editions. They trade and buy books and are happy to special order. If you are content browsing for hours, this is the place for you. The staff is able to help you locate what you are looking for.

Las Cosas Kitchen Shoppe & Cooking School (505-988-3394; DeVargas Center). Probably the best equipped, most reasonably priced, and friendliest cookware shop in town, with a schedule of cooking classes conducted by the irrepressible chef Johnny V.

Tesuque Flea Market, (505-670-2599; 6 miles north of Santa Fe on US 84/285, Exit 171). Operated by Tesuque Pueblo, this flea market is a wonderful example of goods arrayed from as far away as Africa and as nearby as the studios of local artisans. This huge outdoor shopping arena is situated next to the Santa Fe Opera, 10 minutes north of Santa Fe, open Mar.–Dec., Fri.–Sun. 9 AM–4 PM. The shopper can browse for fine jewelry, leather, furniture, masks, and the occasional odd lot. Beneath a turquoise sky and within sight of the Sangre de Cristo Mountains, this is a relaxed place to shop, and it may still be possible to find a bargain, although caution must be applied when selecting goods. Bargaining is acceptable here. Pet friendly, free parking, and free admission.

Kokoman Fine Wine & Liquor (505-455-2219; 34 Cities of Gold Rd., Pojoaque, on US 285, 15 miles north of Santa Fe). One of the largest selections of fine wines, beers, and liquors.

La Montanita Co-op (505-984-2852; 913 W. Alameda St.). Open to the public. Topnotch supplier of natural and organic meats and produce, best selection of gluten-free and other special dietary needs products, plus high-quality bath, body, and nutritional supplements. Be sure to bring your own bags, as plastic bags are banned in Santa Fe.

Barkin' Boutique (505-986-0699; 510 N. Guadalupe St., Ste. N). Outstanding thrift shop benefits Santa Fe Animal Shelter. Designer, vintage, jewelry, collectibles, often donated when the stylish beautiful people clean out their closets.

✳ Entertainment

Santa Fe Opera (800-280-4654; www.santafeopera.org; 301 Opera Dr., Santa Fe, NM 87504; open July–Aug.; expect to pay more than $100 for a good ticket; standing room may be available for less). When the Santa Fe Opera opened in 1957, it filled a musical void and gave the city international stature. *Connoisseur* magazine has called it "the premier summer opera festival in the United States . . . a daring, pioneering enterprise." The ambitious repertoire usually takes chances on lesser-known or new operas, along with a world premiere or nearly forgotten masterpiece.

The opera's elegant amphitheater contributes to the mystique. Seven miles north of Santa Fe on US 285, it sits on a hilltop with views of the Sangre de Cristo Mountains to the east and the Jemez sunsets to the west. The 2,128-seat facility, famous for its architectural design, excellent acoustics, and views of the stage, now has a complete roof. Curtain time is 9 PM in July and 8:30 PM in August. Take a warm coat and blankets; temperatures tend to plummet after dark. Pre-opera gourmet, high-style tailgate picnics are de rigueur summer season highlights. Black tie and jeans will do just fine.

✳ Outdoors and Fitness

Ten Thousand Waves (505-982-9304; lodging 505-992-5003; 3.5 miles up Artist Rd. to Hyde Park Rd.). The legendary Japanese bathhouse with private and community tubs, mind-bending views, massages, facials, and much more, "The Waves" is essential to a Santa Fe visit, although, personally, I find the water a tad too hot. Now with the Japanese restaurant Izanami, featuring small plates.

Nambé Falls Reservoir (about 20 miles north of Santa Fe via US 285 and NM 503; take turnoff to Nambé Falls). For boating information, contact Nambé Pueblo (505-455-4400; 16 Np 102 E., Santa Fe, NM 87506).

Santa Cruz Lake Recreation Area (505-758-8811; Bureau of Land Management, 435 Montano Rd. N.E., Albuquerque, NM 87107). This small no-wake lake and recreation area near Española has a small-boat ramp and a 5 mph speed limit. Swimming is allowed only in the northeast picnic area.

Frank Ortiz Dog Park (505-955-2100; 1160 Camino De Las Crucitas, Santa Fe, NM 87501). Huge off-leash dog park with expansive views, a lot of sociability among people and canines, many walking paths. Exercise for you and the pup.

Santa Fe Spa (505-984-8727; 786 Call Mejila, Santa Fe, NM 87501). Includes free weights, Nautilus and Cybex equipment, treadmills, StairMasters, yoga classes, individual training, sauna and steam rooms, plus an extensive schedule of classes.

Fort Marcy Recreation Center (505-955-2500; 490 Bishops Lodge Rd., Santa Fe, NM 87501). Pool, weight room, cardio equipment, sports leagues, walking track, racquetball courts, and a wide range of classes in yoga, t'ai chi, jazz dance, and more, all operated by the City of Santa Fe Parks & Recreation Department. Open to the public at very reasonable rates.

CERRILLOS ROAD/SOUTHSIDE

Cerrillos Road is a busy thoroughfare that at first glance looks like any suburban roadway clogged with traffic. However, with some careful navigation below the surface, it's possible to search out interesting destinations for dining, entertainment, and lodging, plus experiences that can be found only in Santa Fe. Some of the best bargain motels are found here. Over the past two decades, the town has sprawled to the south, and Cerrillos Road stretches toward this development all the way from its northern, downtown end for about 10 miles to the south, passing strip malls and shopping centers occupied by chain stores and restaurants, then trails on to I-25, where, a few miles south of town, historic sites and hiking trails await. If you head east on Airport Road toward Agua Fria, you'll find an assortment of food trucks catering to the immigrant working population and serving authentic Mexican food.

✳ Restaurants and Cafés

Tiny's Restaurant and Lounge (505-983-9817; 1005 S. St. Francis Dr.; closed Sun. (except during football season), major holidays; inexpensive–moderate; New Mexican, American; L, D; full handicapped access; reservations recommended Wed., Fri., Sat.; special features: take-out, children's portions, patio, full-service lounge). Walter "Tiny" Moore and his son-in-law, Jimmie Palermo, opened Tiny's Dine and Dance in 1950. Since then, the location and name have changed slightly, but Tiny's has maintained its reputation for good food and for being a longtime favorite hangout for local politicos. The *carne adovada* is some of the best in town, and Tiny's is well known for its chicken guacamole tacos, pork chops, and *posole*. Plenty of *banco* seating, country-and-western background music, and hints of Italian proprietorship (including a huge Frank Sinatra picture) add to a comfortable dining experience. The lounge is the heart and soul of Tiny's, and it features one of the largest decanter collections in the Southwest. There's something going on most nights—live music, open mic, karaoke.

New York Deli (505-982-8900; 420 Catron St.; also 505-424-1200; 4056 Cerrillos Rd.; closed Christmas; moderate; New York delicatessen; B, L, D; partial handicapped access; no reservations). The go-to place for a fresh bagel, scrambled eggs with lox and onion, corned beef and eggs, and a pastrami sandwich. Tasty deli food with a southwestern twist, an extensive menu, and reasonable prices make this eatery a local favorite. This Santa Fe standard dishes up family recipes. You'll find chicken soup with matzo balls, cheese blintzes, and a breakfast that's served anytime, with such flourishes as smoked salmon eggs Benedict and blue corn piñon pancakes. They serve excellent coffee, too.

Tortilla Flats (505-471-8685; 3139 Cerrillos Rd.; closed major holidays; moderate; New Mexican; B, L, D; partial handicapped access; no reservations; special features: take-out, children's menu, full bar). Generous portions of everything from the iced tea to the *sopaipillas* make Tortilla Flats a favorite among Santa Feans—not to mention an ideal family restaurant. The chile is traditionally spicy and flavorful, evidenced by the menu's disclaimer: "We are not responsible if chile is too hot." Daily lunch specials include beef brisket tacos, *carne adovada*, Santa Fe Trail steak, and green chile pork chops. Burritos are enormous. The dining area is comfortable, casual, and easy to converse in. And the restaurant's southwestern setting is roomy with an inside-an-adobe feel. Ample booths and tables can accommodate just about any size party. And for those who like to get up late, homestyle New Mexican breakfasts are served until the dinner menu rolls out at 4 PM. A cozy, full-service cantina featuring 16-ounce margaritas connects to the dining room. Fresh ingredients, friendly service, reasonable prices, zesty chile, and hearty servings are the consistent trademarks of Tortilla Flats.

Piccolino Italian Restaurant (505-471-1480; 2890 Agua Fria). Real Italian red sauce, hearty baked pastas, very good chicken marsala and tiramisu, served on red-and-white checked tablecloths. Beer and wine, too. East Coast style.

Lan's Vietnamese Cuisine (505-986-1636; 2430 Cerrillos Rd.). Fine pho, vegetarian versions of traditional noodle soups, and absolutely delicious pan-grilled marinated lamb with lemongrass and ginger, all served at reasonable prices in a serene atmosphere. Culinary joy!

Whoo's Donuts (505-629-1678; 851 Cerrillos Rd.). Fresh-made doughnuts and bagels. Absolutely the best cider doughnuts anywhere! Or try the blue corn strawberry jalapeno or cocoa maple bacon.

El Parasol (505-995-8015; 1833 Cerrillos Rd.). The sibling of the famous taco stand in Española, El Parasol serves the same guacamole-chicken tacos and other beloved northern New Mexican standards at bargain prices that make it a mainstay for locals. Take-out only.

Jambo Café (505-473-1269; 2010 Cerrillos Rd.). Wildly popular and justifiably so. Don't be fooled by the shopping center exterior. This place is authentic down to the bone. Wonderful curries, East African coconut stews, jerk organic chicken, even goat stew. Famously delicious soups.

The Pantry (505-986-0022; 1820 Cerrillos Rd.; B, L, D; inexpensive). Perennially popular local café with hot green chile, homemade corned beef hash, daily specials, and a large menu of American selections. The Pantry comes closer to being Santa Fe's diner than anywhere else. Can get crowded for weekend brunch; if you are on your own, sit at the counter for faster service.

Lulu Chinese Cuisine (505-473-1688; 3011 Cerrillos Rd.; L, D; inexpensive). Located in the Quality Inn, Lulu's serves consistent, familiar Chinese fare; Chinese comfort food, if you will. Nothing challenging here, just flavorful standards that are reliable and crowd-pleasing.

Posa's Tamale Factory and Restaurant (505-820-7672; 1514 Rodeo Rd.; B, L, D; inexpensive). You can't get any more authentic than this place where you can watch the tamales being made according to the proprietor's grandmother's recipes. Big, frosty margaritas, too. They ship all over the country. Caution: These tamales are hot!

Backroads Pizza (505-955-9055; 1807 2nd St. #1; L, D; inexpensive). If you like your pizza thin and crispy, loaded with fresh ingredients, and want to enjoy it in a comfortable neighborhood hangout, this is the place.

Chocolate Maven (505-982-4400; 821 W. San Mateo Rd.; B, L, D; moderate). This longtime bakery-café is known for out-of-this-world confections and luscious soups, brunches, and sandwiches. Possibly the best smoked salmon in town. Parking can be tricky. Try to arrive either early or late to avoid the crush.

Verde Juice (505-983-8147; 851 W. San Mateo Rd.). And now at 105 E. Marcy St., too. The finest cold-pressed organic juices, guaranteed to cure or revive you—for a price. Be prepared to spend about $10 per glass. Also nut milks and all manner of healthy edibles made on the premises.

Whole Foods (505-992-1700; 753 Cerrillos Rd.). Santa Fe's version of the bustling supermarket. Lots of choices for take-out and salads. Now with its own brewpub. Parking madness.

Luna Center (505-982-9692; 505 Cerrillos Rd.). The site of Ohori's Coffee, The Olive Grove with rare and gourmet products, like 100 year-old olive oil and Ta Lin Oriental Market with pop-up dumpling and noodle bars the Luna Center gives visitors many reasons to stop and browse.

Tribes Coffee House (505-473-3615; 3470-A Zafarano Dr.). The cool place to hang out with a good cup of joe and meet up with friends on the south end of town. Pastries and light breakfast and lunch. Serving breakfast all day. WiFi.

Tune-Up Café (505-983-7060; 1115 Hickox St.; B, L; inexpensive). Located in the same funky old neighborhood place as the late, lamented Dave's Not Here, Tune-Up quite possibly serves the best huevos rancheros in town. The heart of the place is Salvadoran. Everything is fresh and fabulous, the only problem is it's often too crowded and parking is not easy to find. Go on the off hours and you won't be disappointed. You may even find a place to sit on the porch.

Santa Fe Brewing Pub and Grill (505-424-3333; 35 Fire Pl.; closed Sun.). In 1988, a wine bottle distributor named Mike Levis opened New Mexico's first commercial brewery on his 65-acre ranch outside Galisteo. Today, the brewery's best-known product is Santa Fe Pale Ale, available in bars, restaurants, and liquor and grocery stores. The company makes seven other beers that are available only at the brewery itself: Fiesta Ale, Porter, Wheat Beer, Barley Wine, Nut Brown Ale, Raspberry Ale, and Russian Imperial Stout. Tour the brewery (no reservations required) and pick up a T-shirt, cap, or poster emblazoned with the company label. Guided tours of the "top of the Turquoise Trail" facility on Saturdays at noon end with tasting samples of their brew at the **Eldorado Taphouse** (505-466-6938; 7 Caliente Rd., Eldorado), about 15 minutes north on I-25 from Santa Fe.

One of the best-loved Mexican food take-out stands in town is **Baja Tacos & Burgers** (505-471-8762; 2621 Cerrillos Rd.), with its healthy ingredients, tasty and ample portions, and "happy-hour" discounts. Specializes in tofu and vegetarian Mexican food. Also excellent for a quick Mexican food fix is **Felipe's Tacos** (505-473-9397; 1711 Llano St.), for healthy, authentic quesadillas, burritos, and tacos, with a choice of fresh salsas to accompany.

If you're after a quick burger, try **Blake's Lotaburger**, a New Mexico chain that's popular for quick-and-easy family outings. Blake's raises its own beef, and if you want a New Mexico chile cheeseburger, this is a good place to find one. There are Lotaburgers in or near Santa Fe (Airport Rd., Cerrillos Rd., St. Michael's Dr., and N. Guadalupe St.), as well as in Pojoaque near Taos (Paseo del Pueblo Sur) and in El Prado, just north of town.

✳ Lodging

Silver Saddle Motel (505-471-7663; www.silversaddlemotel.com; 2810 Cerrillos Rd., Santa Fe, NM 87507; inexpensive; 2 rooms with full handicapped access). Clean and affordable, this budget motel has 25 rooms, 10 with kitchenettes. Despite the nostalgia pitch, you can't get much more basic than this place. Jackalope, a southwestern furniture and import outlet, is located next door. Noise from Cerrillos Road may be offset by the convenience to the shopping experience of Jackalope. Funky, kitschy, western-themed.

Santa Fe Motel & Inn (505-982-1039; 800-930-5002; info@santafemotel.com; www.santafemotel.com; 510 Cerrillos Rd., Santa Fe, NM 87501, 5 blocks south of the Plaza; inexpensive–moderate; no handicapped access). If you're looking for an attractive, affordable motel in a downtown location, this is the place. It's set just far enough off a busy road to have an air of seclusion. In addition to typical motel rooms, it includes 10 adobe casitas with refrigerator, microwave, and patio entrance. Across the street, kitchenettes are available. Many will find this an excellent value and a reasonable way to stay in comfort without breaking the bank.

El Rey Inn (505-982-1931; www.elrayinnsantafe.com; 1862 Cerrillos Rd., Santa Fe, NM 87505; moderate–expensive; 4 rooms with full handicapped access). Built in 1935, El Rey is a classic roadside motel, offering both nostalgia and updated comfort. Many of the 87 rooms have flagstone floors, exposed vigas, Indian rugs, carved furniture, and ornate tinwork. Nine have wood-burning fireplaces; 11 others have gas log fireplaces in

EL REY INN OFFERS VISITORS A BARGAIN WITHOUT SACRIFICING AMENITIES

operation year-round. A large central courtyard is graced with a fountain and several large cottonwoods, creating a special world reminiscent of Mexico. Beautiful tile paintings both inside and out give the motel a Spanish flavor. A unit of passive-solar rooms overlooks a heated pool, and indoor and outdoor hot tubs await. This is one of the most in-demand lodgings in Santa Fe, so book early. A word of caution: I once spent a night here and the in-room antique gas heater was so noisy I could not sleep. Please check the heating system in your room before you accept it; in summer, this should not be an issue. As this motel was recently sold and prices are going up, we cannot say what other changes will occur at this time.

Santa Fe Sage Inn & Suites (866-433-0335; www.santafesageinn.com; 725 Cerrillos Rd., Santa Fe, NM 87501, 6 blocks south of the Plaza, across the street from the Railyard; inexpensive). Surprisingly quiet for a location tucked away on a busy intersection of Cerrillos Road. Also serene, due to what feels like solid construction, and decorated in tasteful southwestern style. Walking distance to many attractions, including the Plaza. Pet friendly, breakfast included, and an on-site bar, Derailed, serving craft beer and comfort food. A seriously great value.

Santa Fe International Hostel and Budget Bed & Breakfast (505-988-1153; www. hostels.com; 1416 Cerrillos Rd., Santa Fe, NM 87505; inexpensive; partial handicapped access; no credit cards). For the most affordable—but not the most private—lodging in Santa Fe (from $20 a night for a dorm room to $25 a night for a shared bath; $35 for a private room), you can't beat this place. In typical hostel style, men and women stay in separate, dorm-style rooms, and the kitchen is available for $1 a day. It's pretty spartan, and there aren't many extras (no TV, no pinball, just a radio), but for little more than a song, you've got a safe, warm place to stay and a great, convenient base of operation. Like most hostels on the worldwide circuit, this is an excellent place for networking and information gathering. This is a "chore hostel," so each guest is required to do a 10- to 15-minute chore per day, such as sweeping the front porch. Reservations must be made well in advance by postal mail with check or money order.

Hotel Santa Fe (505-982-1200; www.hotelsantafe.com; 1501 Paseo de Peralta, Santa Fe, NM 87501, 6 blocks south of the Plaza; very expensive; 4 rooms with full handicapped access). This is the most pet-friendly lobby in town, and this aspect of the hotel gives a homey feel to a luxury stay. In fact, Pampered Pooch packages are offered with every luxury for the beloved companion. This three-story hotel at the southern entrance to Santa Fe's downtown area is the result of a partnership between the Picuris Pueblo and a group of Santa Fe developers. Its terraced, Pueblo-style architecture gives the facade a pleasingly varied appearance. Its 163 rooms are attractively furnished in contemporary southwestern style, and guests will find a hot tub and heated pool. The Hacienda holds 35 luxury rooms, all with fireplace, including 10 suites plus two deluxe spacious suites. The lobby, a matrix of wooden beams and columns, serves as a dining room during the daily breakfast buffet and as a lounge in the afternoon and evening. Free shuttle service to the Plaza (10 minutes away on foot) is available. Emphasizing its Native American aspect, the hotel offers Native American flute music in the lounge as well as storytelling and lectures. Private tepee dining is also available.

Southwest Seminars, best known for its weekly public lectures, holds programs here at 6 PM every Monday in the fields of archaeology, history, Native American culture, and natural sciences, and feature local, regional, and sometimes national scholars. Educational field trips with some of those same scholars are offered periodically or by special arrangement.

✳ Sites

Mountain Cloud Zen Center (505-988-4396; www.mountaincloud.org; 7241 Old Santa Fe Trail, 1 mile south of intersection with Zia Rd., across from electric substation). This Zen center was founded in 1981 by students of Philip Kapleau's Rochester Zen Center. Formal sitting meditations in the Rinzai/Soto tradition are offered early each morning.

Santa Fe Jewish Center (505-983-2000; www.santafejewishcenter.com; 230 W. Manhattan Ave., Santa Fe, NM 87501). Chabad adult education, Torah study, Shabbat dinners, stimulating community, and social gatherings—this Jewish center extends a warm welcome to travelers and locals alike.

KSK Buddhist Center (505-471-1152; 505-471-5336; www.nobletruth.org; KSK Noble Truth Bookstore, 3777 KSK Ln., Santa Fe, NM 87505, off Airport Rd.; open Mon.–Fri. noon–6 PM, weekends 10 AM–6 PM). Buddhist sitting meditations are held in this authentic Tibetan *stupa* (temple). This center of Tibetan Buddhism was founded by the Venerable Kalu Rinpoche in 1975. Its spire is visible as you drive down Airport Road. Visiting lamas and other teachers from many lineages hold prayer and meditation services; they also give talks on Buddhist practices. The bookstore is a friendly, well-stocked place to find books by the Dalai Lama and other Buddhist thinkers. Resident Lama Karma Dorje leads sitting meditations. If you would like to visit the *stupa* at other times, please pick up the key at the bookstore

The **State Records Center and Archives** (505-476-7911; www.nmcpr.state.nm.us; 1205 Camino Carlos Rey, Santa Fe, NM 87507) is a rich collection of primary sources for genealogy and other researchers.

Santa Fe Community College Visual Arts Gallery (505-428-1000; www.sfcc.edu; 6401 Richards Ave., Santa Fe, NM 87508) can be counted on for showing fresh, challenging student work.

Kasha-Katuwe Tent Rocks National Monument (505-331-6259; www.blm.gov/publish/content/nm/en/prog/NLCS/KKTR_NM.html; $5 per car; dogs not allowed). About 40 miles southwest of Santa Fe, just northwest of Cochiti Pueblo. Take I-25 south to the Cochiti exit. This is the site of a fascinating miniature canyon. Soft, compressed volcanic rock has eroded into tent-shaped formations, many with a harder material

HIKING AMONG THE HOODOOS AT KASHA-KATUWE TENT ROCKS NATIONAL MONUMENT

balanced on top. Smaller bases supporting a larger boulder are called hoodoos. A favorite hiking and camping spot, believed by many to be a very spiritual place.

El Rancho de las Golondrinas (505-471-2261; www.golondrinas.org; 334 Los Pinos Rd., Santa Fe, NM 87507, Exit 276 off I-25, 15 miles south of Santa Fe; guided group tours Apr.–Oct.; self-guided tours June–Sept., Wed.–Sun. 10 AM–4 PM; $6 adults, $4 seniors and teens, ages 12 and younger free; festivals slightly more expensive; gift shop). El Rancho de las Golondrinas ("the ranch of the swallows") has seen everything from settlers and traders to bishops and Indian raiders in its nearly 300-year history. Miguel Vega y Coca bought the ranch as a royal purchase in 1710, and it became the last stop before Santa Fe on the Camino Real from Mexico. Caravans of traders, soldiers, and settlers regularly made the six-month round-trip.

Visitors can see an 18th-century *placita* house, a defensive tower, molasses mill, threshing ground, mills, a blacksmith shop, wheelwright shop, winery, weaving rooms, outdoor ovens, and more. The scene is complete with numerous farm animals.

Festivals celebrating weaving, the harvest, historic events, plus a Renaissance fair and more throughout the season. Open summer, spring, and fall.

✳ Shopping

The Flea at the Downs (505-982-2605; I-25, Exit 599, off Cerrillos Rd.). Three markets in one: vintage, artists and artisans, and growers. Open 9 AM–4 PM Sat.–Sun. May–June and Sept.–Oct.; 9 AM–4 PM Fri.–Sun. July–Aug. Shuttle from the Plaza.

Tin-Nee-Ann Trading Co. (505-988-1630; 923 Cerrillos Rd.). The trading company is a quintessential old-fashioned curio shop, with great deals on Indian jewelry, from earrings to squash blossom necklaces. Also features kachina dolls, moccasins, pottery, and sand paintings.

Santa Fe Place Mall (505-473-4253; 4250 Cerrillos Rd.). Once called Villa Linda Mall, Santa Fe Place Mall is the largest in Santa Fe, with 110 stores, including Dillard's. It has movie theaters, a video arcade, a post office, a public library branch, and a food court with carousel.

EL RANCHO DE LAS GOLONDRINAS (THE RANCH OF THE SWALLOWS), AN AUTHENTIC CAMINO REAL HACIENDA IS NOW A LIVING HISTORY MUSEUM THAT HOSTS A FIBER FESTIVAL EACH SPRING

Fashion Outlets (505-474-4000; 8380 Cerrillos Rd., 8 miles south of the Plaza). With more than 40 outlet stores, Santa Fe's Fashion Outlets offers the shopper good prices on many name brands. You'll find leather goods by Coach, housewares from Le Creuset, Ralph Lauren Polo, Nike, Eddie Bauer, Chico's, and more. If you love to shop, this is the place.

El Paso Import Company (505-982-5698; 419 Sandoval St.). For the home decorator looking to add a touch of the warmth of old Mexico, this is the place to shop. El Paso Import Company sells rustic chairs, tables, sideboards, and a wide variety of painted wooden furniture. The store also features pots, pot stands, ceramic candleholders, trunks, ironwork lamps, hardware for doors, and old spurs.

Susan's Fine Wine and Spirits (505-984-1582; 1005 S. St. Francis Dr. #105). Excellent selection of wine, many fine bottles at reasonable prices. Strong Italian and French sections. When I have a dinner party, I shop here for pairing advice.

Design Center (no phone; 418 Cerrillos Rd.). A rich collection of cafés, furniture stores, import shops, galleries, and home design studios, as well as ethnic eateries. Great browsing turf.

✳ Entertainment

Santa Fe Stadium 14 (505-424-0799; 3474 Zafarano Dr.). Cineplex playing first-run flicks.

The Screen (505-473-6494; www.thescreensf.com; 1600 St. Michael's Drive, Santa Fe, NM 87505). When you find The Screen by following the signs on the campus of Santa Fe University of Art

TRADITIONAL CRAFTS AND WAYS OF KNOWLEDGE ARE PASSED ON AT LAS GOLONDRINAS FESTIVALS

and Design, you will discover an intimate setting for independent film. Founded at the university, The Screen showcases the finest in world, art, and independent cinema. Featuring a 16-speaker Dolby Digital 6.1 surround sound system, a high-definition curved screen, and luxurious stadium seating, The Screen is a good place to catch actors' and directors' live presentations.

Meow Wolf (505-395-6369; 1352 Rufina Circle). Cutting-edge art complex located in old bowling alley purchased by author George R. R. Martin and gifted to the youth of Santa Fe. One of the city's newest shining stars. Like an indescribable journey through a gigantic funhouse. It's indescribable, and has become an international attraction.

✳ Wellness

Sunrise Springs: A Wellness Oasis (877-977-8212; 242 Los Pinos Rd., Santa Fe, NM 87507). Newly reopened, this is the last word in posh pampering. They say it best: "We create personalized experiences that incorporate our unique blend

HISTORICAL RE-ENACTORS DEPICT EARLY NEW MEXICANS AT LAS GOLONDRINAS FESTIVAL FOR THE ANNUAL BLESSING OF THE FIELDS

of Eastern and Western therapies enhanced by the ancient wisdom of Native American teachings. Nestled among 70 acres of breathtaking beauty, you'll discover gracious hospitality, tranquil, well-appointed accommodations, vibrant farm-to-table cuisine, our integrative spa, and engaging experiential activities designed to nourish your mind, body, and spirit." You can design a seven-day immersion or simply book a day or half-day. Counselors and medical personnel are also available to help with in-depth personal programs.

✳ Music

Several smaller groups lend variety and flavor to the musical scene year-round. **Serenata of Santa Fe** (505-989-7988) is a professional chamber group that performs at the historic Santuario de Guadalupe (100 S. Guadalupe St.). The **Sangre de Cristo Chorale** (505-455-3707) is an ensemble that performs a repertory of classical, baroque, Renaissance, and folk music. The **Santa Fe Women's Ensemble** (505-954-4922) is a group of semiprofessional singers who present a spring concert and four traditional Christmas concerts in Loretto Chapel. The **Thirsty Ear Festival** www.thirstyearfestival. com), a heralded annual summer event, is an exciting presentation of contemporary blues, roots, and folk music, as well as concerts throughout the year. The **Southwest Traditional and Bluegrass Music Association** (www.southwestpickers.org) keeps the tempo lively with its **Old Time Music Festival** in August. Free concerts all summer long July–Aug. at the Santa Fe Bandstand on the Plaza—with dancing. Check www.santafebandstand.org for schedule.

SANTA FE

Lensic Performing Arts Center (505-988-7050; www.lensic.com; 211 W. San Francisco St., Santa Fe, NM 87501). The Lensic is Santa Fe's arts and music central. From Roseanne Cash to musical comedy to world beat to flamenco, the Lensic is a venue for virtually every kind of sound. The stage is seldom dark. Tickets are available in all price ranges. Originally built as a motion picture palace, the 1930 Lensic is a fantastic creation of ornate sculpted plaster in a faux Moorish–Spanish Renaissance style. It boasts a silver chandelier from New York's Roxy in the lobby, along with the crests of Santa Fe's founding families and murals depicting the European settlement of the New World. State-of-the-art sound equipment makes this an ever-popular performance venue.

Santa Fe Chamber Music Festival (505-982-1890; www.santafechamber music.com; P.O. Box 2227, 208 Griffin St., Santa Fe, NM 87501; open July–Aug.; call for prices). With dozens of internationally acclaimed musicians and a grand concert hall (the St. Francis Auditorium), the Santa Fe Chamber Music Festival is

GRAB A TO-GO FAJITA LUNCH, AND ENJOY PEOPLE-WATCHING ON THE SANTA FE PLAZA

one of the town's biggest summer draws. Those who insist on the best come for the six-week season of more than 80 concerts, master classes, open rehearsals, youth concerts, and more. Through its composer-in-residence program, the festival has brought in some of the foremost composers in the United States. Preconcert lectures by composers, musicologists, and instrumentalists give audiences a deeper appreciation of the music. Daytime rehearsals in St. Francis Auditorium are free.

Performance Santa Fe (505-984-8759; www.performancessantafe.org; 324A Paseo de Peralta, Santa Fe, NM 87501; prices vary with concert; season tickets available). Since 1931, Santa Fe's oldest music organization has brought outstanding musicians from all over the world to perform classical and modern concert music. Association traditions include the Youth Concerts series and the all-Mozart Christmas Eve special. Most concerts are held in the Lensic Performing Arts Center.

Santa Fe Desert Chorale (505-988-2282; www.desertchorale.org; 311 E. Palace Ave., Santa Fe, NM 87501; summer and winter festivals of concerts; call for prices). One of the few professional choruses in the United States, the chorale has been described by the *Albuquerque Journal* as "a definitive choral performing ensemble." Music director Joshua Habermann auditions between 24 and 30 singers each year. Twentieth-century works form the backbone of the chorale's repertoire; however, major music from all periods is performed, particularly from the Renaissance and baroque periods. World premieres have included Dominick Argento's *A Toccata of Galuppi's*, Brent Pierce's *El Pocito*, Steven Sametz's *O'Llama de Amor Viva*, and Grace Williams's *The Call of the Sea*. Santa Fe concerts are performed at several downtown locations. Holiday concerts at the Cathedral Basilica of St. Francis of Assisi are a seasonal high point.

Santa Fe Pro Musica (505-988-4640; www.santafepromusica.com; 1405 Luisa St., Santa Fe, NM 87501; open Oct.–Apr. and Dec.; call for prices). Full orchestral performances are held at the Loretto Chapel and the Lensic Performing Arts Center. The annual candlelight Baroque Christmas concerts in Loretto Chapel are so popular that visitors from all over the world include them in their Santa Fe holiday plans. In addition to concerts by its Chamber Orchestra and Baroque Ensemble, Santa Fe Pro Musica presents world-renowned solo artists such as Yo-Yo Ma, Lang Lang, and Ian Bostridge, while also offering audiences the opportunity to hear up-and-coming young performers.

Santa Fe Symphony (505-983-3530; 800-480-1319; www.santafesymphony.org; 551 W. Cordova Rd., Ste. D, Santa Fe, NM 87505; performances Sept.–May. The Santa Fe Symphony, a lively group founded in 1984, performs under the direction of guest conductors. The season consists of eight subscription concerts of classical and contemporary compositions. Most performances are held at the Lensic Performing Arts Center. Imaginative programming is a hallmark of this professional orchestra.

✳ Nightlife

There's plenty to do, see, and hear during a night out in Santa Fe and Taos. Here are some of the latest hot spots. (For current happenings, check the Friday "Pasatiempo" section of the *Santa Fe New Mexican*, the *Santa Fe Reporter,* or www.santafe.com.)

THE ASTONISHING ART INSTALLATION THAT IS MEOW WOLF HAS CREATED AN INTERNATIONAL SENSATION

If you enjoy flamenco, head to the **Eldorado Court & Lounge** (505-988-4455; 309 W. San Francisco St.) to hear some of the best on weekends, as well as Cuban and Latin sounds. Look to the lovely room that is **Vanessie of Santa Fe** (505-982-9966; 434 W. San Francisco St.) for a cocktail-piano atmosphere and some sophisticated karaoke led by maestro Doug Montgomery.

La Fonda's La Fiesta Lounge (505-982-5511; www.lafondasantafe.com; 100 E. San Francisco St.) is another favorite place for locals and visitors to hear live music nightly while taking a spin on the intimate dance floor. Entertainment ranges from small jazz groups to flamenco guitar to country and western. The website lists the performance schedule. **El Farol** (505-983-9912; 808 Canyon Rd.) is a Santa Fe institution ensconced in an ancient adobe building. Cozy and dark with local landscape murals, it offers tapas bands, both local and national, and dancing in a tight space. Diva Nacha Mendez, salsa, Latin, jazz, open mike—this "heartbeat of Santa Fe" has it all. At **La Casa Sena Cantina** (505-988-9232; 125 E. Palace Ave.), the waitstaff is a young group of professional singers who belt out jazz and the best of Broadway. The cantina offers seating at 5:30 and 8 PM Fri. and Sat. and 6:30 PM Sun.–Thurs.

If you want camaraderie and conversation, popular spots range from the elegance of La Posada de Santa Fe's **Staab House Lounge** (505-986-0000; 330 E. Palace Ave.), with flamenco and South American rhythms, to the funk of **Evangelo's Cocktail Lounge** (505-982-9014; 200 W. San Francisco St.),a dark hangout offering live country, jazz, and rock bands Fri. and Sat. nights. **The Dragon Room Lounge** (505-983-7712; www.thepinkadobe.com/dragonroom.php; 406 Old Santa Fe Trail), located next door to the famous **Pink Adobe** restaurant, is one of the town's best-known see-and-be-seen spots, with dinner service from the Pink Adobe menu. If you just want to relax, head for the **Hotel Santa Fe Hacienda & Spa** (505-825-9876; 1501 Paseo de Peralta) for classical guitar and Native flute music.

Secreto Lounge, Hotel St. Francis (505-983-5700; 210 Don Gaspar Ave.) Garden-to-glass cocktails, housemade syrups, 27 kinds of bitters, and fresh organic fruits make for creative mixology. Vintage cocktails, too!

Skylight Santa Fe (505-982-0775; www.skylightsantafe.com/contact_page; 139 W. San Francisco St.). Now we're talking. Dinner served until midnight, dancing, live music—the place to go if you're young and hip or can manage to look like you are.

Cantina at El Meson (505-983-6756; 213 Washington Ave.) A weekly rotation of tango, jazz, and more jazz complements the tapas and excellent sherry. Love this place! Great food, always lively and festive.

Maria's New Mexican Kitchen (505-983-7929; 555 W. Cordova Rd.), with mariachis nightly during summer, is known for its margaritas, and **Tiny's Dine & Dance** (505-983-1100; 1005 S. St. Francis Dr.) is a fave music and dance scene among locals. The popular **Second Street Brewery** (505-982-3030; www.secondstreetbrewery.com; 1814 Second St.)—and even better at the newer location at the Railyard (505-989-3278; 1607 Paseo De Peralta, #10)—offers a range of contemporary and folk music Thurs.–Sun. A lively hangout and meet-up spot, some would say Santa Fe's best, is the bar and patio at **Cowgirl BBQ & Western Grill** (505-982-2565; 319 S. Guadalupe St.).

OUT AND ABOUT: NOSHING AROUND TOWN

Counter Culture (505-995-1105; 930 Baca St., adjacent to the Railyard neighborhood) is a cool lunch and breakfast stop with grilled sandwiches, Asian noodles, great soups, a patio, and now serves well-prepared, tasty, and reasonably priced dinners. The Chocolate Maven Bakery & Café (505-984-1980; 821 San Mateo, Unit C) offers monster chocolate croissants, breakfasts so good they will make you cry, and unbelievable sandwiches; parking in their narrow lot is the drawback. Downtown Subscription (505-983-3085; 376 Garcia St.) in the Canyon Road neighborhood, the grandma of them all, is a spacious, cheerful bar and patio with rack upon rack of newspapers and magazines to browse, plus good coffees and pastries. Ohori's (505-988-9692; 505 Cerrillos Rd. at the Luna station) serving impeccable coffees and attracting a hip (sometimes "tragically hip") clientele. Harry's Roadhouse (505-989-4629; 98 Old Las Vegas Hwy.) is easy to find. Just look for all the cars parked out front, especially at Sun. brunch time. Delicious, hearty breakfasts, sandwiches, and homemade soups and specials, plus pizzas and salads. The Teahouse (505-992-0972; 821 Canyon Rd.) serves an amazing selection of fine teas, coffees, and light meals with a Zen spin. The hearty oatmeal is popular. Other favorite breakfast spots include the Pantry Restaurant (505-986-0022; 1820 Cerrillos Rd.)—go for the stuffed pancakes, the fresh corned beef and eggs, or anything with chile. Open until 9 PM, it has excellent daily specials. Tecolote Café (505-988-1362; 1616 St. Michael's Dr.) serves up delicious low-cholesterol alternatives to its substantial helpings of French toast and fresh-baked muffins, plus its famous bread basket served with all orders.

For more quick bargain lunches while out and about, try Cleopatra Café (505-820-7381; 418 Cerrillos Rd.) in the Design Center for delicious moussaka, falafel, baba ganoush, and baklava. Back Street Bistro (505-982-3500; 513 Camino de los Marquez) serves up a variety of homemade gourmet soups daily, as well as salads and sandwiches; the Hungarian mushroom is a fave. Ramblin' Café (505-989-1272; 1420 Second St.) has fantastic quesadillas and sandwiches with fresh-roasted turkey; really, when you've got to have a great sandwich, you'll do well here at bargain prices. At Del Charro Saloon (505-954-0320; 101 W. Alameda St.), where you can get a yummy lunch for less than $8, including homemade fries, creamy green chile chicken soup, burgers, and enchiladas that taste far more costly, you can also sip a margarita or Guinness on tap. Dine at the bar or on the heated patio with large outdoor fireplace. Jambo Café (505-473-1269; 2010 Cerrillos Rd.) serves Afro-Caribbean food that wins awards annually. Highly recommended.

✳ Seasonal Events

Unless otherwise noted, admission is not charged for the following events.

SANTA FE

CHRISTMAS Christmas in Santa Fe is a delight that belongs on every bucket list. The Palace of the Governors usually sponsors Las Posadas, a traditional Spanish reenactment of Joseph and Mary's search for shelter on the night Jesus was born. The Plaza is the setting for the pageant, performed by an area church group, wherein the choir and audience members follow the Holy Couple around the Plaza. Other stellar events include Christmas at the Palace of the Governors, with hot cider, *biscochitos*, Christmas music, the annual show of the Gustave Baumann Marionettes, and so much more.

Many area musical ensembles conduct seasonal concerts in Dec.; consult the Santa Fe Convention and Visitor Bureau or local newspapers for schedules. Also, many area pueblos hold special dances around Christmas (see "Pueblos," page 76–81). On Christmas Eve, Santa Fe is alight with thousands of *farolitos*, glowing candles placed in paper bags. The scent of piñon bonfires, or *luminarias*, fills the air as hundreds of people take to the streets in the Canyon Road neighborhood to see the *farolitos*, sing carols, and socialize.

FEAST DAY DANCES Each pueblo has a special Feast Day celebration annually on its patron saint's day.

Indian Market (505-983-5220; www.swaia.org; Southwestern Association for Indian Arts [SWAIA], P.O. Box 969, Santa Fe, NM 87501; weekend following third Thurs. in Aug.; the Plaza and vicinity; free). Indian Market is the biggest weekend of the year in Santa Fe, when more than 1,000 Native American artists exhibit and sell their work at outdoor booths on and around the Plaza. The event is the largest exhibition and sale of Indian art in the world. Begun more than 80 years ago as an effort to help Pueblo Indians revive their pottery and jewelry-making traditions, it has since been the springboard for many successful artistic careers. All participants are carefully screened; they must be Native American, and their work must be totally handmade.

Activity starts before dawn on Sat., with artists unloading work at their booths and eager collectors lining up to get first chance at a coveted pot or necklace when the market officially opens at 8 AM. Irresistible smells of fry bread, coffee, mutton stew, and Navajo tacos fill the air, and the Plaza slowly fills with people. Artists demonstrate skills such as sand painting or basket weaving, and the drums sound for social dances in the courtyard of the Palace of the Governors. The array of artwork is mind-boggling, from pottery, jewelry, beadwork, and weaving to basketry, paintings, drums, and rattles. There's something for everyone, from a $3 corn necklace to a $5,000 Navajo rug. The party begins earlier in the week with special events such as clothing design contests, numerous auctions, and galas. Contact SWAIA for details.

La Fiesta de Santa Fe (800-777-2489 [Santa Fe Convention and Visitors Bureau]; www.santafefiesta.org; weekend after Labor Day; the Plaza and vicinity). The oldest continuously observed festival in the United States, La Fiesta is the quintessential celebration of New Mexico's Hispanic culture. The first Fiesta de Santa Fe was held in September 1712, with processions, sermons, candle lighting, and pomp and circumstance in commemoration of Don Diego de Vargas's reentry into Santa Fe in 1692 following the 1680 Pueblo Revolt (see page 25).

Fiesta preparations begin long in advance, with the selection of a young woman as fiesta queen, along with her court, and a young man as Don Diego de Vargas and his 17-member retinue. All performers play roles in a reenactment of Vargas's return. On the weekend after Labor Day, La Fiesta begins with the Pregón de la Fiesta and Mass at Rosario Church.

An extremely popular addition to La Fiesta is Zozobra, or "Old Man Gloom," a 40-foot-tall papier-mâché puppet that stands in Fort Marcy Park on Thurs. night of La Fiesta. Zozobra was born in 1926, the brainchild of Will Shuster, one of Los Cinco Pintores, founders of the Santa Fe art colony. As fireworks flare and "the Gloomies," as they are known, gyrate wildly around him, Zozobra goes up in flames, symbolically burning away the year's troubles so that the celebrations can begin. The cheering crowd then heads for the Plaza for food, music, and dancing. Plaza festivities continue through the weekend. In recent times, this event has become much, much more commercialized.

Lannan Foundation (505-986-8160; www.lannan.org; 313 Read St., Santa Fe, NM 87501; $6 adults, $3 seniors and students). The Lannan Foundation sponsors the

THE WORK OF MARIE ROMERO CASH IS ON DISPLAY AT SPANISH MARKET IN SANTA FE

Readings & Conversations literary series on various Wed. evenings Sept.–May at the Lensic Theater and at Santa Fe School for the Deaf. National and international literary stars tend to headline. Poets and writers of fiction and nonfiction read and discuss their work. Tickets for these events go fast, so try to book them at least a month in advance by going to www.lensic.com or calling 505-988-1234.

Rodeo de Santa Fe (505-471-4300; www.rodeodesantafe.org; Rodeo Grounds, 2801 Rodeo Rd., Santa Fe, NM 87507; mid-July; call for details). See "Rodeos" on page 58–59.

Santa Fe Film Festival (505-988-7414; www.santafefilmfestival.com; 60 W. San Francisco St., Ste. 307, Santa Fe, NM 87501; Dec.; individual tickets approximately $10, festival pass approximately $300). Independent, international, classic, and animated films; panel discussions; award galas and banquets. The 12th annual festival, held in 2011, showcased an evolving array of filmmaking talent as well as established stars like Emilio Estevez.

Santa Fe International Folk Art Market (505-992-7600; www.folkartmarket.org; second weekend in July, 9 AM–5 PM; Milner Plaza on Museum Hill). The world comes to Santa Fe! The growth of this event has been phenomenal. It now ranks as one of the most popular and best attended of the year, with juried exhibitors and artists from everywhere on the planet attending. The crowds, too, can be overwhelming, so if you have any aversion to them, go early in the day. The earlier the better, even if you pay a premium for your ticket as an Early Bird. The preopening evening gala is exceptional, and again, well worth the expense, if you want first shot at the art. Expect to wait in lines, even for the shuttle buses that leave from various sites around town. World music and entertainment plus an international food bazaar make this event, despite the crowds, a worthy highlight.

Spanish Market (505-982-2226; fax 505-982-4585; info@spanishcolonial.org; www.spanishcolonial.org; Spanish Colonial Arts Society, P.O. Box 5378, Santa Fe, NM 87502; last full weekend in July on the Plaza; free). During the centuries when New Mexico was a Spanish colony, its isolation from Spain and distance from Mexico fostered the growth of unique folk arts. Many of these arts and crafts helped serve the religious needs of the settlers. Beginning in the 1920s, largely due to the interest of writers and

THE ART OF *COLCHA* EMBROIDERY ENDURES AND IS TAUGHT TODAY

artists from the East Coast and California, they experienced a revival, and the work of New Mexican artisans is in great demand by collectors and museums.

At Spanish Market, which celebrated its 65th anniversary in 2016, you can see the finest Hispanic artwork produced in the region today: *santos*, *colcha* embroidery, woolen weavings, straw appliqué, carved and painted furniture, tinwork, forged iron, *reredos*, and more. Hundreds of artists exhibit in booths around the Plaza. The scene is complemented by native New Mexican folk music groups, flamenco dancers, food booths, and artist demonstrations. There's also a Winter Market in Dec.

Don't miss the **Contemporary Market** on Lincoln Avenue just off the Plaza. Exciting, innovative, and affordable work by Hispanic artists, including jewelry, fiber arts, painting, furniture, and crafts, is exhibited and sold at this show, which operates alongside the traditional market. And the artists delight in discussing their work with you.

LOS ALAMOS

Known as the secret city where the atomic bomb was developed during World War II, today Los Alamos remains a city based on defense and research, with a highly educated population and numerous historic sites commemorating the nuclear age as well as the Pajarito Plateau's ancient geology and indigenous populations. It is a pleasant place to spend time and offers golfing, skiing, dining, and shopping; it also serves as a gateway to exploration of Bandelier National Monument and Valles Caldera National Park. A stroll around Ashley Pond, the pretty pond at the city's center, evokes the town's history and shows it to its best advantage.

The Manhattan Project National Historical Park is a brand-new National Historical Park focused on American science, and it includes the noncontiguous locations of Bandelier National Monument and Valles Caldera National Preserve. The park yields interpretations of the social and cultural life of the people who lived and worked on the Manhattan Project. The new portion includes the early structures associated with Los Alamos.

✳ Dining

Blue Window (505-662-6305; www.bluewindowbistro.com; 813 Central Ave.; L, D; moderate). Classy little place with reliable service and New American food.

Ruby K's Bagel Café (505-662-9866; yum@rubykbagel.com; www.rubykbagel.com; 1789 Central Ave., Ste. 2; B, L; inexpensive). A comfortable place for a nosh.

FLAMENCO PERFORMED AT THE GAZEBO ON SANTA FE PLAZA

Pajarito Brewpub & Grill (505-662-8877; www.pajaritobrewpubandgrill.com; 614 Trinity Dr.; L, D; inexpensive; American). More than 30 craft brews on tap.

Viola's (505-662-5617; 1360 Trinity Dr.). Excellent Mexican food. Hot red chile will warm up a cold morning.

✳ Lodging

Hilltop House Hotel and L.A. Suites (505-662-2441; 400 Trinity at Central, Los Alamos, NM 87544; moderate).

✳ Museums

Bradbury Science Museum (505-667-4444; www.lanl.gov/museum; 1350 Central Ave., 35 miles northwest of Santa Fe via US 285 N and NM 502 W; open Tues.–Sat. 10 AM–5 PM, Sun.–Mon. 1–5 PM; closed major national holidays; free; cameras welcome). Photographs and documents give a glimpse of the unfolding of Project Y, the World War II code name for the laboratory that developed the first atomic bomb. But there's more: an impressive display of Los Alamos National Laboratory's weapons research program includes an actual rack for underground nuclear testing and presents an overview of the U.S. nuclear arsenal. You can also view a model of an accelerator and exhibits on the latest research in solar, geothermal, laser, nanotechnology, and magnetic fusion energy. Hands-on exhibits allow you to peer through microscopes, align lasers, and talk to computers. The museum is a clear and excellent window into this vital era of our history.

Films from the laboratory, screened in a small theater, include features on computer graphics, geothermal energy, and the history of the Manhattan Project.

Los Alamos Historical Museum & Shop (505-662-4493; www.losalamoshistory.org; 1050 Bathtub Row, adjacent to Fuller Lodge, 35 miles northwest of Santa Fe via US 285 N and NM 502 W; open winter Mon.–Fri. 10 AM–4 PM, Sat.–Sun. 11 AM–4 PM; summer Mon.–Fri. 9:30 AM–4:30 PM, Sat. –Sun. 11 AM–4 PM; free; bookstore). This museum is housed in a log-and-stone building that was originally part of the Los Alamos Ranch School, the predecessor to the Manhattan Project. It covers a million years, beginning when the Jemez volcano exploded and created the Pajarito Plateau. Exhibits include artifacts of the first known residents, farmers and hunters who lived here about A.D. 1100. Another exhibit, "Life in the Secret City," reveals the story of Los Alamos during World War II, when it was closed to outsiders as the best scientific minds in the nation rushed to make the bomb.

On the museum grounds are the remains of a Tewa Indian settlement of the 1300s. For a small fee, the museum provides a 12-page booklet for a self-guided walking tour of Los Alamos as well as a driving Homestead Tour. Docent-guided tours of Los Alamos Historic District on Mon., Fri., and Sat. at 11 AM, $10. The museum is managed by the Los Alamos Historical Society and was built in 1918 as an infirmary. It housed guests such as Gen. Leslie R. Groves.

Fuller Lodge Art Center (505-662-1635; www.fullerlodgeartcenter.com; 2132 Central Ave.; Mon.–Sat. 10 AM–4 PM; free). The center emphasizes the work of northern New Mexican artists and craftspeople. It is located in the John Gaw Meem–designed building originally built for the boys' school that preceded the Manhattan Project. The center hosts seasonal and holiday arts and crafts events.

✳ Outdoors

Valles Caldera National Preserve (575-829-4100; www.nps.gov/vall; 39201 NM 4, Jemez Springs, NM 87025, about 40 miles northwest of Santa Fe, continue on NM 4 past Bandelier about 15 miles). This vast, astonishing green basin—all that remains of what was once considered the world's largest volcano—is an 89,000-acre caldera, or collapsed volcano, a basin formed during Pleistocene volcanic activity 1.2 million years ago. Located on a 142-year-old land grant, also called Valle Grande ("big valley") or Baca Location, it is home to a herd of 45,000 elk. It is said that lava from the explosion that formed the caldera has been found as far away as Kansas. Since the area was named one of the country's newest national monuments, hiking, cross-country skiing, mountain biking, snowshoeing, sleigh rides, fly-fishing, wildlife viewing, horseback riding, and hunting have become available on a fee basis at various times.

Puye Cliff Dwellings (505-753-7326; www.puyecliffs.com; NM 30 and Santa Clara Canyon Road; call for directions and hours; $5 per adult; for warm weather weekend archaeological tours, call 505-917-6650). About 40 miles northwest of Santa Fe, near Española, the Puye Cliffs are home to Santa Clara Pueblo. The tribe welcomes visitors, who can walk to the top of a mesa where a village once stood and take in the magnificent views, although access has been somewhat limited due to the Las Conchas fire of 2011, which destroyed much of the Pueblo. Here you will find cliff dwellings dating from the 1200s. This ancient pueblo, built 1450 to 1475, was once the center of numerous villages on the Pajarito Plateau. Many of the designs found on pottery here focus on a plumed serpent figure who guarded the springs, which provided life-giving water.

The tourism office of Santa Clara Pueblo offers tours here, which is the only and best way to see the site. Ask for information at the gas station at the intersection above.

Tsankawi Ruin Trail (505-672-3861; open daily except Christmas and New Year's Day; admission included in Bandelier admission, otherwise free). To get to the trail, go about 30 miles west of Santa Fe on US 84/285 to NM 502, then get on NM 4 on the way to Bandelier, immediately south of White Rock. Look for sign and gate on the west side of NM 4, just south of Y-shaped stoplight intersection of East Jemez Road. An easy walk to unexcavated ruins, a visit to the Tsankawi section of Bandelier National Monument offers a spectacular panoramic view across the Rio Grande Valley to Santa Fe and the Sangre de Cristo Mountains. Tsankawi is a simplification of the Tewa Indian name *saekewikwaje onwikege*, which means "village between two canyons at the clump of sharp, round cactus." The enclave protects an important Rio Grande ruin of the Anasazi, a prehistoric Puebloan people. Take the 1.5-mile loop trail that begins at the parking area along NM 4. Descendants of the Chaco Canyon Ancestral Pueblo people lived here about A.D. 1300–1580. Faint petroglyphs and hand- and toeholds of the original Tewa-speaking dwellers are visible along the climb, aided in places by ladders. Please do not disturb the shards of black-on-cream pottery lying on the ground.

Bandelier National Monument (505-672-3861; www.nps.gov/band; 15 Entrance Rd., Los Alamos, NM 87544). The site includes nearly 50 square miles of mesa and canyon country with myriad walking, hiking, and overnight camping opportunities in the land of the ancient indigenous people or Ancestral Puebloans, formerly known as the Anasazi. Automobile permit $20; individual on foot or bike $7. Short trails in Frijoles Canyon lead through ancient ruins and cliff dwellings; longer trails lead south through canyons and west to the Dome Wilderness. Bandelier has more than 70 miles of hiking trails. Due to the massive Conchas Fire of 2011, trail access may be limited. Camping, backcountry camping.

Pajarito Mountain Ski Area (505-662-5725 information; 505-662-SNOW snow report; www.skipajarito.com; 7 miles west of Los Alamos via NM 502 and FR 1; 10,441 feet peak elevation; 1,200-foot vertical drop; 153 inches average snowfall; no snowmaking; 37 downhill trails [20 percent beginner, 50 percent intermediate, 30 percent advanced]; no cross-country trails; lifts: 5 chairlifts [3 double, 1 triple, 1 quad], 1 rope tow; terrain park; $49 adults, $39 half-day, $42 teens and seniors, $34 children, free for ages 6 and younger and 70 and older). Pajarito was started in 1957 by a group of Los Alamos National Laboratory employees who wanted a convenient place to ski. The area is owned and operated by the Los Alamos Ski Club, whose members are mainly Los Alamos employees or residents; however, it's also open to the public.

Pajarito is geared toward the serious day skier. Its runs are steeper, shorter, and rougher than most areas, which can be frustrating for beginners. On the other hand, some experts consider its runs the most challenging in the state. "If you can ski bumps, you're in heaven," says a friend. "If you're a novice who gets stuck on a bumpy run or goes into the trees, it's just hell." In recent years, there's been an effort to increase grooming to accommodate all levels of skiers.

There's no resort atmosphere at Pajarito—you won't find bars, lounges, or daycare for the kids—but you will find a three-story lodge with ski rentals and a nice cafeteria. You'll also find one of the rarest pluses of any ski area: no lift lines. Also, with only three skiing days a week, the snow at Pajarito lasts a relatively long time. Because of this and its small-town family atmosphere, many consider it an undiscovered gem.

In May, Pajarito converts to a biker's wonderland with lift service and trails galore.

Los Alamos County Golf Course & Community Center (505-662-8139; 4250 Diamond Dr., Los Alamos, NM 87544). This course is 18 holes, par 71, 6,500 yards. It includes a driving range, putting green, bar, and snack bar. The pro on duty is Donnie Torrez. Greens fees $31–$35.

THE HIGH ROAD

Little has changed over time along the 56-mile winding High Road between Santa Fe and Taos. Descendants of original settlers still farm and live sustainably, getting by with bartering, cutting wood, hunting, and fishing on land granted their ancestors by the Spanish crown. Ancient crafts of woodcarving and weaving still thrive, along with cultivating small sustainable farms. Isolated in tiny villages within high mountain ranges, people are polite but not overly friendly to outsiders. The mission churches of Truchas and Las Trampas are not to be missed; the Santuario de Chimayó, the "Lourdes of America," is a pilgrimage site that attracts more than 30,000 on Good Friday and many more throughout the year. It is a sacred site emblematic of New Mexico's deep Catholic faith. Newer arrivals, artists and craftspeople who have settled here since the 1960s, now also make pottery, create art, and farm, coming to town to sell their produce at farmers' markets in Santa Fe. The entire trip along the High Road takes about 2½ hours. From Santa Fe, take US 68 north to Española. From Española, go right on NM 76 on up the High Road about 11 miles to Chimayó.

✳ Dining

El Paragua (505-753-3211; 603 Santa Cruz Rd., Española; Mon.–Fri. L, D; Sat.–Sun. B, L, D; moderate; northern New Mexican; partial handicapped access; no reservations). For a half-century, El Paragua has served some of the finest New Mexican food (some would say the finest) in the land, including top-notch chips and salsa and luxurious *natillas*, a creamy custard dessert. Walk into its rathskeller-like dining room and bar and find someone fashioning fresh tortillas on a wood stove and a tree growing through the roof. The place is packed with locals, especially on weekend nights. If you want authentic—and delicious—this is the place to find it.

When traveling to and from Santa Fe and Taos, do as the locals do and stop next door to El Paragua at **El Parasol** (505-753-8852; 603 Santa Cruz Rd., Española; inexpensive) for the take-out version. There's no better place to take in the local color or the red chile; the chicken-guacamole tacos made them famous, and they are the best. Also with locations in Santa Fe and Pojoaque. Lowriders and movie stars alike flock here.

Rancho de Chimayó (505-351-4444; 300 Juan Medina Rd., Chimayó; closed Mon., Nov.–May; moderate; northern New Mexican; L, D; full handicapped access; reservations recommended; special features: fireplaces, patio dining, musicians in summer). This is the single most important northern New Mexico restaurant to bring your visiting family and friends. It provides the ultimate New Mexico experience in both food and décor. This beautifully remodeled ranch house has been in the Jaramillo family since the 1880s. A restaurant since 1965, it still has the feel of old northern New Mexico, including wood floors, whitewashed adobe walls, hand-stripped vigas, and a lushly terraced patio. Moreover, the food is prepared from recipes that have been in the Jaramillo family for generations.

After many visits over the years, we've found the food consistent, the portions generous, and the service friendly and efficient. And despite their busy-ness, both service and food remain up to their consistent quality standards. It's lovely in wintertime to sip a margarita beside the blazing piñon fire. The menu includes about a dozen traditional northern New Mexican plates plus steak and trout amandine. The nachos are particularly crisp. A huge, flaky *sopaipilla relleno* is stuffed to bursting with beef, beans, and Spanish rice. And the Chimayó chicken is moist and flavorful. For dessert, we recommend the flan, a rich, creamy caramel custard with a pleasing tapioca consistency. A visit to the Santuario de Chimayó followed by a lunch at Rancho de Chimayó will give you a better feeling for New Mexico tradition than just about anything else, as well as a true sense of well-being. In 2016, the restaurant received a James Beard Foundation American Classic Award.

Sugar Nymphs Bistro (575-587-0311; 15046 State Rd. 75, Penasco; moderate; New American; L, D, Sun. brunch; partial handicapped access; reservations recommended; special features: patio dining). Please don't leave the High Road without dining at this unpretentious, little spot. In fact, it's worth the drive just to eat here. Reviewers from top national magazines have awarded their highest commendations. Local, seasonal fare. Famous chocolate maple pecan pie and towering triple layer chocolate cake aside, the homemade soups, burgers, and special international dinners are the best around, made with love by two ladies from San Francisco who have been dishing out this grand fare for 20 years. Fresh baked bread baskets that accompany Sunday brunch. Call for hours, which may vary by season.

Lodging

Casa Escondida (505-351-4805; info@casaescondida.com; www.casaescondida.com; CR-100, Chimayó, NM 87522, 28 miles north of Santa Fe; moderate; 3 rooms with partial handicapped access); moderate–expensive. The beautiful simplicity of northern New Mexico awaits the visitor at the secluded and serene eight-room Casa Escondida, or "hidden house." Built in the Spanish colonial adobe style typical of this region and situated on 6 beautiful acres, this is the perfect place to rest deeply; go for long, undisturbed country walks; and enjoy the pleasures of the brilliant light, the scent of a piñon fire, and the profound sense of history and the sacredness of the land that characterize northern New Mexico. Lovingly decorated with antiques and rustic southwestern-style furnishings, this inn wraps you in its sense of tradition. A scrumptious hot breakfast is served in a light-filled room with French doors, and a large hot tub is tucked into a stand of trees. Pets and children are welcome. If you want to be away from the crowd yet not too far away from the attractions, this could be your spot. Pet friendly.

Hacienda Rancho de Chimayó (505-351-2222; 298 Juan Medina Rd., Chimayó, NM 87522, 25 miles north of Santa Fe; moderate; 1 room with partial handicapped access; moderate). This charming place is located in the heart of the ancient village of Chimayó, known for its historic church and its tradition of fine Spanish weaving. The inn was converted from a 19th-century, 150 year-old rural hacienda in 1984. The plasterless, straw-streaked adobe walls are adorned with red chile *ristras*, and the enclosed courtyard is bursting with fruit trees. Seven guest rooms, predominantly Spanish in appearance but with an air of the Victorian, feature dark massive vigas and heavy, handwoven curtains, the work of a local artisan. Antiques, wallpaper, and high ceilings give the rooms an almost American Colonial touch. Some have a private balcony and all have fireplaces. The seven-room hacienda is directly across the road from the acclaimed Rancho de Chimayó restaurant also owned by Florence Jaramillo and her family.

Rancho Arriba (505-689-2374; rancho@ranchoarriba.com; www.ranchoarriba.com; P.O. Box 338, Truchas, NM 87578, 40 miles north of Santa Fe; inexpensive; handicapped access; no credit cards; reservations required). You won't find a setting much more spectacular than this. Located on the Truchas Plateau above 8,000 feet, this

ROADSIDE AND STREET STANDS OFFERING BRILLIANT CHILE RISTRAS FOR SALE SHOW OFF THE ESSENCE OF AUTUMN IN NEW MEXICO

hacienda-style adobe B&B sits at the foot of the southern Rockies with amazing views of the Sangre de Cristos. A mile to the west is the centuries-old Hispanic village of Truchas, one of the more picturesque of northern New Mexico's mountain communities.

The four guest rooms are fairly small; one has a private bathroom, but all are authentically decorated in Spanish colonial style. The inn, also a small working farm and ranch, is organized around a central courtyard big enough to qualify as a plaza. Family-style breakfasts, cooked up on a woodstove, are served in a cozy common area with a fireplace and viga-and-*latilla* ceilings. Frank knows the mountains well and can recommend hikes. A winter or spring visit should not be attempted without a four-wheel-drive vehicle or tire chains. Here's a place to unwind for those with a bit of a sense of adventure.

Rancho Manzana (505-351-2227; 888-505-2227; ranchomanzana@gmail.com; www.ranchomanzana.com; 26 Camino de Mision, Chimayó, NM 87522, 24 miles northeast of Santa Fe; inexpensive; no handicapped access). Set on 4 lush acres, this ecofriendly establishment is a working farm. Highlights include an adobe with 29-inch-thick walls from the 1700s reclaimed from the ancient Plaza del Cerro, fruit orchards, fields of New Mexico chile, lavender that blooms in June and September, and an age-old *acequia*. Hostess Jody Apple established this wonderland in 1995. The full organic breakfasts can be enjoyed under a grape arbor in warm weather. An outdoor fire pit made of river rock and flagstone inlaid with mosaic is a splendid place for a BBQ, and a bubbling hot tub offers a relaxing spot to contemplate Chimayó's starry sky. There are two guest rooms downstairs in the ancient adobe. It's possible for one party with as many as six people to rent the entire lower level. A garden cottage with a two-room guest suite overlooking the lavender fields is available. Not only is there a hot tub, but a pond (for dipping) graces the grounds as well. Rancho Manzana is known as a spot for many special events, particularly weddings, and cooking classes are offered. Looking for heaven on earth? It's right here.

✳ Sites

Holy Cross Church (Iglesia de Santa Cruz de la Cañada) (126 S. McCurdy Rd., Santa Cruz, NM 87567). Tucked away just up the road from the turnoff to NM 76 up to Chimayó, this 1733 mission church stands in the shadow of El Santuario de Chimayó but ought not be overlooked by those interested in Spanish colonial art. The work of some of the earliest master santeros hangs here, and New Mexico history breathes through the walls.

El Santuario de Chimayó (505-351-4889; www.elsantuariodechimayo.us; 6 Santuario Dr., Chimayó, NM 87522; Sun. Mass, noon; weekday Mass, Oct.–May 7 AM, June–Sept. 11 AM; open daily in summer 9 AM–5 PM, winter 9 AM–4 PM). This chapel is located about 25 miles northeast of Santa Fe on US 84/285 to Española; turn east on NM 76. Follow signs to Chimayó. The site of this chapel is believed to be a former healing place of Pueblo Indians. The church was built 1813–16 by Bernardo Abeyta and other residents of El Potrero. They later finished the adobe chapel honoring Nuestro Señor de Esquipulas. There are at least two versions of the legend of its origin: Abeyta, while deathly ill, received a vision that beckoned him to a spot on the ground beneath the cottonwoods, where he was immediately cured. Or, in another variation of the story, he was saying his Friday evening prayers for healing when he saw a nearby illumination. At any rate, he built the chapel on that spot. For generations, Hispanic villagers in these remote mountains have attested to the miraculous healing powers of the "holy dirt" from a certain spot in the chapel floor. Testimonials and crutches lining the walls of the anteroom to the chapel give weight to the Santuario's reputation as the "Lourdes of America." Pilgrims bring prayers for healing to the Santuario all year long, but on Good Friday it is the destination of a pilgrimage when approximately

SAN JOSE DE GRACIA CHURCH AT LAS TRAMPAS IS CONSIDERED ONE OF THE MOST BEAUTIFUL MISSION CHURCHES OF THE HIGH ROAD

30,000 walk to Chimayó from all over the state to receive blessings. The twin-towered Santuario, a classic example of Spanish-Pueblo church architecture, is also a favorite subject of artists.

San Jose de Gracia de Las Trampas (Las Trampas, NM 76, 40 miles northeast of Santa Fe; open 8 AM–5 PM daily in summer; donations accepted). This structure, built between 1760 and 1780, is frequently described as the most beautiful Spanish colonial church in New Mexico. The village of Las Trampas was established in 1751 by 12 Santa Fe families led by Juan de Arguello, who received a land grant from Governor Tomas Velez Capuchin. In summer, the church is usually open 8 AM–5 PM; in winter, you'll probably find it locked. Ask at one of the gift shops for the person who keeps the key.

Sikh Dharma of New Mexico (505-753-6341; www.espanolaashram.com; 1 W. Sombrillo Rd., Española, NM 87532). Hacienda de Guru Ram Das, named for the builder of the Golden Temple in India, is the location of this spiritual center, which is open to visitors. The annual Peace Prayer Day, which begins a weeklong celebration, is held on the Saturday before summer solstice. A recent theme was "Activating Compassion through Sacred Sound." Certain practices, yoga, classes, and meals are open to the public. To get to Sikh Dharma, take US 84/285 north from Santa Fe 26 miles. Before Española, go right on NM 106 at the stoplight, then take the first right onto Sombrillo Rd. Go up and over the hill. Look for the gold dome of the gurdwara (temple) on the left; the parking lot is on west side of street.

Cleveland Roller Mill Museum (575-387-2645; Cleveland, NM 87115). The last working water-driven mill in the state operates during Mill Fest, held annually on Labor Day weekend. This area used to be a breadbasket, supplying wheat to the U.S. military and the Indians. The museum, actually the mill house, with equipment of the era and vintage photographs of the area, is generally open on weekends. Call for hours. Operated by Dan Cassidy, a descendent of 19th-century settlers.

✳ Shopping

El Portrero Trading Post (505-351-4112; 17A Santuario Rd., Chimayó). Also known as Vigil Store, here find chile, *milagros, santos*, books, tinwork, *retablos*, folk art, and much else that makes this area around the Santuario de Chimayó so special and unique. Founded in 1921 as a local grocery, it has grown into the humble gallery of some very well-known artists.

Galeria Ortega and Ortega's Weaving Shop (505-351-2288; 55 Plaza de Cerro, Chimayó). Watch Andrew Ortega, a seventh-generation weaver, at work in his studio. Authentic 100 percent woolen blankets, rugs, coats, vests, and purses made in the Chimayó weaving style. This is an excellent place to find a "lifetime" garment. Also Santa Clara Pueblo pottery and southwestern books. Snacks are available at the adjoining Café Ortega.

High Road Marketplace Artists' Co-Op & Gallery (888-343-5381; 1642 State Road 76, Truchas). Traditional and contemporary arts and crafts by more than 70 northern New Mexico artists, from whimsical sage dolls to tinwork and fine woodcarving. A good overview introduction to traditional arts and contemporary interpretations of those traditions. A nonprofit community store.

Theresa's Art Gallery (505-753-4698; NM 76 between Española and Chimayó). A small, welcoming gallery operated out of the home of Theresa and Richard Montoya, artists who paint Spanish colonial folk art. They also carry wood carvings, *retablos* and *bultos* made by area artists, Santa Clara Pueblo pottery, and more. Reasonably priced.

THE LIGHTS ARE OUT AT THE ROADSIDE BROKEN ARROW MOTEL ON ESPAÑOLA

Chimayó Trading and Mercantile (505-351-4566; NM 76 at Chimayó). Chimayó weavings, New Mexico folk art, Indian art, pottery and jewelry, antiques and furniture. Open daily.

Salman Raspberry Ranch (575-387-2900; NM 518 and NM 422, Buena Vista). During raspberry season, generally late Aug.–Sept., a visit to this family-run farm is an annual pilgrimage for many locals. Then the ranch is serving its luscious raspberry sundaes and raspberry lemonade; you can pick your own raspberries or purchase them to bring home. During the off-season, the ranch store stocks all things raspberry: jams, jellies, vinegars, plus other fine food and kitchen products. You can take in the old church and hacienda on this historic site by booking a private tour.

Victory Ranch (575-387-2254; Mile Marker 1, NM 434, Mora). Even if you're not shopping for an alpaca to bring home with you, you can enjoy looking at the fine yarns, weaving supplies, and alpaca hats, gloves, and sweaters. And you can feed the alpacas.

Centinela Traditional Arts (505-351-2180; 976 NM 76, Chimayó). This studio-gallery of Irvin and Lisa Trujillo, traditional Rio Grande weavers, is absolutely lovely and deserves an attentive stop. In addition to their own fine work, they display outstanding work of other weavers.

Cardona-Hine Fine Art Gallery (505-689-2253; 82 CR 75, Truchas). Originally from Los Angeles, Alvaro Cardona-Hine and Barbara McCauley, contemporary fine artists, have exhibited and sold their paintings from this idyllic location to collectors for 30 years. An illuminating stop.

Ojo Sarco Pottery (505-689-2354; 82 CR 73, Ojo Sarco). Whether you are shopping for a set of new dinnerware or a new baking dish, the hand-thrown pottery here, fashioned in knock-out colors by two master potters in this studio-gallery, is the gift of a lifetime. Kathy Riggs and Jake Willson have made this their home business for decades. Open by appointment 10 AM–5 PM.

✳ Outdoors

Sipapu Ski and Summer Resort (800-587-2240; www.sipapunm.com; 5224 NM 518, Vadito, NM 87579, 25 miles southeast of Taos via NM 68 and NM 518; 9,225 feet peak elevation; 1,055-foot vertical drop; 190 inches average snowfall; snowmaking 70 percent of area; 42 downhill trails [20 percent novice, 40 percent intermediate, 40 percent advanced]; cross-country trails available in nearby Carson National Forest; lifts: 2 triple chairs, 1 pomas, 2 Magic Carpets, 1 new quad and quad trail; $45 adults, $34 half-day, $29 ages 7-12 and free 6 and younger, $29 ages 61–69, free for seniors 70 and older; rates subject to change; ask about the new Power Pass). Sipapu was started by Lloyd and Olive Bolander, who first brought a small portable rope tow to the area in 1952. The next year they offered 30 pairs of rental skis with bear-trap bindings. Now, more than 50 years later, Sipapu is many times its original size. The area's laid-back atmosphere helps everyone feel at home, and the terrain parks are a haven for locals.

This refreshingly small, quiet ski area focuses mainly on beginner and intermediate fun, though they have added trails to appeal to experts, too. It is also known as a telemark mountain. Lots of times after a pleasant run, you can jump right back on the lift with no wait at all. The area includes a restaurant and a snack bar, about 750 pairs of rental skis, on-slope lodging for nearly 200, and another 375 beds nearby. Delightful Sipapu is just about custom-made for families on a budget. Many new summer activities, including fly casting clinics and disc golf.

✳ State Parks

Please visit www.emnrd.state.nm.us/SPD for information on state parks in the area.

TAOS

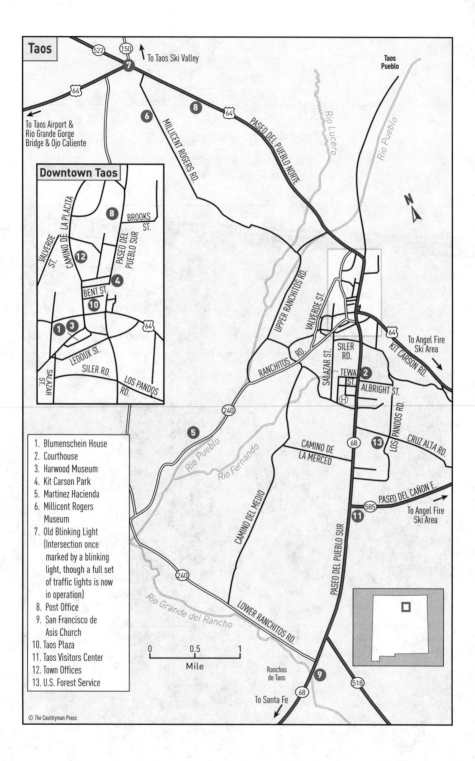

Taos

522
150
↑ To Taos Ski Valley

7

64

Taos
Pueblo

To Taos Airport &
Rio Grande Gorge
Bridge & Ojo Caliente

6

8

64

PASEO DEL PUEBLO NORTE

MILLICENT ROGERS RD.

Rio Lucero

Rio Pueblo

N

Downtown Taos

VALVERDE ST.

CAMINO DE LA PLACITA

8

12

BROOKS ST.

PASEO DEL PUEBLO SUR

4

BENT ST.

10

1 3

64

LEDOUX ST.

SALAZAR ST.

SILER RD.

LOS PANDOS RD.

UPPER RANCHITOS RD.

VALVERDE ST.

RANCHITOS RD.

SALAZAR ST.

SILER RD.

TEWA ST.

H

2

ALBRIGHT ST.

64

To Angel Fire
Ski Area

KIT CARSON RD.

LOS PANDOS RD.

CRUZ ALTA RD.

240

5

Rio Pueblo

Rio Fernando

CAMINO DE
LA MERCED

68

13

U.S. Forest Service

CAMINO DEL MEDIO

CAMINO DEL MEDIO

PASEO DEL PUEBLO SUR

PASEO DEL CAÑON E.

585

11

To Angel Fire
Ski Area

1. Blumenschein House
2. Courthouse
3. Harwood Museum
4. Kit Carson Park
5. Martinez Hacienda
6. Millicent Rogers
   Museum
7. Old Blinking Light
   (Intersection once
   marked by a blinking
   light, though a full set
   of traffic lights is now
   in operation)
8. Post Office
9. San Francisco de
   Asis Church
10. Taos Plaza
11. Taos Visitors Center
12. Town Offices
13. U.S. Forest Service

240

Rio Grande del Rancho

LOWER RANCHITOS RD.

Ranchos
de Taos

9

68

518

To Santa Fe

0   0.5   1
Mile

© The Countryman Press

TAOS

aos—the Place of Red Willows—is as old as the 1,000-year-old Taos Pueblo, a World Heritage Site, and as new as the people who just moved here from California to retire. It retains a bit of all it has ever been throughout its long history—trade center, hippie refuge, and community of artists. What we call Taos is actually the merging of three separate districts: Taos Pueblo, Ranchos de Taos to the South, and the central Don Fernando de Taos plaza area. It is today a place of diversity and creativity as well as a place of turmoil and struggle between old and new ways. Taos treasures its past, and it is not always kind to newcomers. Yet the Taos society of artists, including Mabel Dodge Luhan, D. H. Lawrence, and Millicent Rogers, were all newcomers at one time. One thing is certain: mythical beauty rules every bend in the road, and the mountain rules over all. They say you don't come to Taos—you are called. Adventure calls. Taos offers an unbeatable combination of white-water rafting, ballooning, fly-fishing, hiking, and skiing.

Lively shopping, recreation, art and music, food consciousness, and spiritual questing live in every nook and cranny of this funky, unpredictable, irresistible, unforgettable place.

✳ Taos—stroll

For a pleasant tour of Taos, start at the Kit Carson Home and Museum and go half a block north of the Plaza. Then walk toward the Plaza. Just before you get there, turn north onto NM 68, Taos's main street. A short stroll away is the historic Taos Inn, a popular gathering place for Taoseños and visitors. After you've poked your head in or sat for a bit, cross Paseo del Pueblo Norte and amble down Bent Street. It's filled with art galleries, alluring boutiques, and fabric and kitchenware shops. Then make your way to the Plaza and the Hotel La Fonda. From the Plaza, go west one short block and turn south onto Placitas Road. Follow Placitas until you come to Ledoux Street, then turn west again. Here is the former home of Ernest Blumenschein, one of the founding members of the Taos Society of Artists. A beautiful example of southwestern architecture, it too has been renovated, and the famous artist's private collection—including paintings by his wife, Mary, and daughter, Helen, accomplished artists in their own right—is open for public viewing.

✳ Dining

Taos Diner (575-758-2374; 908 Paseo del Pueblo Norte, Taos; inexpensive; open daily; contemporary American; B, L; partial handicapped access; no reservations). Although Taos Diner has opened a second kitchen on the south end of town, I prefer the original location for huevos rancheros with red chile, Cobb salad, local natural burgers, and general deliciousness. You can order half a salad. Much of the food is locally sourced. The red chile is good and hot. No wonder locals flock here. Check out the upscale food emporium next door for goodies for your special picnic and extra-healthy snacks.

Lambert's of Taos (575-758-1009; 123 Bent St., Taos; open daily; expensive–very expensive; contemporary American; D; partial handicapped access; reservations recommended; special features: private dining, patio dining, take-out). Lambert's delivers a fine meal in a relaxing atmosphere conducive to high enjoyment. This is one of those rare places that will feel like a bargain despite the considerable tab. Appetizers featuring fresh lobster, like lobster gazpacho, and other seasonally available ingredients are creative, light, and scrumptious, like the vanilla saffron poached pear salad. The house special of ancho espresso–rubbed lamb loin with red wine demi-glace, the Harris Ranch all-natural filet mignon, and the Maple Leaf duck two ways are but a few examples of the grace and flair demonstrated here. The menu changes seasonally. Sitting at the Treehouse Lounge, open at 2:30 PM daily, is where you're likely to find locals. Dinner over budget? Lunch served daily, while Sunday brunch is legendary.

Michael's Kitchen Restaurant & Bakery (575-758-4178; 304C Paseo del Pueblo Norte, 0.3 mile north of the Plaza; open daily 7 AM–8:30 PM, closed Nov., major holidays; inexpensive; American, New Mexican; B, L, D; partial handicapped access; no reservations; special features: fresh-baked pastries and desserts, counter seating, children's menu, take-out). You can't avoid Michael's Kitchen while in Taos. The menu has something for everyone, the doughnuts are beloved, the red chile is just right, and parking is no problem. And the price is right, too. Don't be put off if there is a line. It moves quickly. Michael's Kitchen serves delicious hearty dishes from fried chicken to enchiladas, chosen from a tabloid-sized menu. As you walk in the door, you will notice the large display cases full of breakfast pastries, breads, pies, and other mouthwatering desserts baked fresh daily at the restaurant. Once you finish gawking at the salad-plate-sized cinnamon rolls with cream cheese icing and confetti sprinkles on top, have a seat at the counter or at a table in one of the main dining rooms and settle in for a while.

Bearclaw Bakery & Café (575-758-1332; 228A Paseo Del Pueblo Norte, Taos, 0.3 miles north of the plaza; open daily 8 AM-3 PM; inexpensive–moderate; American, New Mexican; B, L; partial handicapped access; reservations; special features: fresh-baked pastries and desserts, gluten-free selections, take-out). The former pastry chef from Taos Inn has gone out on her own and is serving gorgeous baked goods, including fabulous pastries as big as actual bear claws and specializing in gluten-free cookies, coffee cakes, and other assorted goodies. The creative menu includes spins on local traditional dishes like breakfast fajitas with organic eggs and includes an alternative serving of greens for carbs, a delicious dish of lightly sautéed chard and kale. Omelets and blue corn pancakes star at breakfast; lunch starts at 11 AM and features salads, homemade soup of the day with housemade bread, bison burgers, and lamb gyros. Anthony's Bearclaw Reuben is the best!

Hunan Chinese Restaurant (575-751-0474; 1023 Paseo del Pueblo Sur, Taos; closed Tues., major holidays; inexpensive; Chinese; L, D; partial handicapped access; non-smoking section; no reservations; special features: take-out). This is the place to refresh your palate after all your New Mexican dining experiences. Here you can indulge in delicious pot stickers, hot-and-sour soup, pepper steak, moo shu duck, and imperial shrimp, and there's a great bargain-priced lunch special served 11 AM-3 PM daily. Those who know and love Chinese food will be able to appease their cravings at Hunan.

Orlando's New Mexican Café (575-751-1450; 1114 Don Juan Valdez Ln., 1.8 miles north of the Plaza on left; closed Sun., Christmas; inexpensive; northern New Mexican; L, D; no handicapped access; no reservations; no credit cards; special features: patio). If you're in the market for authentic northern New Mexico cooking without the lard, you can't do better than Orlando's. The décor of colorful Mexican folk art in lime and hot pink, accentuated with punched tinwork, and the scrumptious desserts all contribute to a delightful experience. Try the chile bowl "with everything," or go for one of the best Frito pies in northern New Mexico. Summer dining on the patio is a joy, though it can be very crowded during peak times, so plan accordingly. Success has not spoiled Orlando's, and it has come far from its humble beginnings as a hot dog cart on the Plaza.

Hero Handcrafted Fine Food (575-751-4444; 103 Juan Largo Ln. at North Plaza; open daily 11 AM–2:45 PM; inexpensive–moderate; American, global, New Mexican; L; partial handicapped access; no reservations; special features: patio seating, take-out). Hero is a new addition to the Bent St. district that is already a hit. Handcrafted fine food includes *carnitas* tacos with handmade, organic, non-GMO corn tortillas, bowls with international flair like the Seoul Bowl of Korean meatballs over sticky rice with hot and sweet glaze and hoisin mayo and hot pots, as well as delicious sandwiches like the turkey and Brie with cranberry red chile jam.

Gutiz (575-758-1226; 8128 Paseo del Pueblo Norte, Taos, 1.5 miles north of the Plaza on left; closed Mon., open Tues.–Sun. 8 AM–3 PM; moderate; Latin-French; B, L; no handicapped access; reservations; special features: children's menu). A local favorite with fabulous crepes and French toast for breakfast and outstanding soups and salads at lunch. The place for a croque monsieur, paella, or specialty sandwich. A little pricey but worth it.

Five Star Burger (575-758-8484; 1032 Paseo del Pueblo Sur, Taos; open daily; inexpensive). Get your burger in bison, lamb, turkey, veggie, or the old-fashioned way, with green chile, cheese, and Harris Ranch beef. Go for the crispy sweet potato fries. A bit pricier than your chain burger, but oh so worth it. Truly satisfying and, ultimately, a reasonable place to take the family for lunch or dinner. Money can't buy happiness, but it can buy satisfaction. At least here it can. The décor is a bit sterile and chainlike, but don't let that deter you.

The Love Apple (575-751-0050; 803 Paseo del Pueblo Norte, Taos; D; no handicapped access; check hours; expensive; reservations strongly recommended; special features: patio). The food is quirky, the menu limited, and everything served from the tiny kitchen in this crumbling adobe, a former chapel, is delish, from the cornbread all the way to the chocolate mousse. Free-range and locally sourced ingredients, intriguing salad combinations, traditional New Mexican dishes made with nontraditional ingredients, all served with casual elegance by candlelight make this one romantic adventure. Some interesting deconstructed dishes. Call ahead to be sure the menu is diverse enough for your party. The steaks are scrumptious and, for the daring, so is the wild boar. The menu changes often. Wines are excellent, and save room for the homemade desserts, particularly whatever is chocolate. One memorable evening guaranteed. The "love apple" refers to an antique moniker of the tomato.

The Bavarian Ski Restaurant & Lodge (575-776-8020; 100 Kachina Rd., Taos Ski Valley; open daily during winter, call for summer hours; expensive; German; L, D, après ski; handicapped access; reservations recommended). This is one hopping place at lunchtime during ski season. Warm and cozy as a German beer hall, it is the place to dine and unwind. You can ski to this midmountain European log lodge or call for a van to pick you up at Taos Ski Valley. Featuring German and European specialties such as Wiener schnitzel, bratwurst, Hungarian goulash, apple strudel, and beer imported from the oldest brewery in Munich. Bask in the winter sunshine on the beautiful sundeck surrounding this re-creation of an Alpine ski lodge.

Ranchos Plaza Grill (575-758-5788; 6 St. Francis Plaza, Ranchos de Taos; closed Mon.; inexpensive; traditional American with southwestern flavor; B, L; partial handicapped access; reservations recommended; no credit cards; special features: patio, fireplace). Sit on the patio in view of the most painted and photographed church in

THE BAVARIAN ATOP TAOS SKI VALLEY INVITES SKIERS TO WARM UP WITH ITS EUROPEAN-STYLE HEARTY FOOD AND DRINK

America, the old Ranchos San Francisco de Asis Church made famous by Georgia O'Keeffe and Ansel Adams. Then dig into some of the most savory red chile you'll find anywhere. The blue corn cheese enchiladas with red chile are pure New Mexico. The Ranchos Plaza Grill specializes, most appropriately, in classic New Mexico cooking, served in an ancient rambling adobe hacienda.

Old Martina's Hall (575-758-3003; 4140 State Road 68, Ranchos de Taos; open 7 AM–8:30 PM Mon., 7 AM–8:30 PM Wed.–Sat., Sunday brunch 9 AM–3 PM, closed Tues.; American, Continental, New Mexican flair; expensive; partial handicapped access; reservations recommended; special features: Fri. evening dancing or dinner theater, historic building). The varied menu includes Kobe steak salad, steamed mussels, and duck enchiladas for lunch; at dinner look for braised buffalo short ribs, local Tierra Amarilla lamb chops, green chile flan, and French onion soup. A romantic place suitable for a celebration, across the street from the famous Ranchos Church.

Taos Pizza Out Back (575-758-3112; 712 Paseo del Pueblo Norte, Taos; closed Thanksgiving, Christmas; inexpensive–moderate; pizza; L, D; partial handicapped access; no reservations; special features: take-out). Don't miss this funky little pizza joint slightly outside the Taos town limits. Don't be put off by its "back in the day" appearance. The undisputed local favorite pizzeria, Out Back is one of the hippest pizza parlors you've ever seen, complete with an old-fashioned gas pump in the corner and customers' crayoned works of art hanging on the walls. It specializes in "Taos-style gourmet pizza," lovingly made to order from organic Colorado wheat. Because the place is so often packed, you might want to order in advance or do take-out. Try the Florentine, with chicken, garlic, and herbs sautéed in white wine, or the portobello mushroom pie. Servings are more than generous, and they don't scrimp on the toppings. One slice will fill you up, but it's so delicious you'll want more. The salads are fresh and generous as well.

Trading Post Café Italian Restaurant (575-758-5089; 4179 NM 68 at NM 518, Ranchos de Taos; closed Sun., Christmas, New Year's; moderate–expensive; European; L, D; partial handicapped access; reservations recommended for parties of five or more; special features: fireplace, patio dining). Don't get confused. Despite the "Italian" sign out front, this is still the same Trading Post Café serving a freewheeling mix of Continental fare. Located along the Taos Highway, this bustling, well-run eatery opened in November 1994 on the old Ranchos Trading Post. Until 1981, the trading post had been the largest general store in the Taos area and was also the area's most popular meeting place. Today the owners of the Trading Post Café have revived that community spirit, inviting residents and travelers alike to come in and warm their feet by the kiva fireplace, nestle into a comfy corner table, or sit counterside on tall, wrought-iron swivel stools. If you are dining solo, this is a most comfortable place to sit at the bar and watch your food being prepared.

The menu includes a wide array of lunch and dinner offerings—generous portions to suit everyone's palate, at a variety of prices. Salads, fish, pastas, soups—including the house special chicken noodle soup—Creole pepper shrimp, roast duck, chicken Vesuvio, and *bistecca Fiorentina*, a 10-ounce rib eye. How about a paella with a glass of Vouvray? The pasta specials are reliable, and the menu is always varied with daily specials. Do ask about the price in advance, however, as some of the special salads can be surprisingly pricey. Service is professional, and there's an excellent and moderately priced list of red and white wines by the glass, as well as an array of wonderful, homemade desserts. The patio is glorious in warm weather.

Taos Common Fire (505-803-9113; 88 Calle Margarita (88 NM 150), El Prado, (L, D, Sun. brunch; Thurs.–Sun. noon–9 PM; moderate; special features: Wednesday night special events often scheduled; patio). The venture of experienced restaurateurs is creating superb classic American and Asian-influenced dishes plus fire-finished flatbreads with a well-curated wine and beer list. Menu is not expansive, but casual entries are spot on. The enormous hearth lights up the evening; in warmer weather, the patio is the place to be, especially in fall as the aspens shimmer gold.

✳ Breweries, Wine Bars, and Wineries

Taos offers a number of craft breweries, including **Taos Ale House** (575-758-5522; 401 Paseo del Pueblo Norte, Taos) and **Taos Mesa Brewing** Mothership (575-758-1900; approximately 11 miles west of the Town of Taos off US 64 near the historic Rio Grande Gorge Bridge), or their Taos Downtown Tap Room at 210 Paseo del Pueblo Sur with crazy good pizza lunch specials, a dozen draught brews, and a happening music scene. If you just want to relax with a microbrew, you can't beat **Eske's Brew Pub** (575-758-1517; 106 Des Georges Pl.; closed Christmas), the oldest microbrewery in the state. Ever try a green chile beer or an apricot ale? This is the place, where the fresh home-brewed beers are served with a menu of green chile stew, bratwurst, and delicious grilled sandwiches. A hangout where you really can kick back.

Wine bars of note are **Black Mesa Winery Tasting Room and Gallery** (505-852-2820; 241 Ledoux St.), serving New Mexico wine and live music, and **Parcht Bottleshop & Bites** (575-758-1994; 103 E. Plaza), which opens at 2 PM.

LOCATED JUST OUTSIDE OF TOWN, TAOS MESA BREWING IS A POPULAR SPOT FOR MICROBREWS AND LIVE MUSIC

Kyote Club Culinary Bar (575-751-3302; 330A Paseo del Pueblo Sur, Taos). Could be the best happy hour in town, with 50 percent off appetizers and drinks every day 3–6 PM.

✳ Wineries Near Taos

The first grapevines in the Rio Grande Valley were planted by missionaries in the 1500s, from cuttings originally brought from Spain to make sacramental wine. Thanks to the valley's long, warm days and cool nights, winemaking flourished here for hundreds of years—all the way up to prohibition in the 1920s. Finally, in the early 1970s, after a hiatus of 50 years, commercial wine production began making a comeback—partly with the help of French, German, and Swiss investments. Today, New Mexico has dozens of wineries scattered throughout the state, a few of them located in the mountainous Santa Fe–Taos area. Most have tasting rooms and welcome visitors.

Black Mesa Winery (505-852-2820; www.blackmesawinery.com; 1502 NM 68, Velarde; closed major holidays). Jerry and Lynda Burd live on the road to Taos in fruit country, where grapes have grown for four centuries. Perhaps too well known for their Black Beauty, a chocolate-scented red, Black Mesa has matured into a producer of a grand range of highly respectable wines. Their tasting room is a comfortable place to get acquainted and "nose some juice."

La Chiripada Winery (505-579-4437; NM 75, Dixon, about 3 miles east of NM 68; open daily). Sometime when you're shuttling between Santa Fe and Taos on NM 68, take a quick detour at the Dixon turnoff for a taste of heaven in a traditional adobe and viga tasting room. Mike and Patrick Johnson started this little family vineyard in 1977 and began making wine in 1981. At 6,100 feet, La Chiripada is the highest commercial vineyard in the United States, where they successfully cultivate the heartiest of grapes (two pinot noir hybrids, for example) that ripen into intense flavors. Each year they crush 20 to 30 tons of fruit. The combined results, several of which have won bronze medals in the *Dallas Morning News* National Wine Competition, speak for themselves.

These wines are surprisingly good. We recommend the Primavera, a blend of riesling and French hybrids, served at the Santa Fe School of Cooking. They also operate a wine shop in Taos on Bent Street, a block from the Plaza.

✳ Casinos

Taos Mountain Casino (575-737-9777; 700 Veterans Hwy., in Taos Pueblo). Slots and live entertainment in the only nonsmoking casino in the state.

✳ Cafés

Good sipping spots in Taos include the **Bent Street Cafe** (575-758-5787; 120 Bent St. in the John Dunn House Shops complex), with adequate, not knockout, soups, salads, and sandwiches; and the classic **Caffe Tazza** (575-758-8706; 122 Kit Carson Rd.), with its ramshackle patio. **World Cup Café** (575-737-5299; 102 Paseo del Pueblo Norte, Ste. A, on the Plaza) serves only one kind of coffee—a strong, dark, espresso roast, and it is grand. And the grown-up feeling **Elevation Coffee** (575-758-3068; 1110 Paseo del Pueblo Norte, El Prado) pours a fabulous cup and beautifully foams its lattes. But **Wired? Coffee Cyber Cafe** (575-751-9473; 705 Felicidad Ln.), behind Albertson's, is probably the numero uno coffee/hangout spot, with its rambling garden and multi-leveled work spaces. However, the **Coffee Spot** (575-758-8556; 900 Paseo del Pueblo Norte, open 6 AM–6 PM daily, is coming on strong as a competitor, with small plates, breakfast and lunch all day, fine baked goods, and decadent desserts, including fudge and Rice Krispies Treats, cheesecake, and pie. **El Gamal** (575-613-0311; 112 Dona Luz St.) is a Middle Eastern café serving fresh bagels, pita sandwiches, and hummus.

YES, YOU CAN GET FRESH HOT BAGELS IN TAOS, AT EL GAMAL

✳ Nightlife

An excellent place to begin or end your evening is Taos's "living room"—the Taos Inn's **Adobe Bar** (575-758-2233; www.taosinn.com; 125 Paseo del Pueblo Norte). The inn itself is a lovingly restored historic landmark. There's live entertainment nightly. There's live music Fri. and Sat. at the **Sagebrush Inn** (575-758-2254; www.sagebrushinn.com; 1508 Paseo de Pueblo Sur), where some of the best local country-and-western performers play. Local bands also play weekends at the **Best Western Kachina Lodge** (575-758-2275; 413 Paseo del Pueblo Norte). At **Ally Cantina** (575-758-2121; 121 Teresina Ln.), tourists and locals crowd into this funky old space until the wee hours for live music nightly. **KTAO Solar Center** (575-9758-5826; NM 150) has evolved into a super venue for touring musicians and performers (think reggae, afro-beat), with happy hour Wed.–Sun. 5–7 PM, a full bar, food service, and local bands on Thurs. evenings. Very reasonable ticket prices, kid-friendly, and the coolest place in town to hang out. **Caffe Tazza** (575-758-8706; 122 Kit Carson Rd.) is the place to hear poetry readings and more offbeat performers.

✳ Lodging

Air B&B and VRBO offer numerous listings in Taos.

Taos Lodging Vacation Properties: 575-751-1771; 109 Brookes St., Taos, NM 87571.

American Artists Gallery House B&B (800-532-2041; aagh@newmex.com; www.taosbedandbreakfast.com; 132 Frontier Lane, P.O. Box 584, Taos, NM 87571, 1 mile south of the Plaza; inexpensive–expensive; 1 room with partial handicapped access). As the name implies, artists and their art are celebrated at this peaceful B&B on a secluded Taos lane. The hosts are warm and the breakfast scrumptious. The inn displays more than 300 works of art, and artists are sometimes invited to discuss their work. Kiva fireplaces and knockout views of Taos Mountain contribute to your developing love of place. With 10 rooms and three very private, luxurious Jacuzzi suites in the southwestern-style complex, this B&B offers an ideal opportunity to relax and catch up on some genuine R&R.

Best Western Kachina Lodge, Resort and Meeting Center (575-758-2275; 413 Paseo del Pueblo Norte, Taos, NM 87571, 4 blocks north of the Plaza; inexpensive; 7 rooms with partial handicapped access). Learn to time travel in Taos. Just north of the city center, this Best Western is a classic roadside motel straight out of the 1950s. Don't miss the circular Kiva Coffee Shop, dominated by a bizarre hand-carved totem pole. Hot breakfast is included. All 118 guest rooms look onto a spacious courtyard with a broad lawn, tall pine trees, and a large heated swimming pool. The grounds have a country club feel. The Indian décor is laid on a bit thick, and there are even Indian dances on summer nights, but that's how they did things 40 years ago. What makes this place is that it evokes nostalgia without really trying. Close to town, homey, and the price is right.

Casa Benavides Historic Inn (575-758-1772; www.casabenavides.com; 137 Kit Carson Rd., Taos, NM 87571; 1 block east of the Plaza; moderate–expensive; 1 room with full handicapped access). Airy, light, and colorful, this sprawling B&B boasts 38 guest rooms in six different buildings on 5 downtown acres. Five of the buildings are traditional southwestern adobe, and one is a western Victorian home. The rooms are spacious and modern with all the usual southwestern accents: Navajo rugs, flagstone floors, ceiling fans, skylights, Indian pottery, and kiva fireplaces. There are even a few surprises, including deerskin drums and an authentic Indian tomahawk. Owners Tom and Barbara McCarthy are native Taoseños who've headed a number of different retail businesses in town. Return for afternoon tea to the aroma of freshly baked cookies. The big breakfasts include homemade tortillas and waffles, Mexican eggs, and homemade muffins. A short walk to the Plaza. Guests are inevitably pleased.

Cottonwood Inn (575-776-5826; cottonwoodinn@gmail.com; 2 State Road 230, El Prado, NM 87529; moderate–expensive; 1 room with full handicapped access). Located just off the route to Taos Ski Valley, Cottonwood Inn is the brainchild of two delightful and charming California refugees who are very much in love with their renovated classic and live on-site at this pueblo estate, formerly the residence of flamboyant local artist Wolfgang Pogzeba. Cottonwood Inn is now a two-suite rental. With kiva fireplaces, balconies, viga ceilings, Jacuzzis, wet bars, and skylights in most rooms, all guests need to do is kick back and enjoy the spectacular views and fabulous breakfasts. Winters bring the warmth of a roaring fire, while summer is the time to enjoy the lovely gardens on 4 acres of paradise.

Dreamcatcher Bed and Breakfast (575-758-0613; 888-758-0613; dream@dreambb. com; www.dreambb.com; P.O. Box 2069, 416 La Lomita Rd., Taos, NM 87571; about 1 mile southwest of the Plaza; moderate; 2 rooms with full handicapped access). Done up in true southwestern style, the seven cozy rooms, each with fireplace, have some unusual touches, like an aqua-colored tile floor (with radiant heat, most appreciated in winter). Big country breakfasts are served. Within walking distance of the Plaza, this casual B&B with hot tub, tucked away in a country-like setting, makes for a most comfortable stay. The emphasis here is on green; much of the produce is garden fresh, grown in the garden on the premises. And there is no more delightful hostess than Prudie. She and husband John exited the corporate world for Taos, and they are now "living the dream."

El Monte Sagrado Living Resort & Spa (575-758-3502; 855-846-8267; elmontesagrado@hhandr.com; www.elmontesagrado.com; 317 Kit Carson Rd., Taos, NM 87571; very expensive; 3 rooms with full handicapped access). The phrase *green grandeur* might best describe the ecofriendly opulence of this resort. Some might find it a bit over the top. It feels like a tropical jungle transplanted to the high desert, and it is known for its claims of environmental purity and innovative recycling. The 84 lodgings include six historic casitas, each with its own private courtyard, and twelve deluxe Global Suites, each with a wet bar, private courtyard, and gas-burning fireplace, 48 Taos Mountain rooms and 18 Native American suites. Here the Old West merges with Native American and Eastern aesthetics. You may stroll the exquisitely landscaped grounds studded with cascading waterfalls and crystal ponds. In addition to the Living Spa, with exotic body treatments you've never even heard of, this oasis offers a fabulous Aqua Center with pools, including a salt water pool, hot tub, and fitness center. The restaurant, De la Tierra, strives for elegance. The Anaconda Bar is famous as a hangout for movie stars. If money truly is no object, this is the place to check in. Pets may stay for a $50 pet fee; a recently added Resort Fee covers valet parking and many of the conveniences ordinarily supplied without cost, such as coffee and newspapers in the lobby and use of the business center. The property's most recent manager is Heritage Hotels, a small but growing local "constellation" of venues.

Hacienda Del Sol (575-758-0287; stay@taoshaciendadelsol.com; www.taoshaciendadelsol.com; 109 Mabel Dodge Ln., Taos, NM 87571; moderate–expensive; 1 room with full handicapped access). Shaded by giant trees, this B&B was chosen by *USA Weekend* as one of America's 10 most romantic inns. Two of the 11 guest rooms are located in the main house, a beautiful 180-year-old adobe; five are in a casita, with an additional room found in a separate casita; and three are attached to the main house. Brick floors, Saltillo tiles, and hardwood floors are found in the main building, as are Pueblo-style archways, viga-and-*latilla* ceilings, *bancos*, *nichos*, and stained-glass windows. Four rooms have their own steam bath, while the honeymoon suite has a double-sized black Jacuzzi with a skylight for stargazing. The luxurious level of comfort provided by the hosts, who have experience as an executive chef and cruise director, is superlative. You could easily wake up here from a restful night on the most comfortable bed in the world, look out at Taos Mountain and weep for joy, have a vision, and decide to move to Taos! Super-romantic.

Hotel La Fonda de Taos (575-758-2211; 800-833-2211; info@lafondataos.com; www.hotellafonda.com; 108 S. Plaza, Taos, NM 87571, on the Plaza; moderate–expensive; 1 room with full handicapped access). If you want to be in the thick of the action, here's the place for you, directly on the Plaza. The historic 1937 La Fonda, the grande dame known for years as the gallery of D. H. Lawrence's paintings, underwent a complete renovation awhile back. The art-embellished lobby is still sheltered by giant vigas, and the mezzanine, where continental breakfast is served, retains a mood of old-fashioned comfort. Many of the 24 beautifully redecorated rooms now have kiva fireplaces and a view of the Plaza below. To stay here is to travel back in time (without sacrificing any contemporary amenities) and experience the nostalgia of Taos's heyday, when such movie stars and celebrities as Gary Cooper, Judy Garland, and Tennessee Williams visited here.

Inn on the Rio (575-758-7199; info@innontherio.com; www.innontherio.com; 910 Kit Carson Rd., Taos, NM 87571, 1.5 miles east of the Plaza; moderate; 4 rooms with partial handicapped access). Brilliant flower gardens and brightly painted flowers adorn this charmingly renovated 1950s-style motor court inn with heated outdoor swimming pool and hot tub, all beautifully tended by Robert and Julie Cahalane, who will do whatever it takes to make your stay perfect. Julie is a master baker who provides fresh-baked quiche, lemon poppy-seed cake, and blueberry blue corn muffins each morning to accompany a full, hot, hearty breakfast. This vintage inn, with baths whimsically hand decorated by Taos artists, is a superb place to really kick back and relax—and a great family spot as well. Featured as a choice destination in numerous national magazines with an AAA Three Diamond rating.

La Doña Luz Inn (575-758-9000; 800-758-9187; info@stayintaos.com; www.stayintaos.com; 114 Kit Carson Rd., Taos, NM 87571, half a block east of the Plaza; inexpensive–expensive; 1 room with full handicapped access). If you want to be surrounded by colorful folk art and have the Plaza right out your front door, this 200-year-old inn is the place for you. These walls contain enough history and stories to keep you intrigued during your entire visit. The five guest rooms in this centrally located—practically on the Plaza—inn are all dazzlingly different, decorated with a collection of angels from around the world, filled with authentic Indian artifacts nestled in *nichos*, or displaying a Franklin stove, claw-foot tub, blacksmith tools, or a Winchester rifle. One room features hand-carved teak woodwork, Afghani rugs, a Kuwaiti chest, and a Balinese fertility goddess suspended over the queen-sized bed. Much of this amazing array comes from a trading post on the property. Rooms are located in three different buildings, including an adobe compound with its own courtyard. Four rooms have their own hot tub and seven have whirlpools.

La Posada de Taos (575-758-8164; 800-645-4803; laposada@laposadadetaos.com; www.laposadadetaos.com; 309 Juanita Ln., Taos, NM 87571, 2½ blocks west of the Plaza; moderate–expensive; limited handicapped access). Opened in 1982 with the claim of being Taos's "first B&B," this inn has an air of romantic seclusion, perhaps because it's located at the end of a quiet dirt road that might take a bit of patience to find. Or maybe it's the honeymoon suite, with a skylight directly over the bed. Whatever it is, this is an especially wonderful place to stay. The house, built by a founding member of the Taos Society of Artists, is replete with kiva fireplaces and private patios. The owners have installed their personal antique collection from England, making the six-room inn a distinctive blend of Southwest style and English country. The two styles make an amazingly harmonious blend.

Blue Sky Retreat at San Geronimo Lodge (575-751-3776; sgl@newmex.com; www.sangeronimolodge.com; 1101 Witt Rd., Taos, NM 87571, 1.4 miles from the Plaza east off Kit Carson Rd./US 64; moderate–expensive; two wheelchair-accessible rooms). To immerse in the essence of Taos and to float in Taos's only chile-shaped swimming pool, book a stay in this 1925 inn, the town's first resort. If you have the heart of a time traveler, if you yearn for old New Mexico as it was in the heyday of the Taos Society of Artists, this 18-room lodge is your place. Thick adobe walls and viga ceilings envelop the visitor in a sense of the past as authentic as the imagination fancies. Authentic period art and New Mexican wooden furniture contribute to the well-worn elegance while kiva fireplaces create a glow at day's end. It's off the beaten path, but once you know the way, it's close to town, on its northern end toward Taos Ski Valley. Situated beside an *acequia*, with a clear view of Taos Mountain amid ancient cottonwoods and lush apricot and pear trees, San Geronimo is a place to escape, relax, and wrap up in the romance of the distinctive locale that is Taos. A labyrinth and prayer path trail, open to guests and to the public, enhance meditative moments. Dog-friendly rooms may be shared with your beloved pooch, and dietary needs are graciously honored—advance notice requested. A luscious hot breakfast, included in the price of a stay, is highlighted by fresh fruit and housemade jams, salsas, and chutneys. Specialties like blue corn–blueberry pancakes, apricot scones, and green chile strata make breakfast an event every day. No wonder guests are known to break into song when the host plays the piano!

Mabel Dodge Luhan House (575-751-9686; 800-846-2235; mabel@MabelDodgeLuhan.com; www.mabeldodgeluhan.com; 240 Morada Ln., Taos, NM 87571, 1 mile north of US 64; moderate; partial handicapped access). Set on 5 acres at the edge of a vast open tract of Taos Pueblo land, this rambling, three-story, 22-room adobe hacienda *is* Taos history. This is primarily because of Mabel Dodge Luhan, famous patroness of the arts who arrived in New Mexico in 1918, and let's face it, if people are still telling stories about you 50 years after you're gone, you've lived quite a life. She came at the urging of her husband at the time, artist Maurice Sterne, who was in Taos to paint Indians. Sterne eventually left, but Mabel stayed, married Taos Pueblo Indian Tony Luhan, and bought and renovated this 200-year-old structure. It quickly came to be known as the Big House, where she lived, wrote such classics as *Winter in Taos*, and entertained.

From the 1920s through the 1940s, the Big House was visited by artistic and literary figures, including D. H. Lawrence, Georgia O'Keeffe, Carl Jung, Aldous Huxley, and Willa Cather. After Mabel died in 1962, the property was bought by actor-producer Dennis Hopper, who lived there during the filming of *Easy Rider*. In 1977 it was bought by a group of academics as a center for seminars and study groups. It became a B&B in the early 1980s, although workshops are still held here.

The house is filled with viga-and-*latilla* ceilings, arched Pueblo-style doorways, fireplaces, and dark hardwood floors. Just to curl up in the living room is to inhale the essence of what makes Taos Taos. Mabel's Bedroom Suite still contains her original bed; Tony's Bedroom opens out onto a sleeping porch; and the Solarium, accessible only by a steep, narrow staircase, is literally a room of glass (Mabel sunbathed in the nude here). There are nine rooms in the main house, a cottage for two, and a guesthouse containing eight southwestern-style rooms. Breakfast, included in the room rates, is served in the spacious dining room. If you want to immerse in Taos history, sleep here.

Old Taos Guesthouse Inn (575-758-5448; oldtaos@newmex.com; www.oldtaos.com; 1028 Witt Rd., Taos, NM 87571, 1.8 miles east of the Plaza; moderate; no handicapped access). Nestled amid a stately grove of trees in a rural area just east of Taos, this 200-year-old adobe hacienda has plenty of rural Spanish charm—not to mention wonderful views of the nearby Sangre de Cristo range and Taos Plateau, a nature trail of its own, and a traditional *acequia* (irrigation ditch). Its nine guest rooms, with handmade aspen furniture and all sorts of thoughtful little touches, look out onto a lovely courtyard, and the century-old central living area is classically southwestern in design and décor, with a red oak floor. Spa services and facials now available on-site in the new massage room.

Adobe & Pines Inn Bed & Breakfast (575-751-0947; www.adobepines.com; 4107 Road 68, Taos, NM 87557; moderate). A highly acclaimed 1830s adobe where rooms have a kiva fireplace and soaking tub. Lovely gardens surround the flagstone courtyard, and there is a labyrinth to walk and meditate in that is also open to the public. Full gourmet breakfast included. Although just off the highway south of Ranchos de Taos, the place retains a serene, secluded feel. A top choice.

El Pueblo Lodge (575-758-8700; www.elpueblolodge.com; 412 Paseo del Pueblo Norte, Taos, NM 87571, half a mile north of the Plaza; inexpensive–moderate). My family, which includes an English springer spaniel and an Airedale terrier, loves staying in this convenient, unpretentious 1940s-style motel with hot tub and pool. A simple breakfast is included in the warm breakfast room. Popular with skiers. Great location—you can walk everywhere.

Sagebrush Inn & Suites (575-758-2254; 800-428-3626; sagebrush@newmex.com; www.sagebrushinn.com; P.O. Box 557, 1508 Paseo del Pueblo Sur, Taos, NM 87571, 2 miles south of the Plaza; inexpensive–moderate; 2 rooms with partial handicapped access). The Sagebrush has recently changed hands and the rooms have been refreshed. The posh Sagebrush has some amazing deals for you, with surprisingly reasonable

ADOBE & PINES B&B OFFERS A LABYRINTH RIGHT OUTSIDE YOUR DOOR

rates. Opened in 1929 to cater to the trade between New York and Arizona, the Sage-brush Inn is one of Taos's oldest hotels. It's also one of the town's nightspots, with live music and dancing, where you'll be treated to some of the best local bands. Built in Pueblo Revival style, the inn is a sprawling structure with 97 rooms, two restaurants, a famously friendly bar, a swimming pool, and two indoor hot tubs. The décor, both Indian and Spanish, includes a fabulous collection of paintings by southwestern masters, along with Navajo rugs. You might want to stay in the third-floor room where Georgia O'Keeffe painted. The separate Executive Suites offer alternative family lodging, including spacious suites (sleeping up to six people each) with fireplaces. A complimentary breakfast is included in the rate. Ski packages with reduced rates are also available. The inn is pet-friendly, with pet fee and advanced booking. Restaurant and cantina on the premises.

Taos Inn (877-807-6427; taosinn@newmex.com; www.taosinn.com; 125 Paseo del Pueblo Norte, Taos, NM 87571, just north of the Plaza; all price ranges; 1 room with full handicapped access). If immersion in the colorful atmosphere of New Mexican arts, crafts, history, and legend is your cup of tea—or shot of tequila—you can do no better than to stay at the 1936 Taos Inn. You would join a guest register that includes the likes of Greta Garbo, Thornton Wilder, and D. H. Lawrence. It has National Landmark status and was thoroughly restored and modernized in the early 1980s. The lobby is both an art gallery and a people-watcher's paradise, and the Adobe Bar is fondly known as "Taos's living room," with events from Dia de los Muertos community altars to open mic and live music every night. Doc Martin's Restaurant, winner of the Wine Spectator Award of Excellence, is popular and atmospheric, but to be honest, the menu is not one of my favorites. Do check the menu before committing to dining here.

Each of the 44 guest rooms in four separate buildings at the inn is graced with a distinct personality. Most have pueblo fireplaces, Taos-style antique furniture, bathrooms with Mexican tile, handwoven Indian bedspreads, and even cable TV. Several rooms open onto a balcony overlooking the lobby, while several more open onto a quiet courtyard in the rear. You may have to choose between the character of the main inn and the updated amenities of the back properties. The inn offers specials, such as stay three nights get the fourth one free. A swimming pool is available in warm weather, and for weary skiers a Jacuzzi bubbles invitingly in the plant-filled greenhouse.

Touchstone Inn Spa & Gallery (575-779-1174; 800-758-0192; info@touchstoneinn.com; www.touchstoneinn.com; 110 Mabel Dodge Ln., Taos, NM 87571, 1 mile north of the Plaza; moderate-expensive; no handicapped access). Located on the edge of Taos Pueblo lands, bordered by tall trees, with splendid views of Taos Mountain from the 2-acre grounds, Touchstone Inn is a lovingly restored historic adobe that fulfills every fantasy of Taos. Optional breakfast is vegetarian and gluten-free; artist studio space is available for rent. In-room Jacuzzi tubs, outdoor hot tub, lovely gardens, historic associations with salon diva Mabel Dodge Luhan, and spa treatments more than complete an already perfect experience. Most of the nine rooms, named for artists, have fireplaces. Spa packages available.

ARROYO SECO

Arroyo Seco, the little village with a collection of pretty and distinctive shops, galleries, and cafés, is just 10 minutes up NM 150 en route to Taos Ski Valley. It is best explored on foot when you have an hour or two to ramble.

Taos Cow Café & Deli (575-776-5640; 485 NM 150; closed Thanksgiving, Christmas, New Year's; inexpensive; no handicapped access; special features: patio). There is such a thing as going to the source, and if you're an ice cream lover, you'll want to make the

SCOTT CARLSON FASHIONS HIS POTTERY WARES OUTDOORS IN THE FRONT YARD OF HIS ARROYO SECO STUDIO

pilgrimage up the Taos Ski Valley Road to the ice creamery known as Taos Cow for the creamiest, most exquisite ice cream you've ever tasted in delectable seasonal flavors like lavender and peach. Great breakfasts, delicious sandwiches, home-made soups, and snacks, plus relaxed, Taos-funky riverside tables.

Arroyo Seco Mercantile (575-776-8806; 488 NM 150). Vintage textiles, including quilts, Saltillo weavings, Indian trade blankets, toys, gifts, *santos*, books, and garden ornaments. A shopping experience in an 1895 general store.

TAOS SKI VALLEY

At the time of this writing, Taos Ski Valley is undergoing big changes. The recent shift in ownership from a locally owned ski area to ownership by a larger corporation is resulting in much renovation, starting with the highly anticipated ski lift to Kachina Peak, now complete. TSV is very much a work in process, with major expansion of the Snakedance Lodge and other facilities, meaning we can't offer much in the way of review at this time. The brand new 80 room ski-in/ski-out Blake Hotel is scheduled to open during the 2016-17 ski season, and new base area retail and restaurant establishments are promised. The Taos area is holding its breath, waiting to ascertain the impact of the change on the character of the place. Taos remains a great place to ski, however.

Known for abundant snow, challenging runs, and, after much controversy, the addition of snowboarding terrain, TSV also offers daycare, kids' ski school, ski patrollers, rentals, views, as well as plenty of intermediate and novice slopes. Snow-makers crank out the white stuff during dry years. Famous for the quality of its light dry powder, TSV has 110 downhill runs and 15 lifts.

❋ Lodging

The Abominable Snowmansion (575-776-8298; www.snowmansion.com; snow-mansion@newmex.com; 476 NM 150, Arroyo Seco, NM 87514, off NM 150, half-way to Taos Ski Valley; inexpensive; partial handicapped access). Located in the old Hispanic village of Arroyo Seco, the

DECISIONS, DECISIONS. SOMETIMES IT REALLY IS HARD TO CHOOSE AMONG THE FABULOUS FLAVORS AT TAOS COW ICE CREAM

Abominable Snowmansion wins, hands down, the contest for the best-named ski lodge in the Taos area. It's also tops when it comes to informality, fun, and affordability. The Snowmansion is a youth hostel and campground in summer; in winter, a hostel and budget B&B with a wide selection of tepees, private rooms with private baths, and dorm rooms. You can prepare your own meals here if you like. The bedding is surprisingly high quality. Though it attracts mainly young people, old-timers are more than welcome. Most of the quarters are dormitory style with bunk beds, and the sexes are segregated. There are four private rooms for couples. The lodge offers a continental breakfast in winter. The common area is a social hub. This clean, well-run lodging makes a vacation totally affordable. Pet friendly with adherence to strict guidelines.

Austing Haus Hotel (505-776-8751; austing@newmex.com; www.theausting haus.com; 1282 NM 150, Taos Ski Valley, NM 87525; 1.5 miles west of Taos Ski Valley; moderate; 24 rooms, 11 with lofts, 2 rooms with full handicapped access).

AUSTING HAUS HOTEL IS MINUTES FROM TAOS SKI VALLEY LIFTS

More than 70,000 board feet of timber with 3,000 interlocking joints were used in the construction of this hotel, making it the tallest timber-frame building in the United States. An impressive feat. A large continental breakfast is included. Pets are allowed and ski packages are available. The hotel caters to groups and families. Offers a free shuttle to the slopes.

The Bavarian Lodge & Restaurant (575-776-8020; www.skitaos.com/bavarian; bavarian@thebavarian.net; 100 Kachina Rd., Taos Ski Valley, NM 87525; very expensive; no handicapped access). Completed in 1996, this is the last word in ski lodging, conceived "as a private high Alpine retreat for a few precious guests." The midmountain log mansion is perched at 10,200 feet in the Wheeler Wilderness Area, surrounded by mountain peaks. Modeled on high-Alpine guesthouses of Austria and Bavaria, the Bavarian invites you to ski to its exquisite restaurant. Or you may be driven up from the lower Ski Valley. The luxurious guest suites feature marble-tiled bathrooms, Bavarian antiques, and hand-carved and -painted appointments. The slopeside restaurant, with a real European feel, is definitely the place to be during the day or après ski.

Hotel St. Bernard & Condominiums (575-776-2251; stbhotel@newmex.com; www. stbernardtaos.com; 112 Sutton Pl., Taos Ski Valley, NM 87525; moderate–expensive [weekly all-inclusive ski packages only]; no handicapped access; no credit cards). Closed outside ski season. Jean Mayer, owner of Hotel St. Bernard (named for the patron saint of skiers), is the maestro ski instructor of Taos Ski Valley Ski School. All guests accepted at the hotel are those on the ski school's six-day plan. The package includes three meals a day, including seven-course gourmet dinners prepared by French chefs, as well as lift tickets and lessons. The hotel's 28 rooms are located in three buildings and include attractive A-frame units with sundecks at the bottom of the slopes. The ski season is often booked by July, so planning ahead to avoid disappointment is essential. The hotel's staff is exceptionally professional and helpful, and the Rathskeller Bar is a well-known après-ski spot. A top choice for anyone serious about skiing and having a good time. Spa and fitness center on the premises.

The Little Tree B&B (575-776-8467; www.littletreebandb.com; 226 Hondo Seco Rd., Arroyo Hondo, NM 87513, 10 miles northeast of Taos; moderate–expensive; partial handicapped access). Located about halfway between Taos and Taos Ski Valley, this charming Pueblo-style adobe B&B looks as if it's been part of the landscape for decades. In fact, it was built in the early 1990s. The owners have added private courtyards as well as a two-person air-massage Jacuzzi. They offer a two-course breakfast served on china and crystal. Four guest rooms, arranged around a courtyard bursting with flowers in springtime, are named for four species of small trees native to the Taos region: piñon, juniper, aspen, and spruce. Each room has its own private entrance, two have kiva-style wood-burning fireplaces, two have glazed adobe mud floors, and one has an outdoor

HOTEL ST. BERNARD IN TAOS SKI VALLEY IS FAMOUS FOR FINE FOOD AND DRINK

private hot tub. An allergen-free environment is maintained. In summer the place is alive with hundreds of hummingbirds. The owners' favorite season is fall, but this facility is also a favorite of cross-country skiers.

Ojo Caliente Mineral Springs (505-583-2233; www.ojospa.com; 50 Los Banos Dr., Ojo Caliente, NM 87549, US 285, 35 miles southwest of Taos; moderate–expensive; 1 room with full handicapped access). In the 1500s, Spanish explorer Cabeza de Vaca chanced upon these desert hot springs, a favorite bathing spot of local Indians, and described them as "wonderful waters bursting out of a mountain" (see "Spas and Hot Springs," page 66–67). Locals have come to "take the waters" for more than half a century. Today the springs are the focus of this 36-room resort, and the place still retains the air of a dusty, old-fashioned sanatorium. The resort offers special rates for overnight stays with a soak. You may stay in the somewhat drafty old lodge or rent a private cottage. Campsites are available, and a restaurant featuring healthful offerings is located in the lodge. There's a little wine bar, too. Ojo is no longer the sleepy little getaway it once was. Hot springs open 8 AM–10 PM daily, with 11 mineral pools, a mud pool during warmer weather, private pools, hiking and mountain biking trails, yoga classes, and personal growth and renewal programs.

Snakedance Condominium Hotel (575-776-2277; 800-322-9815; info@snakedancecondos.com; www.snakedancecondos.com; 110 Sutton Pl., Taos Ski Valley 87525; expensive). The Ski-Better-Week package, two-person minimum, with seven nights' lodging, six days' lift tickets, and morning lessons, is by far the best deal in this posh, comfortable resort. As of this writing, a big addition is in process.

Taos Mountain Lodging & Retreat Center (575-776-2229; 1346 NM 150, Taos Ski Valley, NM 87525; moderate; partial handicapped access). Two lodging options, one of which offers shared bathroom and common areas suitable for retreats. This is a great deal for friends or family. Fireplaces in most rooms. Suites are equipped with satellite television and outfitted kitchens. All rooms are done in tasteful, if typical, southwestern décor. Indoor and outdoor whirlpools can relieve your aches, and there is a steam room. Walking distance to Arroyo Seco village. Outdoor gas grills are available. Completely surrounded by national forest. You can have serenity plus a seven-minute trip to the lift! Summer rates are a great bargain.

✳ Galleries

New Directions Gallery (575-758-2771; 107-B North Plaza). Some of the deepest and most challenging contemporary art is on display here, including the work of Taos artists Larry Bell and the late sculptor Ted Egri.

Taos Artisans Cooperative Gallery (575-758-1558; 107 Bent St.) Silverwork, tile, woven sculpture, watercolors, and acrylics from the hands of 14 local artists, priced for any budget.

Total Arts Gallery (575-758-4667; 122-A Kit Carson Rd.). One of the oldest and certainly finest galleries, featuring work from traditional to contemporary. Exquisite figurative and landscape work.

Taos Community Center's Co-op (575-758-1054; 121 N. Plaza). Handmade and imaginative work, much of it rustic, from the hands of the crafters and artists of Taos.

Open Space: An Artist-Owned Gallery (575-758-1217; 103-B E. Plaza). Extremely well-executed work in all media—paint, ceramic, metal, glass, fiber, and more. Lovingly tended by the artists themselves, this gallery has been in place a good long while for good reason.

R. B. Ravens (505-758-7322; 4146 NM 68, Ranchos de Taos, south of Taos in St. Francis Church plaza). Even if your budget can't handle an antique Navajo weaving, you'll enjoy viewing the museum-quality Pueblo, vintage Navajo, and Rio Grande textiles here. The beautiful adobe building also houses antique Indian jewelry, paintings by Taos founders, pottery, kachina dolls, and pre-Columbian pottery.

Earth and Spirit Gallery (575-770-3390; 132 Bent St.). Hand-painted drums and artwork by Shari Ubechel in sensational seasonal colors, reasonably priced. Also special 3-D metaphysical and cosmic scenes, as well as interesting jewelry.

✳ Museums and Sites

Harwood Museum (575-758-9826; www.harwoodmuseum.org; 238 Ledoux St.; open Mon.–Sat. 10 AM–5 PM, Sun. noon–5 PM; closed Mon. Nov.–Mar. and major holidays; $8 adults, $4 ages 6–16, under 6 free; free First Friday 5–7 PM June–Sept.; museum shop). The Harwood Museum, New Mexico's second oldest, is a treasury of Taos art. Founded in 1923, it contains paintings, drawings, prints, sculpture, and photographs by the artists who made Taos famous. Included are works by Victor Higgins, Ernest Blumenschein, Andrew Dasburg, Patrocinio Barela, Earl Stroh, Joe Waldrum, Larry Bell, and Fritz Scholder. There is also a collection of 19th-century *retablos*.

The museum is housed in a 19th-century adobe compound that was purchased by Burt and Elizabeth Harwood in 1916 and transformed into an outstanding example of Pueblo Revival style architecture by John Gaw Meem, the leading practitioner of the style. Notable is the relatively new, utterly minimalist Agnes Martin Gallery, dedicated to the work of a leading American minimalist and Taos resident. The Arthur Bell Auditorium is an important Taos arts venue.

Millicent Rogers Museum (575-758-2462; www.millicentrogers.org; 1504 Millicent Rogers Rd., 4 miles north of Taos Plaza, go left before the "old blinking light" to Millicent Rogers Rd.; open daily 10 AM–5 PM; closed Mon. Nov.–Mar. and major holidays; $10 adults, $8 seniors; $4 ages 6–16, under 6 free; gift shop). This outstanding private museum was founded in 1953 by relatives of Millicent Rogers, a stunning blond *Vogue* model, Standard Oil heiress, and style-setter who moved to Taos in 1947. Her study of regional architecture and Indian and Spanish colonial art resulted in an extensive collection of Native American jewelry, textiles, basketry, pottery, and paintings. Today it forms the core of a display that has been expanded to include religious and secular artwork of Hispanic New Mexico. The museum also holds one of the most important collections of pottery by famed San Ildefonso artist Maria Martinez and her family, as well as rare Penitente artifacts. The gift shop is the place to purchase that special heirloom piece of jewelry.

San Francisco de Asis Church (575-758-2754; 60 St. Francis Plaza, Ranchos de Taos, about 4 miles south of Taos on NM 68; open Mon.–Sat. 9 AM–4 PM; Mass Sat. at 6 PM, Sun. at 7 AM [Spanish], 9 AM, 11:30 AM [English], and Mon., Tues., Wed., Fri. at 6:45 AM; Parish Hall open Mon.–Sat. 10 AM–4 PM; call for winter hours; $3 to see video and Mystery Painting in Parish Hall; gift shop next door). The most frequently painted and photographed church in the United States was built sometime between 1776 and 1813 and was in use by Franciscans in 1815. This iconic mission church symbolizes the purity and essence of New Mexico history and spirituality. Viewed from the west, its massive adobe walls change appearance hourly as the light changes, posing an irresistible challenge to artists. Visitors are also intrigued by artwork in the Parish Hall (found across the driveway to the right), including Henri Ault's *The Shadow of the Cross*.

D. H. Lawrence Ranch (575-776-2245). Call for seasonal hours, but it is likely open 10 AM–4 PM Tues., Thurs., Sat. Apr.–Oct. The 160-acre ranch is located 20 miles north of Taos, off NM 522 near San Cristobal at 8,600 feet. The place where the British author wrote *Mornings in Mexico* and where his ashes rest. Supposedly

TAOS EXERTS A MAGNETIC PULL ON ARTISTS FROM ALL OVER THE WORLD. MANY COME TO TOWN AND OPEN GALLERIES TO SHOWCASE THEIR WORK

THE SAN FRANCISCO DE ASIS CHURCH IN RANCHOS DE TAOS IS SAID TO BE THE MOST PAINTED AND PHOTOGRAPHED CHURCH IN THE UNITED STATES

Mabel Dodge Luhan swapped this Kiowa Ranch, crossed by the Kiowa Peace Path, a sanctuary where war was forbidden, for the original manuscript of *Sons and Lovers*. Owned and managed by the University of New Mexico and recently reopened to visitors.

Southern Methodist University-in-Taos (575-758-8322; P.O. Box 314, Ranchos de Taos, about 8 miles southeast of Taos on NM 518; open June–Aug., varies with class). SMU is located in Fort Burgwin, an 1852 U.S. cavalry fort set in a small valley on a tributary of the Rio Grande. Now it's an archaeological research and training center for SMU, which is based in Dallas, Texas.

During summer, SMU-in-Taos offers cultural programs and a lecture series that emphasizes archaeology. Visit www.smu.edu/taos for current class listings.

Ernest L. Blumenschein Home (575-758-0505; www.taoshistoricmuseums.org; 222 Ledoux St., Taos, just south of the Plaza; open summer, Mon.–Sat. 10 AM–5 PM, Sun. noon–5 PM [call for winter hours]; $8 adults, $6 seniors, $5 under 16; Saver Card grants admission to two museums for $12; gift shop). Ernest and Mary Greene Blumenschein were among the founders of the famous Taos Society of Artists around 1915. Their home, a 1797 Spanish colonial adobe, is open for tours and exhibits of area artists' work. The restored home appears much as it did in the Blumenscheins' day: You'll find the original adobe plaster inside and out, with replication of the Blumenscheins' color scheme, as well as traditional Taos furniture, European antiques, and artwork from around the world.

Kit Carson Home and Museum (575-758-4945; www.kitcarsonhome.com; P.O. Drawer CCC, 113 E. Kit Carson Rd., Taos, half a block east of the Plaza; open daily 10 AM–5 PM Mar.–Oct., daily 10 AM–4 PM Nov.–Feb., closed Thanksgiving, Christmas, New Year's, and Easter; $7 adults, $6 seniors, $5 teens, $2 children, under 6 free; gift shop). Kit Carson was the consummate mountain man, scout, and soldier. He was also a family man. In 1843 he married Josefa Jaramillo, and the couple raised a large family in this 12-room adobe. Kit and Josefa both died in 1868, a month apart. Three rooms of the house are furnished as they might have been during the quarter-century the Carsons lived there. Other rooms are filled with exhibits on Taos's colorful frontier history.

Carson was an active Mason, and the Masons now operate this museum. Reenactors guide visitors through.

Hacienda de los Martinez (575-758-1000; www.taoshistoricmuseums.org; 708 Hacienda Way, Taos, off Ranchitos Rd., 2 miles south of the Plaza on NM 240 or 4 miles west of Ranchos de Taos on NM 240; open Mon.–Fri. 10 AM–4 PM, Sun. noon–4 PM, closed Christmas and New Year's Day; $8 adults, $4 ages 6–16; gift shop). This 19th-century hacienda features thick adobe walls and a windowless exterior, with 21 rooms enclosing two central *placitas*. This fortresslike building was designed to keep out Comanche and Apache raiders. Livestock were driven through the gates and into the *placitas* when raiders threatened.

This is perhaps the only hacienda in the Southwest that has been restored to its original condition. Rooms are furnished in Colonial style, reflecting a time when goods were either made by local artisans or hauled by oxcart from Mexico City. Exhibits tell the story of trade on the Camino Real and of the Spanish colonial culture of New Mexico. Demonstrations of contemporary and traditional crafts are presented on a regular basis. The Taos Trade Fair, held here each Sept., includes mountain men–style goods and historic reenactments.

Taos Art Museum at Fechin House (575-758-2690; frontdesk@taosartmuseum. org; www.taosartmuseum.org; 227 Paseo del Pueblo Norte, Taos, 2 blocks north of the Plaza; open May–Oct., Tues.–Sun. 10 AM–5 PM; Nov.–Apr., Tues.–Sun. 10 AM–4 PM; $10 adults, $9 seniors, $8 students, under 12 free). This distinguished adobe home was designed in the Russian style by renowned artist Nicolai Fechin, a Russian immigrant. Built 1927–1933, the house features Fechin's hand-carved woodwork. Exhibitions feature Fechin's own paintings, his collections of Asian and Russian art, and many fine works by Taos founders. Monthly talks by director V. Susan Fisher are not to be missed!

The **Taos Public Library** (575-758-3063; 402 Camino de la Placita) is housed in a beautiful new building. The 30,000-volume collection is strong in southwestern literature and history.

Rio Grande Gorge Bridge (no phone). At intersection of NM 68 and NM 150, go left 17 miles on US 64. Completed in 1965 at 650 feet above the Rio Grande, this is the nation's second highest span, and it carries dark, tragic histories associated with such heights. Always windy, regardless of the season. Best observation point of the Rio Grande rift, or "New Mexico's Grand Canyon." Craft booths. Free.

Earthship Biotecture (575-751-0462; www.earthship.com; 2 Earthship Way, Tres Piedras). An earthship is a radical sustainable home built of recycled materials such as aluminum cans and tires. You can rent one for a night or two to try out the experience, or just tour the visitor center. Tours are offered. Check on times, or if you are more interested, look into the seminars in permaculture, global housing, green building, and related subjects. Off the grid and sustainable.

Lama Foundation (575-586-1269; info@lamafoundation.org; www.lamafoundation. org; 1895 Lama Mountain Rd., Questa; open weekdays 10 AM–noon; please write or call for calendar of summer events). Founded in 1967, the Lama Foundation has endured beyond the "be here now" revelations of the 1960s to become an ecumenical spiritual center where teachers of many paths offer workshops. Since the Hondo Fire swept through the Ponderosa pines on Lama Mountain in 1996, Lama has lengthened its offerings of workshops on permaculture, creativity, sustainable agriculture, gender, and architecture. All are invited to share a vegetarian meal and participate in Dances of Universal Peace on visitors days, which occur on scheduled Sundays during the summer season. The mountain, long reputed to be a link on the Kiowa Peace Path, where all could pass freely and safely, is still recovering from the 2006 fire that transformed the landscape from a forested mountain with meadows of wildflowers and stands of aspen

MEDITATION CIRCLE IN THE DOME AT THE LAMA FOUNDATION

shaping a new ecology. The name *Lama* comes from *la lama*, meaning "mud." A key Lama offering is the opportunity to make a solo self-sufficient retreat, or hermitage, in a secluded cabin on the mountain.

Neem Karoli Baba Ashram (575-751-4080; www.nkbashram.org; 416 Geronimo Ln., Taos; open daily 7 AM–9 PM, in winter 7 AM–8 PM; chanting Tues. 7 PM, Sun. 11 AM; morning and evening devotions). Inspired by the teachings of the Indian guru Neem Karoli Baba and his American disciple, Ram Dass (Richard Alpert), this ashram offers a quiet meditation room with an impressive statue of Hanuman, the monkey-faced Hindu god of service. The annual cycle of celebrations culminates with Majaraj-ji's Mahasamadhi Bhandara on the weekend in Sept. closest to the full moon. Chanting begins Sat. at 4 AM; that afternoon, around 4 PM, a vegetarian Indian feast is served to all. The ashram continues to evolve and expand, with the addition of a permaculture farm and more facilities.

Montefiore Cemetery (www.nmjewishhistory.org). This cemetery is located about 65 miles north of Santa Fe. Take I-25 to second Las Vegas exit. Go left to large cemetery. Jewish section is in back on right. In the old Jewish cemetery in Las Vegas, New Mexico, it is possible to be touched by the lives of Jewish pioneers of the West. You can also begin to get a sense of the strength of the Jewish merchant-rancher community instrumental to the development of the life of culture and commerce in northern New Mexico during the late 19th and early 20th centuries. The New Mexico Jewish Historical Society holds an annual cemetery-cleaning celebration. People of all ages tend the graves, and a picnic lunch is served.

For those who would like to learn more about Jewish pioneer life, contact the New Mexico Jewish Historical Society at 505-348-4471 or 5520 Wyoming Boulevard N.E., Albuquerque, NM 87109, about their archive located at the State Road Center and Archives, Cerrillos Rd. and Camino Carlos Rey in Santa Fe.

Taos Pueblo (575-758-1028; www.taospueblo.com; 120 Veterans Highway, Taos, 2 miles north of Taos off NM 68; Tewa language; feast days: Sept. 29–30, San Geronimo; fees: $16 adults, $14 students, $5 students, under 10 free; parties of eight or more, $14 per person; sketching, painting, still camera fees additional; pueblo may be closed to non-Indians during Feb., Mar., and Aug. [inquire at tribal office]; no photography during feast days). Taos was well established long before Europe emerged from the Dark Ages. The present pueblo of multistoried adobe apartment buildings has been occupied since about A.D. 1450. Today, as then, the clear waters of the Rio Pueblo flow through the area from sacred Blue Lake in the Sangre de Cristo Mountains, and residents draw their water from the stream. To honor their traditions, they live without indoor plumbing or electricity, just as their ancestors did. Beyond the borders at the village wall, these conveniences are available.

Architecturally, Taos Pueblo is the most spectacular of the area's pueblos, capturing the imaginations of countless artists. Its beauty is the outward manifestation of its spiritual strength. Taos was the seat of the Pueblo Revolt of 1680, when the Spaniards were driven out of New Mexico. It also played an active role in the 1847 uprising of Hispanics and Indians against the U.S. government.

TAOS PUEBLO POW WOW

Taos Pueblo is governed by the governor and war chief. The economy is based on government services, tourism, arts and crafts, ranching, and farming. The Feast of San Geronimo is a highlight of the year, with a sunset dance on Sept. 29, footraces, an arts-and-crafts fair, a ritual pole climbing, traditional dances, and food. During the festivities, Chifonetes perform humorous acts.

Visitors are also welcome at the Taos Pueblo Pow Wow, held the second weekend of July each year. Native Americans from many tribes join in this colorful and popular social dance event. (The powwow is a Plains Indian tradition, but Taos has been influenced by contacts with Plains tribes for centuries.) Other dances open to the public (no cameras) are the Turtle Dance, Jan. 1; Buffalo or Deer Dance, Jan. 6; Feast of Santa Cruz Corn Dance, May 3; San Antonio Corn Dance, June 13; San Juan Corn Dance, June 24; and Deer Dance or Matachines, Christmas Day. Christmas Eve is a special time to visit, with bonfires and processions. July 25–26, the Feast of Santa Ana and Santiago, is an excellent time to visit and observe dancers from many tribes.

Taos Pueblo artists are noted for their mica-flecked (micaceous) pottery, tanned buckskin moccasins, and drums made of hides stretched over hollowed cottonwood logs. Many shops on the pueblo plaza sell these goods, along with fragrant breads freshly baked in outdoor adobe ovens called *hornos*.

OUTDOOR ADOBE BEEHIVE OVENS CALLED *HORNOS* ARE STILL USED THROUGHOUT NEW MEXICO TO BAKE DELICIOUS BREADS AND PIES

✳ Shopping

Brodsky Bookshop (575-758-9468; 226 Paseo del Pueblo Norte). An almost "legacy" intimate shop with a wide range of western and southwestern fiction and nonfiction, general interest titles, and used books—plus maps and cards. The scent of the old days wafts through. An indie bookstore of 40 years.

Twirl (575-751-1402; 225 Camino de la Placita). Those who say there are not enough activities for kids in Taos have not been to Twirl. Part playground, part activity and crafts center, and mostly just the most magical toy store—for all ages—you have ever seen, Twirl gives kids the world from their point of view.

Overland Fine Sheepskin & Leather (575-758-8820; 1405 Paseo del Pueblo Norte). Shearling coats to see you through the coldest winters, plus hats, slippers, mittens, and more. Imported fine Italian leathers and gorgeous beaded leather jackets. Find something fine to fit the budget—belts, gloves, slippers, wallets—or splurge on a lifetime purchase. Items sold here will never go out of style. Look for the spring sales starting around Valentine's Day.

Steppin' Out (575-758-4487; 120 Bent St.). Two floors of fine leather goods, from shoes to belts to handbags, are the last word in style. Some high-end waterproof boots make bad weather not only endurable but a chance for chic. Also a selection of stylish clothing to flatter the world traveler.

Country Furnishings of Taos (575-758-4633; 534 Paseo del Pueblo Norte). You want local? We got local. Unique and appealing folk art furniture painted by local artists. Home accessories, jewelry, and a panoply of gifts by some of the state's top craftspeople.

Starr Interiors (575-758-3065; 117 Paseo Del Pueblo Norte). Step into Starr and bring home the aura of the Southwest. Known for handcrafted Zapotec Indian weavings "to

BOTH YOU AND YOUR LITTLE ONES WILL FALL IN LOVE WITH THE OUTDOOR PLAY SPACE AT TWIRL

last a lifetime," this shop also features benches, tables, and *trasteros* (cabinets) hand-carved and hand-painted by Taos artisans. Oaxacan masks and more. A reliable décor source since 1974. Columbian art and an excellent selection of books on Navajo textiles.

At Home in Taos (575-751-1486; 117 S. Plaza). Everything you didn't know you wanted but simply must have! Housewares, clever gifts, jewelry, pottery, cards, accessories in a huge space for browsing. Can be dangerously addicting and very difficult to leave.

Moxie: Fair Trade & Handmade (575-758-1256; 216 Paseo del Pueblo Norte). OK, this is where I shop. Imports from Africa, Latin America, Nepal, cottons, felts, wearables, unusual décor, socks, hats, toys—all that is colorful and comfortable.

Garden & Soul (575-751-1825; 137 N. Plaza). Art and things from New Mexico and beyond. Luscious journals and bound books, cards, local art, exquisite chocolate truffles by Jennifer Loves Chocolate—what's not to like?

Wabi-Sabi (575-758-7801; 216 Paseo del Pueblo Norte). As serene as a tea ceremony. Japanese aesthetics and the goods you need to create "less is more" Zen beauty on your person or in your home.

Made in New Mexico (575-758-7709; 104 W. Plaza). The official home of real New Mexico products, this is the place, right on the Plaza, to purchase salsa, blue corn pancake mix, chokecherry syrup, foodstuffs, and any New Mexico memorabilia you want to bring home. Good for souvenirs and gifts.

Monet's Kitchen (575-758-8003; 124 Bent St.). A nicely apportioned kitchen shop with espresso makers, woks, pottery, aprons, and table linens. Some gourmet foods and coffees as well, for a complete gift basket.

Taos Cookery (575-758-5435; 113 Bent St.). Besides featuring general kitchenware, Taos Cookery also represents many local potters. Among the most eye-catching designs are the multicolored productions of Ojo Sarco Pottery, whose husband-and-wife team creates dishwasher- and microwave-safe pottery emblazed with patterns taken from the New Mexico landscape.

Artwares Contemporary Jewelry (575-758-8850; 129 N. Plaza). Known for its stylized Zuni bears executed in precious metals and used to adorn earrings, necklaces, and pins. There is fine lapidary work and a mix of Native American and contemporary-style jewelry in a reasonable price range.

FX/18 (575-758-8590; 103 Bent St.). Whimsical sculptures, retro items, silver jewelry, and dining and household wares with a playful touch. The store shows the work of younger cutting-edge local jewelers as well as locally made soaps, notecards, and gifts.

Taos Blue (575-758-3561; 101 Bent St.). Saints and angels brush halos and wings in this gift shop specializing in objects with divine inspiration—from pottery to paintings on wood to luscious hand-knit sweaters. The place to find a unique gift by a local craftsperson.

Artemesia (575-737-9800; 117 Bent St.). Definitely the place to splurge on a hand-woven chenille wrap or hand-dyed silk top. It's all wearable art and fabulous, made by locals and other well-selected artists. Seriously to die for and the quickest way to look like a knockout at the big event on your calendar.

Taos Book Gallery (575-751-7161; 117A Kit Carson Rd.). One block east of the Plaza, this newest bookstore in town has inspired selections of new and fine used books. It feels like an old-fashioned bookstore. Lots of regional western literature.

Francesca's Clothing Boutique (575-776-8776; 492 NM 150, Arroyo Seco). Voted the favorite shop of Taos women, packed with colorful and relaxed pieces to mix and match in unusual ways. Perfect for après-ski fun. Totally geared to the Taos imagination and look, perhaps best characterized as something of a "gypsy-cowgirl-nostalgia princess."

Spotted Bear (505-758-3040; 127 Paseo del Pueblo Sur). One of the most extraordinary clothing stores anywhere, Spotted Bear is worth a pilgrimage. Women's clothing here is exotic and exquisite, from velvet animal-print scarves to amusing flowered hats. There are dresses of hand-painted silk and vintage designer outfits, as well as unique raincoats in rich materials. Choose your era, from a period look to right-now metallic and faux leopard. If you shop here, it's guaranteed no one else will be wearing anything at all resembling your outfit. And you can do well on the sale racks, especially if you are short in stature.

OptiMysm (575-741-8545; 129 Kit Carson Rd. Ste. E.). Taos's metaphysical bookstore has a lovely atmosphere and outstanding service. Go slowly along Kit Carson or you might miss it. The shop is tucked away in an alley.

Twining Weavers & Contemporary Crafts, Ltd. (575-758-5040; 103 Bent St.). The stock here includes handwoven wool rugs, pillows made from hand-dyed yarns, Guatemalan cotton runners, place mats, napkins, and baskets from around the world. They will work directly with the customer to customize colors and designs.

Cid's Food Market (575-758-1148; 623 Paseo del Pueblo Norte; closed Sun., major holidays). Since Cid's opened in 1986, owners Cid and Betty Backer have made it a point to purchase the freshest, purest food available. In addition to an array of organic, locally sourced fruits and vegetables and gourmet items, Cid's offers natural soaps, herbs, vitamins, non-animal-tested cosmetics, and biodegradable cleansers. At the same time, it has a great selection of treats such as Lindt chocolates and locally made salsas. Cid's has a first-rate meat department with bison, fresh fish, and the best cuts of lamb, beef, and pork. Those looking for sugar-free or gluten-free products will find them here. It's also the place to run into everyone you know in town and catch up on the latest. There's a salad and hot food bar where you can eat in or take out. You can sip your smoothie in the little glassed-in café space out front.

Taos Farmers Market (575-751-7575, the Plaza). Runs Mid-May–late Sept., Saturday mornings 8 AM–12:30 PM. A bonanza of local growers, bakers, beekeepers, and crafters.

ARTIST ED SANDOVAL'S TRUCK MAKES ITS WAY DOWN KIT CARSON ROAD

✳ Music, Theater, Visual and Literary Arts

Taos Community Auditorium (575-758-4677; www.tcataos.org/calendar; 145 Paseo del Pueblo Norte, Taos; open year-round; prices vary with performers, most $10–$15). An enormous spectrum of fine, cutting-edge, innovative, multicultural music, drama, comedy, dance, and theater performances with regional and national talent.

Taos School of Music Summer Chamber Music Festival (575-776-2388; www.taosschoolofmusic.com; P.O. Box 2630, Taos, NM 87571; open mid-June–early Aug.; $25 individual, $10 under 18; $100 season tickets). Established in the 1960s, this chamber music academy draws an international group of talented young chamber music performers to study piano and stringed instruments at Taos Ski Valley. Weekly performances at Taos Community Auditorium feature the young artists as well as world-renowned faculty and groups such as the American String Quartet and Brentano String Quartet. Dinners followed by chamber music concerts at Hotel St. Bernard, the group's summer headquarters, are a Taos summer highlight.

Music from Angel Fire (575-377-3233; 888-377-3300; www.musicfromangelfire.org; P.O. Box 502, Angel Fire; Aug.–Sept.; $30–$35; series tickets available). Internationally known musicians perform superb renditions of classical, Romantic, Baroque, and contemporary works in a series of concerts in Angel Fire, Taos, Raton, and Santa Fe. Some concerts are free.

Taos Chamber Music Group (575-770- 1167; nancy@taoschambermusicgruup.org). Season May–Sept., season tickets $132. Concerts held at Harwood Museum of Art. A blend of classic, contemporary, and "music that reflects life in Taos." Now almost a quarter-century old.

Metta Theater (575-758-1104; 1470 Paseo del Pueblo Norte, El Prado). Quality live theater, staged readings, improv classes, youth outreach.

SOMOS (575-758-0081; 108 Civic Plaza Dr., Taos). Claiming to be the literary society of Taos, the Society of the Muse of the Southwest (SOMOS) has expanded its headquarters, and along with it activities, to showcase readings, open mics, local writers, classes, summer camps for kids, and much more.

UNM Taos (575-737-6200; 1157 County Road 110, Ranchos de Taos). The Taos branch of the University of New Mexico is a campus south of town with a complete schedule of classes.

Taos Art School (575-758-0350; www.taosartschool.org). Located on "the Left Bank" of the Rio Grande, this two-decades-old art institute offers classes and workshops in painting, Navajo weaving, photography, and more, as well as tours of Chaco Canyon, Georgia O'Keeffe

EVERY SUMMER TAOS SCHOOL OF MUSIC ATTRACTS SOME OF THE MOST TALENTED UP-AND-COMING CLASSICAL MUSICIANS TO ITS YOUNG ARTISTS PROGRAM

country, and just about any place in northern New Mexico worth exploring deeply.

Taos Center for the Arts (575-758-2052; www.tcataos.org; 133 Paseo del Pueblo Norte, Taos). The Taos Center for the Arts has been in existence for more than 50 years and sponsors more than 50 performing arts events annually in the Taos Community Auditorium. At this cultural wellspring, find exciting dance, performance art, film, music, and all manner of well-executed entertainment designed to stimulate and uplift, usually at reasonable prices. Check out the packed schedule at www.taosartcalendar.com/events.

Taos Plaza Live (575-751-8800, Taos Plaza, Taos). A wide assortment of local music and performances, May–Sept., 6–8 PM every Thurs. evening on Taos Plaza. Everything from country swing to alternative to traditional New Mexican music. Dance into the night on the Plaza. All performances are free.

✳ Fitness

Northside Health and Fitness (575-751-1242; 1307 Paseo de Pueblo Norte, El Prado). A friendly, accessible, community-oriented fitness center with indoor and outdoor pools, four tennis courts, Cybex weight equipment, aerobics classes, cardiovascular room with Cybex rowers and NordicTrack skiers, physical therapy, kids' activities, and great drumming classes! Day passes available for $10.

Taos Spa & Tennis Club (575-758-1980; 111 Dona Ana Dr., Taos, across from Sagebrush Inn). Includes racquetball, tennis, indoor and outdoor pools, aerobics, weight room with free weights and machines, personalized instruction, hot tubs, sauna, steam rooms, and child care. Day passes available for $12.

✳ Outdoors

Taos offers every level of trail, from moderate to difficult, and all of them have their own distinctive character. Divisadero Loop makes for a great early hike before the heat of the day, offering high altitude views of the valley and 70-mile western vistas; South Boundary Trail, originally a sheep trail, is a shuttle-type, downhill walk though fir forests deep into Taos Canyon. Italianos Canyon, near Taos Ski Valley, is rated as difficult, and the easy-to-moderate Williams Lake Trail delivers you to the base of Wheeler Peak. As with all hikes in the area, be prepared for sudden weather changes and carry plenty of water. For more recommendations and information, contact the U.S. Forest Service at its local Taos office.

Rio Grande del Norte National Monument (Taos Field Office, 575-758-8851; Wild Rivers Visitor Center, 575-586-1150; Rio Grande Gorge Visitor Center, 575-751-4899; www.blm.gov/publish/content/nm/en/prog/NLCS/RGDN_NM.html for information and interactive map; 226 Cruz Alta Rd., Taos, NM 87571). Encompassing much of the outdoor adventure land around Taos, this new 242,500-acre national monument was established in 2013. Recreational opportunities galore with hiking, biking, fishing, camping, and climbing.

Carson National Forest (575-758-6200; 208 Cruz Alta Rd., Taos, NM 87571). A million and a half acres of four-season recreation that includes Wheeler Peak, the state's highest at 13,171 feet. Within the Carson is an 86,000 acre-designated wilderness motor-free area—travel by foot and horseback only. Recent fires have restricted use in some areas. Call for specifics.

Wild Rivers Back Country Byway (800-733-6396, ext. 42371; 26 miles north of Taos, west on NM 378 off NM 522, north of Questa). This stupendous 13-mile drive parallels the Rio Grande and Red River along NM 378, accessing Wild Rivers Recreation Area, which is located within the Rio Grande Del Norte National Monument and along the Rio Grande and Red Rivers. Warning: If you are thinking of hiking down to the river, wear stout shoes and take plenty of water and sunscreen. Not too bad going down, but every step on the return is demanding. No mules to the rescue a la Bright Angel Trail in the Grand Canyon, though the sensation on the way back up is similar. You're on your own. Think rugged and steep.

Rio Grande Gorge West Rim Trail. Access this biking trail from the Rio Grande Gorge Bridge rest area on US 64. An easy 9-mile one-way trip with mind-bending views of both mountains and gorge. Very popular with locals and visitors for both hiking and mountain biking. Caution: The area is known for rattlesnakes on the trail during hot summer months. Some years produce more snakes than others. Talk to people before you go—and if you have pets, get them inoculated for anti-venom rattlesnake bites if you intend to take them. It won't eliminate the effects of the bites, but it will make it less painful for them and give you more time to get them to the vet.

Williams Lake. Great hiking spot with trailhead above Taos Ski Valley, about 1.3 miles past the Bavarian Lodge & Restaurant. July–Aug. is the best time to view wildflowers.

Taos Box and Racecourse (www.blm.gov/nm/st/en/prog/recreation/taos/river_segments_rio.html). River rafting at its best. Two of the most popular whitewater stretches on the Upper Rio Grande. Good runoff can mean a season from May–July. Be prepared for Class IV rapids.

Costilla Creek. If you love to fish, Costilla Creek offers catch-and-release of native cutthroat from Latir Lakes. This expedition requires a 4-mile moderate hike to reach the nine glacier lakes and their trophy cutthroats at the headwaters of the Rio Costilla. Located north of Questa.

Cimarron Canyon State Park (575-377-6271; 28869 US Highway 64, Eagle Nest, NM 87718, 3 miles east of Eagle Nest). A 33,000-acre mountainous preserve with numerous wonderful trails, camping spots, and picnic areas. Known for the German browns in the Cimarron River that flows through it. A narrow canyon bisected by a two-lane road.

RAFTING THE RIO GRANDE BELOW TAOS IS AN EXCEPTIONAL ADVENTURE

Kit Carson Memorial State Park (575-758-8234; 211 Paseo del Pueblo Norte, Taos, NM 87571). The in-town park offers short walks and a playground on 22 acres, along with an immensely interesting historic cemetery.

Rio Grande Gorge State Park (Visitor Center 505-751-4899). 16 miles southwest of Taos on NM 570). Includes shelter, barbecues, trails, drinking water, and campgrounds along the road.

✳ Annual Taos Events

Fiestas de Santiago y Santa Ana (575-758-3873; 800-348-0696; www.new-mexico-visitor.com or www.fiestasdetaos.com; 1139 Paseo del Pueblo Sur, Taos, NM 87571; late July; the Plaza; free). In the 1930s, the newly incorporated Town of Taos started the Fiestas for Santiago (St. James) and Santa Ana (St. Anne). Still celebrated today, Las Fiestas de Santiago y Santa Ana continues to preserve and celebrate the cultures that have lived together in this valley for four centuries.

This event honors Taos's patron saints. The joyous celebration begins with a Friday night Mass and candlelight procession to the Plaza. The weekend is filled with a satirical parade on local history, crowning of a Fiesta Queen, kids' parade, arts-and-crafts fair, and food booths. The event is not only a celebration; it is a way to pass on rich traditions.

Taos Pow Wow (www.taospueblopowwow.com). Generally held the second weekend in July on Taos Pueblo Pow Wow grounds, this event is a brilliant gathering of tribes from throughout the hemisphere, and the dancing, color, and tradition are transporting. Abundant food and arts-and-crafts booths expand the event's fascination.

Old Taos Trade Fair (575-758-0505; www.taoshistoricmuseums.org; 222 Ledoux St., Taos, NM 87571; late Sept.; $5 one day; $8 both days adults, $4 children under 16, Sun. free for Taos County residents). This two-day fair, which coincides with San Geronimo Day at Taos Pueblo (see "Pueblos," page 76–81), brings to life Spanish colonial culture in the 1820s. Held at the Martinez Hacienda (see "Cultural Attractions," page 42), the fair features mountain men, frontier life, traditional craft demonstrations, native foods, caravans, muzzle-loading rifle demonstrations, and Hispanic and Indian music.

Taos Solar Music Festival (575-758-9191; www.solarmusicfest.com; late June; Kit Carson Park, Paseo del Pueblo Sur and Civic Plaza Dr.; $20–$80). Wow! This is the place to be to hear headliners and emerging artists in an atmosphere of pure fun. Plus, you can get an education on the latest in solar energy. Performers have included Michelle Shocked, Leo Kotke, Los Lobos, Robert Mirabal, Ottmar Liebert, Ani DiFranco, and the Indigo Girls playing a variety of reggae, folk, western swing, Spanish, rock, and acoustic music. Also, a showcase for the latest in sustainable energy innovations.

San Geronimo Days (575-758-1028; Taos Pueblo, 120 Veterans Highway, Taos, NM 8757; $16 per person, children under 10 free; photo permit extra). Very strict restrictions on photography and video. Be sure to follow the rules. Taos Pueblo feast day, held each Sept. 29–30, features the famous pole climbers. Mon.–Sat. 8 AM–4:30 PM, Sun. 8:30 AM –4:30 PM.

Taos Fall Arts Festival (505-758-4648; www.taosfallarts.com; P.O. Box 675, Taos Convention Center, 120 Civic Plaza Dr., Taos, NM 87571; late Sept.–early Oct.; free). A roundup of arts festivities, this yearly event celebrates the history, cultures, and art of Taos County. Events include gallery openings, invitational and juried art exhibitions, and an arts-and-crafts fair. High-quality exhibits of art celebrating the region are always worthwhile. Plus, it is a glorious time of year to be in town.

Yuletide in Taos/Lighting of LeDoux Street (575-751-8800; www.taos.org; Taos County Chamber of Commerce, 1139 Paseo del Pueblo Sur, Taos, NM 87571; mid-Dec.; free). Imagine Taos Plaza edged in snow on a clear, crisp winter night, the scent of piñon smoke flavoring the air. This celebration incorporates Taos's Hispanic and Indian traditions in a series of community events: *farolito* tours, candlelight dinners, dance performances, ski area festivities, ethnic holiday foods, a crafts fair, caroling, and a Christmas parade and tree lighting on the Plaza. This is truly a meaningful and precious experience of the season with the community, starting with the lighting of LeDoux Street with hundreds of dazzling *farolitos*.

SACRED TAOS MOUNTAIN AS SEEN FROM THE MARTINEZ HACIENDA

Taos Wool Festival (800-684-0340; www.taoswoolfestival.org; P.O. Box 2754, Taos, NM; held first full weekend in Oct. at Kit Carson Park.) From live alpacas and churro sheep to demonstrations of weaving and needle arts to exquisite for-sale items such as hand-dyed wools, felt hats, scarves, and handmade sheepskin boots, this event is pure paradise for the crafter or wannabe. You can also enroll in classes. You'll find an outstanding regional wool market featuring juried vendors displaying their wool fiber, yarns, and artistic creations. In other words, do not miss! This is one very family-friendly festival, and every year it just keeps getting better.

ENCHANTED CIRCLE SCENIC BYWAY

Aspens turn shimmering gold in September, but this 83-mile loop between Taos, Questa, Red River, over Bobcat Pass to Eagle Nest, and back through the Moreno Valley to Angel Fire, then winding up the mountains back to Taos makes a fine excursion year-round. Both Red River and Angel Fire have ramped up their warm weather activities with ziplines, ropes courses, and summer lift rides. You never know when you'll spot the elusive bighorn sheep or even a brown bear up here, so keep cameras ready for wildlife. Be prepared for high mountain driving, big temperature drops, and plenty of opportunities to jump out of the car and explore. Many fun events that have now become traditions are on the calendar, from Fourth of July fireworks over Eagle Nest Lake to Mardi Gras in the mountains at Red River to the shovel race at Angel Fire, where entrants have a blast skiing down the mountain on adapted shovels. The holidays feature torchlight parades as skiers glide down the mountains carrying torches on New Year's Eve. Wine and beer festivals are popular, too—check town websites for details. Memorial Day weekend sees a huge influx of motorcyclists at Red River as many make a pilgrimage to the Angel Fire Vietnam Veterans Memorial.

✳ Dining

Texas Red's Steakhouse & Lost Love Saloon (575-754-2922; 400 E. Main St., Red River; L, D; moderate–expensive). The go-to restaurant in Red River, with peanut shells on the floor and classic red-checkered tablecloths. Steaks aren't bad, but they are not the quality advertised. The place is tourist-rustic and fun. Expect steakhouse prices.

    Shotgun Willie's (575-754-6505; 403 W. Main St., Red River; B, L; inexpensive). Tasty, casual BBQ, burger—fresh, never frozen—and breakfast joint that is a longtime favorite. A good choice for lunch, but try not to arrive during prime time.

    Pub 'n Grub (575-377-2335; 52 N. Angel Fire Rd., Angel Fire; D; inexpensive–moderate; no handicapped access; special features: patio, gluten-free options). Daily specials, decent steaks, chicken pot pie is a house favorite.

    Zeb's (575-377-6358; 3431 Mountain View Blvd., Angel Fire; L, D; inexpensive). Whatever you're in the mood for, you ought to be able to find it here. Burgers, fried chicken, salads to satisfy the family. Don't expect gourmet fare. A bit cavernous, but usually can provide a decent default stop. Plenty of brewskis.

    Hail's Holy Smoked BBQ & More (575-377-9938; 3400 Highway 434, Ste. F, Angel Fire; L, D; inexpensive). Very modest café, good for take-out. Reliable local favorite. Has been around long enough to know. Homemade desserts; tender, well-seasoned BBQ; daily specials.

    Enchanted Circle Brewery (505-507-8687; 20 Sage Ln., Angel Fire; inexpensive; limited handicapped access; special features: patio). A dozen craft brews on tap, grade A pub fare, live music, just what Angel Fire needed. Call for hours of operation.

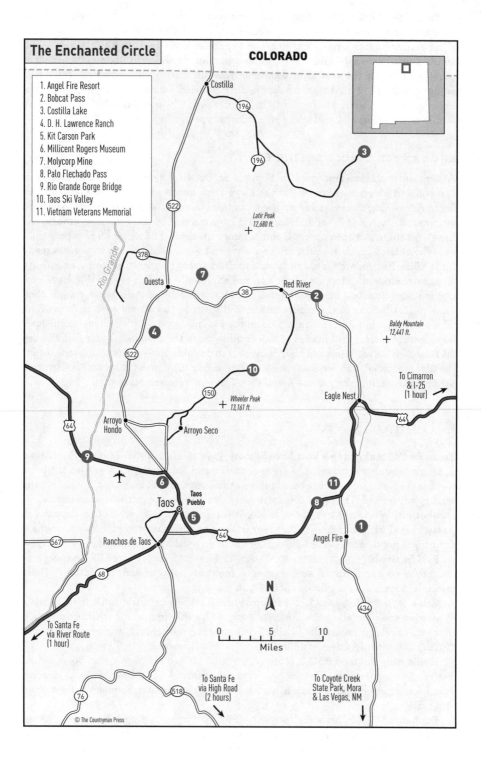

The Enchanted Circle

COLORADO

1. Angel Fire Resort
2. Bobcat Pass
3. Costilla Lake
4. D. H. Lawrence Ranch
5. Kit Carson Park
6. Millicent Rogers Museum
7. Molycorp Mine
8. Palo Flechado Pass
9. Rio Grande Gorge Bridge
10. Taos Ski Valley
11. Vietnam Veterans Memorial

Costilla

196

196

3

Latir Peak
12,680 ft.

522

Rio Grande

378

7

Questa

38

Red River

2

Baldy Mountain
12,441 ft.

4

522

10

To Cimarron
& I-25
(1 hour)

150

Wheeler Peak
13,161 ft.

Eagle Nest

64

Arroyo
Hondo

Arroyo Seco

64

9

6

11

Taos
Pueblo

8

Taos

5

1

567

Ranchos de Taos

64

Angel Fire

68

434

To Santa Fe
via River Route
(1 hour)

N

0   5   10
Miles

76

518

To Santa Fe
via High Road
(2 hours)

To Coyote Creek
State Park, Mora
& Las Vegas, NM

© The Countryman Press

TIME OUT FOR A BURRITO ON A CLASSIC TAOS MORNING

✳ Lodging

Angel Fire Resort (844-218-4107; www.angelfireresort.com; 10 Miller Lane, Angel Fire, NM 87710, at the ski area; expensive; 2 rooms with full handicapped access). Steps away from the Chile Express chairlift, with 157 rooms, each with two queen beds, Angel Fire Resort is by far the biggest lodging establishment in Angel Fire. The décor is contemporary southwestern, and the ski area is right outside the window. Legends Grill has seven flat-screen TVs and serves burgers, pizza, chicken-fried steak, and microbrews on tap. Pet-friendly rooms available, as well as a business center, indoor pool, hot tub, and fitness room. Golf, zipline, cycling packages available in summer; ski packages in winter. State-of-the-art RV resort, too. Something for everyone.

Laguna Vista Lodge (575-377-6522; www.lagunavistalodge.com; 51 E. Therma Dr., Eagle Nest, NM 87718). Legend has it that a betrayed housemaid from the 1930s era haunts the premises. The food is nothing to write home about; however, not much else is open in Eagle Nest during the winter, and you can get an adult beverage here.

Alpine Lodge Red River (575-754-2952; info@alpinelodgeredriver.com; www.alpinelodgeredriver.com; 417 W. Main St., Red River, NM 87558 at the ski area; inexpensive–moderate; 3 rooms with full handicapped access). On the banks of the Red River at the base of the main ski lift, Alpine Lodge was run by native German Ilse Woerndle and her family for more than 30 years. The current owners have spruced up some of the 46 rooms, located in cabins, condos, or the hotel, and are keeping the lodge open year-round. Full kitchens are available. Four-acre private park adjacent to Carson National Forest. Riverside campfires. A pretty perfect place to get away.

Arrowhead Lodge (575-754-2255; 800-299-6547; arrowhead@newmex.com; www.arrowheadlodge.com; 405 Pioneer Rd., Red River, NM 87558; inexpensive; no handicapped access). This quiet, no-frills lodge is located on a side street off Red River's main drag, within easy reach of the ski area. There are 19 units, most with kitchens, plus a few larger accommodations; some have fireplaces. In warm weather, a sundeck, barbecue pit, and several picnic tables are available for your use. The lodge prides itself on being family oriented and offering good value.

Angel Nest RV Retreat (575-377-0533; 28418 US 64, Eagle Nest, NM 87718; inexpensive). Paved road to Eagle Nest Lake, fantastic views. However, there was a time when prairie dogs were shot from the RVs. Just sayin'.

Weathers RV Park (575-377-2276; US 64, Eagle Nest; inexpensive). The Weathers family is well known to my family, are long-standing members of the community with a lot of integrity, and they provide a quality, clean, and quiet environment well situated on Eagle Nest Lake.

Horseshoe Motel and Cabins (575-377-6966; 350 E. Therma Dr., Eagle Nest, NM 87718; inexpensive). Basic motel comforts. However, the owner, who was also the mayor, passed away recently, so who knows what the future holds for this property.

Golden Eagle RV Park Campground (575-77-3188; 540 W. Therma Dr., Eagle Nest, NM 87718; moderate). Very popular, somewhat crowded, busy place. Gift shop, grocery store, craft room, club room, fitness room. A home away from home.

❋ Museums and Sites

Enchanted Circle Gateway Museum (575-377-5978; located on US 64 [north side across from Fifth Street], Eagle Nest, NM 87718; open every day except Christmas and Thanksgiving Day, Mon.–Sat. 9:30 AM–4 PM, Sun. 11 AM–4 PM; museum subject to close in inclement weather, so please call in advance). Gold excursions, chuckwagon dinners.

Elizabethtown (575-377-3420; ghost town 5 miles north on NM 38, Eagle Nest). This is the gold rush town, aka E-town, that kicked off settlement of the Moreno Valley. Hard to believe several thousand people once lived here. A truly haunted feeling.

Vietnam Veterans Memorial State Park (575-377-2293; www.angelfirememorial.com/the-memorial; 34 Country Club Rd., Angel Fire, NM 87710; $5 per vehicle). This deeply moving memorial to those who perished in the Vietnam conflict was built by Dr. Victor Westphall, who lost his son, David Westphall, there. Thousands of motorcyclists converge here each Memorial Day in the "Run for the Wall" pilgrimage. Reflection Room open 24 hours; visitor center open 9 AM–7 PM daily Memorial Day–Labor Day, 9 AM–5 PM daily otherwise.

❋ Outdoors

GOLF **Angel Fire Resort** (575-377-3055; www.angelfireresort.com; 10 Miller Ln., Angel Fire, NM 87710). 18 holes (see "Recreation", page 49–50).

HIKING Red River is surrounded by 138 miles of marked hiking trails. Marked hikes range from short nature trails along the Red River to day trips through the Wheeler Peak Wilderness Area.

Short hikes: Red River Nature Trail, Middle Fork Lake, Pioneer Trail, Mallette Park Nature Trail

Long hikes: Goose Creek Canyon, Columbine, Lost Lake, Horseshoe Lake, Wheeler Peak

QUESTA

This is where you'll find the rare river access down into the gorge, in the Wild Rivers area of the Rio Grande del Norte National Monument. (Turn left/west onto NM 378 about 2.6 miles north of Questa's traffic light.) Enjoy the dramatic open scenery, well-marked trails, and facilities along the paved loop road. The Big Arsenic Springs trail leads down to where the spring flows into the Rio Grande; a perfect picnic spot with petroglyphs just another quarter-mile upriver. La Junta Trail is a very steep route to the joining of the Red River and Rio Grande, but a stunning hike.

Meadows, streams, wildflowers, and cool forests define the Forest Service trails east of Questa, turning toward Red River on NM 38. Columbine Canyon is a favorite for short or long excursions.

Cabresto Lake, just northeast of Questa, is a jewel of a mountain lake with ideal fishing, canoeing, and hiking. It is the southern approach to the broad vistas of the Latir Lakes area, which can also be reached by driving north, then east at Costilla, for Rio Costilla Park. Farther on are the remote and beautiful valleys of Valle Vidal.

ANGEL FIRE

Angel Fire recreation trails are open four seasons for hiking, biking, cross-country skiing, and snowshoeing. The trails are maintained by the Trekkers, kept free of hazards, and are well marked using signs, cairns, and diamond markers. Posts and mileage from trailhead have been added on all trails.

Angel Fire trailheads: Bobcat, Solar Loop, Sendero del Sol, Deer Elk Bear, Coyote, Oeste Vista, Lake, and Lady Slipper. Angel Fire also has entrances to the Elliot Barker trails.

SNOWMOBILING There's an exhilarating network of trails for snowmobilers through both the Santa Fe and Carson National Forests. Many of these regularly groomed mini-highways twist and turn through thick forests to high-alpine meadows where speedsters can zoom across wide-open spaces to their hearts' content. Remember to slow down and stay clear of skiers and snowshoers. For maximum safety and fun, choose a trail that's designated for snowmobiles only. Three of the best are Fourth of July Canyon, Old Red River Pass, and Greenie Peak in the **Questa Ranger District** (575-758-6200) near Red River. A number of businesses in Red River also provide safe, guided snowmobile tours, complete with mountaintop hot dog cookouts. And in January, the **Angel Fire Ski Area** (575-377-3055) hosts the Angel Fire Snowmobile Festival, with races, free rides, buffet dinner, and prizes.

Angel Fire Excursions (575-377-2799; NM 434, Angel Fire, NM 87710). Guided snowmobile trips on scenic trails of the Carson National Forest.

HORSEBACK RIDING **Nancy Burch's Roadrunner Tours** (575-377-6416; US 64 Headquarters, Angel Fire, NM 87710). Family favorites including gold panning day trips and horse-drawn wagon/sleigh rides that feature cozy fireside and chuckwagon meals, as well as sunset dinner rides and overnight camping tours. Open year-round, covering Taos, Red River, Angel Fire, and Cimarron.

CROSS-COUNTRY SKIING For cross-country ski instruction and tours in the Taos area, call **Millers Crossing** (575-754-2374; 800-966-9381; 417 W. Main St., Red River, NM 87558). The place to go touring near Taos is the **Enchanted Forest Cross Country Ski Area** (575-754-2374; 29 Sangre de Cristo Dr., Red River, NM 87558). Just east of

Red River atop Bobcat Pass, it offers 30 km of groomed and ungroomed trails amid 600 forested acres. Here, you'll find not only dog-friendly trails and prime ski terrain for classical, freestyle, and telemark, but also instructors, patrols, warming huts, rentals, snowshoeing, and special events. $18 a day, $15 for seniors and teens, $9 for children 12 and younger; rentals $16 a day, $13 for seniors and teens, $8 for children 12 and younger.

Angel Fire Resort (575-377-6401; 800-633-7463 information, snow report, and reservations; www.angelfireresort.com; 10 Miller Ln., Angel Fire, NM 87710, 22 miles east of Taos via US 64 and NM 434; 10,677 feet peak elevation; 2,077-foot vertical drop; 210 inches average snowfall; snowmaking 52 percent of area; 67 downhill trails [31 percent beginner, 48 percent intermediate, 21 percent advanced]; groomed 35 km cross-country track; lifts: 5 chairlifts [2 high-speed quads, 3 doubles, 2 SunKid Wonder Carpets]; $64 adults, $48 half-day, $44 ages 7–12, free for ages 6 and under and 70 and older; sightseers may purchase a single lift ride to the summit for $20). Texan Roy H. Lebus started Angel Fire Resort in 1967 with little more than a dream and a handful of dedicated workers. Today it is known as a family resort and a "cruiser's mountain," featuring a variety of long, well-groomed trails (the longest is 3.5 miles). Angel Fire is predominantly tailored to beginning and intermediate skiers; however, it also offers a number of outstanding expert runs, including the addition of a new expert trail called C-4. A short 15-minute hike from the top of the Southwest Flyer chairlift, C-4 will top the adventurous skier's and boarder's must-hit list on any fresh powder day. And they are so confident of their conditions and snowmaking machines, that if you are dissatisfied they will automatically return your ticket within one hour if you want to come back another day. Widespread snowmaking guarantees 2,000 vertical feet of skiing even in the driest of years, and only at the very busiest of times does the lift line require more than a 5- or 10-minute wait. Another plus is the large picnic pavilion on the mountain that can accommodate several hundred skiers at a time.

With 3,000 beds, Angel Fire has one of the largest, most affordable lodging bases in the state. The resort also boasts more major (and offbeat) events than almost any other area—for example, the world shovel race championships, featuring the wild antics of riders careening down the mountain at more than 60 mph on scoop shovels.

Angel Fire Resort has also bolstered its freestyle parks with exciting new features, helping cement Angel Fire's position as snowboarding capital of the state. They have added more than a dozen high-quality freestyle rails and fun box features, including the most popular flat rails, rainbows, double-kinks, C-rails, tabletops, and a few surprises—open challenges to freestyle skiers as well as boarders. Angel Fire Resort was the site of the USASA Snowboard Nationals in 2004, and Liberation Park was picked as the 2008 Terrain Park of the Year in North America by *OnTheSnow*.

What's new at Angel Fire is the Angel Fire Resort Nordic Center, offering 10 km of groomed classic and skate cross-country ski trails, plus snowshoeing lanes and a family snow play hill for sledding. Lessons, equipment rental, retail, and pull-sleds are available in the full-service winter sports shop downstairs. When you're done playing outside and need to warm up, come into the club, grab a hot chocolate, and enjoy the beautiful views of the Sangre de Cristo Mountains. Snowboarding lessons are available at the ski school. Snowboarding, terrain park, zipline.

Red River Ski Area (575-754-2223 information, snow report; 800-331-SNOW reservations; www.redriverskiarea.com; P.O. Box 900, Red River, NM 87558, 37 miles north of Taos via NM 522 and NM 38; 10,350 feet peak elevation; 1,600-foot vertical drop; 214-inch average snowfall; snowmaking 85 percent of area; 57 downhill trails [32 percent beginner, 38 percent intermediate, 30 percent advanced]; cross-country trails available nearby at Enchanted Forest; 7 lifts [2 double chairs, 3 triple chairs, 2 surface tows]; $73 adults, $55 half-day; $67 teens; $57 children and seniors, free for seniors over

70 and children under 3). Red River was started in 1961 by a well-loved oilman and character named John Bolton, and its first lift consisted of used derricks and cables Bolton imported from an oil field in Texas. Located in the northern arc of the Enchanted Circle, Red River is another family-friendly ski area, a great place to learn, with extensive snowmaking and numerous wide beginner and intermediate trails. Runs such as Kit Carson and Broadway allow plenty of room for everybody to fall down, while expert speedways like Cat Skinner and Landing Strip are enough to get anyone's adrenaline pumping. The area rents about 1,000 pairs of skis, with another 2,000 pairs available in Red River. It also hosts on-slope bars and restaurants.

The Pioneer Flyer, an accelerated reverse chairlift newly opened in 2015, is a thrill akin to bungee jumping. It pulls you backward, then releases you to fly over some of the most spectacular scenery in the West. And the new Emerald Quad will virtually eliminate lift lines at Summit Camp by doubling the uphill capacity and traveling at nearly twice the speed of the current lift.

Red River features a 4,500-bed lodging base less than a block from the ski area. During February's Mardi Gras in the Mountains, the whole town turns to cooking Cajun food and dressing in festive Southern garb. There's a moonlight ski and snowshoe event, and a Spring Break Torchlight Parade & Fireworks show. Red River has a Kinderski school for ages 4 to 10 and Buckaroo Child Care for ages 6 months to 4 years.

Great powder, a variety of challenges, and plenty of facilities for the young ones make affordable Red River more attractive than ever.

BOATING At **Eagle Nest Lake State Park** (east of Taos on the edge of the Enchanted Circle), **Eagle Nest Marina** (575-377-6941; 28386 US 64, Eagle Nest, NM 87718) can provide information on boat rentals and activities. Eagle Nest Lake, a 2,400-surface-acre lake, offers some of the best trout and kokanee salmon fishing in the state. Seasonal recreation includes boating, hiking, picnicking, and cross-country skiing, with opportunities to see an abundance of birds and other wildlife, including elk, deer, bears, and eagles. Set in the scenic Moreno Valley and surrounded by two of the state's highest peaks, Baldy Mountain and Wheeler Peak. At 8,300 feet in elevation, the park offers a cool retreat from the summer heat for fishermen, boaters, campers, and wildlife enthusiasts. A state-of-the-art green visitor center features exhibits, a classroom, and an expansive patio overlooking the lake, making Eagle Nest Lake an ideal location for wildlife viewing. In the winter, ice fishing and snowmobiling are popular sports when ice thickness permits. Snowmobiling is limited to the lake surface.

ABIQUIU

A little outside the area to the west on US 84 sits the Hispanic village of **Abiquiu**, where artist Georgia O'Keeffe lived. You'll see why when you get a look at the landscape with its spectacularly colored cliffs and mesas. This place provided the artist with so much inspiration she said, "In New Mexico, half your work is done for you." A few miles up the road, you'll come to spacious Abiquiu Lake. The nearby Chama River, a federal Wild and Scenic River, flows through some of the most gorgeous desert scenery on the planet. A bit farther north, you can take a trip on the Cumbres and Toltec Scenic Railroad, an old-fashioned, steam-powered narrow-gauge that runs between Chama and Antonito in southern Colorado. Snaking back and forth along the border through the San Juan Mountains, it's a wonderful way to see knockout mountain scenery from the comfort of a railroad car. About 40 miles north on US 84 find Los Ojos, a tiny mountain village that is home to Tierra Wools (575-588-7231; 91 Main St., Los Ojos, NM 87551), a weaving cooperative that produces locally dyed Rio Grande textiles.

To find out what is going on in Abiquin, El Rito, and the area, see *Abiquiu News* (www.abiquiunews.com; info@abquiunews.com.), an Internet newsletter that comes out each Friday.

✳ Restaurants and Cafés

Bode's General Store (505-685-4422; 21196 US 84, Abiquiu). Café open 10:30 AM–3 PM daily, but takeout items ready all day. WiFi. Landmark trading post and gas station with the flavor of the place, stocking groceries, cookware, hardware, books, and hand-made gifts by local artists. Famous breakfast burritos, pastries, stellar New Mexico home cooking. An essential stop.

Café Abiquiu (888-735-2902; www.abiquiuinn.com; 21120 US 84, Abiquiu). Located in the Abiquiu Inn, this small, lovely, full-service restaurant serves authentic northern New Mexico cuisine along with wine and craft beer. Packed with books on the area, colorful clothing, jewelry, crafts—much of it locally made. A good place to shop.

Purple Adobe Lavender Farm (505-685-0082; www.purpleadobelavenderfarm .com, US 84, Private Road 1622, Gate 31, Abiquiu; open Apr.–Oct., 10 AM–5 PM Tues.–Sat.). Coffee, tea, gluten-free scones. Lavender labyrinth, greenhouse, Lavender Shoppe. Serving lunch in the lavender fields. Lavender Festival held early July, with crafts, goodies, and all things lavender.

El Farolito (575-581-9509; CR 156, El Rito). Out of the way, inconvenient, with uncertain hours and only eight picnic tables in the place, this is a mecca of great green chile, which is why it is included. Anyone who loves New Mexican food ought to eat here at least once. Call ahead.

Three Ravens Coffee House (575-588-9086; www.threeravenscoffeehouse.com; 15 NM 531, Tierra Amarilla). WiFi. Great coffee where you'd least expect to find it, in the shadow of the Tierra Amarillo Courthouse.

✳ Lodging

Abiquiu Inn (888-735-2902; www.abiquiuinn.com; 21120 NM 84, Abiquiu, NM 87510). Charming and comfortable casitas with kiva fireplaces and gardenlike setting. Book your Georgia O'Keeffe tour here.

Old Abiquiu Bed & Breakfast (505-685-4784; US 84, Abiquiu, NM 87510). Located on the Rio Chama, here you may take your choice of two cozy rooms or a campsite on the river at this bicycle-friendly abode.

✳ Museums and Sites

Florence Hawley Ellis Museum of Anthropology (505-685-4312, ext. 4118; www. ghostranch.org/explore/museums/museum-of-anthropology; Ghost Ranch Conference Center, US 84, Abiquiu, NM 87510, 35 miles northwest of Española; open Mon.–Sat. 9 AM–5 PM, Sun. 1–5 PM; suggested donation $2 adults, $1 children and seniors). Dr. Florence Hawley Ellis was a pioneer anthropologist who conducted excavations and research in Chaco Canyon and elsewhere. She initiated the archaeological digs at Ghost Ranch. The museum specializes in excavated materials from the Ghost Ranch Gallina digs. The little-studied Gallina culture of northern New Mexico comprised the people who left Mesa Verde, Chaco Canyon, and the Four Corners area during a long drought around A.D. 1200. Other exhibits feature the Spaniards of the area, Pueblo Indian clothing, and prehistoric pottery making.

The adjacent Ruth Hall Museum of Paleontology houses a copy of the *Coelophysis* dinosaur skeleton. The original was found near Ghost Ranch, one of the five best dinosaur quarries in the world. This sharp-toothed, birdlike carnivore, extinct for some 200 million years, is the official state fossil.

Dar al Islam (505-685-4515; www.daralislam.org; off County Rd. 155 at Sign 42A, above Ghost Ranch; visitors are restricted, so call for hours). Designed by Egyptian architect Hassan Fathy, reputed to be the world's foremost adobe architect, this imposing mosque is the center of a long-standing local Muslim quarter.

Echo Amphitheater (4 miles beyond Ghost Ranch on US 84). Many legends, mostly dark, are associated with this natural amphitheater, though it is fun to get out and hear your voice echo.

Poshuouinge: Village Above the Muddy River (Located off US 84; call Santa Fe National Forest, 505-438-7840, for directions). This 500-year-old pueblo ruin is accessible only by foot; the path is a steep, unpaved half-mile to a hilltop overlook.

✳ Retreats

Ghost Ranch Education and Retreat Center (505-685-1000; www.ghostranch.org; 280 Private Dr. 1708, Abiquiu, NM 87510, US 84 between Mile Markers 224 and 225). When Georgia O'Keeffe discovered Arthur Pack had sold Ghost Ranch to the Presbyterian Church, she said, "Why didn't you offer it to me?" She also said of her beloved Pedernal mesa, "God told me if I painted it often enough, he would give it to me." If you want to experience the magic of New Mexico and you are on a budget, it's a good bet you'll love Ghost Ranch. Here you will find classes and seminars in photography, writing, pottery, silversmithing, watercolor, weaving, traditional arts such as natural indigo dyeing, history, spirituality, bodywork, renewable energy, health, and music year-round, with

ON A HIKE AT GHOST RANCH, THERE ARE NO BAD SHOTS

PEDERNAL, AS SEEN FROM GHOST RANCH, WAS ONE OF GEORGIA O'KEEFFE'S FAVORITE SUBJECTS. SHE SAID, "GOD TOLD ME THAT IF I PAINTED IT OFTEN ENOUGH, I COULD HAVE IT."

the biggest concentration of offerings during the summer months. Located in the heart of O'Keeffe's breathtaking red-rock country, rustic Ghost Ranch is a center of diversity. Visit the website for a downloadable catalog.

Modest lodging, as well as trailer camping, is available at Ghost Ranch. In addition, Ghost Ranch has three noted high desert hiking trails of various difficulty—Kitchen Mesa, Chimney Rock, and Box Canyon—each photogenic in its way. A $5 admission entitles you to hike and covers museum entrance fees. Special tours are available, notably the O'Keeffe Landscape tour, where the guide takes you on a restricted part of the ranch to see the actual sites O'Keeffe painted, such as "Gerald's Tree," comparing the place with the painting. Cost $34.

Monastery of Christ in the Desert (801-545-8567; www.christdesert.org; P.O. Box 270, Abiquiu, NM 87510, 75 miles north of Santa Fe on US 84/285, go west on US 84 past Ghost Ranch Visitor Center, turn left on Forest Service Rd. 151; Sun. Mass 9:15 AM, open to all; gift shop and bookstore open daily). A 13-mile winding dirt road takes you to the monastery grounds with its glorious rock-and-adobe church. This remote Benedictine monastery built along the Chama River was designed by Japanese architect George Nakashima. Visits give guests the opportunity to share in the life of this 40-member Benedictine order with the key elements of love, prayer, reading, study, silence, and manual labor. To reserve guest rooms for silent retreats, write the guest master (by postal mail or email via the website) well in advance, especially for Christmas and other Catholic holidays.

Ojo Caliente Mineral Springs Resort & Spa (505-583-2233; 800-222-9162; www.ojospa.com; 50 Los Banos Dr., Ojo Caliente, NM 87549, southwest of Taos or north of Española on US 285; closed Christmas; reservations required for private tubs). A delightful getaway for all. This is the most popular mineral springs spa in northern New Mexico, featuring natural hot waters with therapeutic iron, arsenic, and lithium.

Attendants in separate men's and women's locker areas pamper and guide you either to individual cubicles with fresh water for 15-minute arsenic soaks (great for arthritis and rheumatism) or to a large, enclosed outdoor grotto area with hot iron water. There's also a coed bathhouse with individual rooms for couples. After your soak, an attendant will put you on a table and cover you head to toe with steaming hot cotton blankets (aka the mummy wrap) for further relaxation or in preparation for a full-body massage.

Before returning to the world, you're invited to take a shower, a swim in the heated outdoor pool, or a peaceful walk beside giant cottonwoods—hike up to see the petroglyphs or to fill canisters with any of the three mineral waters. You can even go riding if you want.

Ojo used to be rather latter-day-hippie funky, but gentrification has definitely set in. Although they bill themselves as "unpretentious," those of us who soaked here back in the day beg to differ. Locals find it disappointingly pricey, and prices keep going up here. As of 2016, they were $18 for an all-day pass Mon.–Thurs.; $28 for the same on weekends and holidays; $16 sunset rate (after 6 PM) on Mon.–Thurs. and weekends. Expect to pay between $100–$200 for body work. The inn here also offers overnight packages for couples, including breakfast and two mineral baths apiece. If you are a local New Mexican, you are eligible to purchase the New Mexico Club card, entitling you to nine soaks for $119, Mon.–Thurs., the best deal you can get.

✳ Outdoors

Abiquiu Lake (505-685-4371; about 65 miles northwest of Santa Fe on US 84). This large, scenic reservoir behind Abiquiu Dam offers a little of everything, from canoeing and windsurfing to fishing and waterskiing. No boat rentals are available. Managed by U.S. Army Corps of Engineers.

GERALD'S TREE, ONE OF O'KEEFFE'S BEST LOVED WORKS, IS ONE OF MANY MARVELOUS SITES FEATURED ON THE GHOST RANCH LANDSCAPE TOUR

Heron and El Vado Lakes (505-476-3355; 888-667-2757; near the town of Chama). Both lakes, administered by the New Mexico State Parks Division, have boat ramps and camping facilities. Heron is a no-wake lake, especially popular for small sailboats and Hobies. Waterskiing is allowed at El Vado. For further information, contact the **Stone House Lodge** (575-588-7274; HC 75, Box 1022, Los Ojos, NM 87551). Stone House rentals, available Apr.–Nov., include 24-foot pontoon boats with awnings and outboard engines, 20-foot Bass Buggies, 14-foot fishing trollers, and 17-foot canoes.

✻ Events

Lavender Festival (505-685-0082; www.purpleadobelavenderfarm.com). Held mid-July. Lavender harvest, lavender treats and products. All things lavender. Teahouse open seasonally; call for schedule.

Abiquiu Studio Tour (505-685-4454; www.abiquiustudiotour.org). Columbus Day Weekend. Visit artists' studios from 10 AM–5 PM; meet them and learn about their work one-on-one. Huge variety of media—pottery, painting, photography, textiles. More than 70 local artists participate.

FURTHER READING

For the traveler who enjoys reading about a region as well as visiting it, we've put together a list of some of the many books that have been written on the Santa Fe–Taos area.

✳ Autobiographies, Biographies, and Reminiscences

Berke, Arnold. *Mary Colter: Architect of the Southwest*. New York: Princeton Architectural Press, 2002. 320 pp., $35.

Burns, Cherie. *Searching for Beauty: The Life of Millicent Rogers, The American Heiress Who Taught the World about Style*. New York: St. Martin's Griffin, 2013. 280 pp., $19.99.

Cabeza de Baca, Fabiola. *We Fed Them Cactus*. Albuquerque: University of New Mexico Press, 1954, 1994. 186 pp., $9.95.

Chavez, Fray Angelico. *But Time and Chance: The Story of Padre Martinez of Taos 1793–1867*. Santa Fe: Sunstone Press, 1981. 171 pp., $11.95.

Church, Peggy Pond. *The House at Otowi Bridge: The Story of Edith Warner and Los Alamos*. Albuquerque: University of New Mexico Press, 1959. 149 pp., $9.95.

Cline, Lynn. *Literary Pilgrims: The Santa Fe and Taos Writers Colonies 1917–1950*. Albuquerque: University of New Mexico Press, 2007. 184 pp., $19.95.

Horgan, Paul. *Lamy of Santa Fe*. New York: Noonday Press, 1975. 523 pp., $17.95.

Luhan, Mabel Dodge. *Winter in Taos*. Taos: Las Palomas de Taos, 1935. 237 pp., $14.95.

Magoffin, Susan Shelby. *Down the Santa Fe Trail and into Mexico: The Diary of Susan Shelby Magoffin, 1846–1847*. Lincoln: University of Nebraska Press, 1982. 284 pp., $6.95.

Rudnick, Lois Palken. *Mabel Dodge Luhan: New Woman, New Worlds*. Albuquerque: University of New Mexico Press, 1984. 400 pp., $22.

Russell, Marian. *Land of Enchantment: Memoirs of Marian Russell Along the Old Santa Fe Trail*. Albuquerque: University of New Mexico Press, 1954. 163 pp., illus., index, $10.95.

✳ Cultural Studies

Bullock, Alice. *Living Legends of the Santa Fe Country*. Santa Fe: Lightning Tree—Jene Lyons Publishers, 1978. 96 pp., illus., $7.95.

Cajete, Gregory. *Native Science: Natural Laws of Interdependence*. Santa Fe: Clear Light Publishers, 2000. 315 pp., $14.95.

Chavez, Fray Angelico. *Origins of New Mexico Families: A Genealogy of the Spanish Colonial Period*. Revised edition. Santa Fe: Museum of New Mexico Press, 1992. 441 pp., $33.

Curtin, L. S. M. *Healing Herbs of the Upper Rio Grande: Traditional Medicine of the Southwest*. Santa Fe: Western Edge Press, 1997. 235 pp., $12.

Dickey, Roland F. *New Mexico Village Arts*. Albuquerque: University of New Mexico Press, 1990. 266 pp., $24.95.

Edelman, Sandra A. *Summer People, Winter People: A Guide to the Pueblos in the Santa Fe Area*. Santa Fe: Sunstone Press, 1986. 32 pp., index, $4.95.

Gibson, Arrell Morgan. *The Santa Fe and Taos Colonies: Age of the Muses, 1900–1942*. Norman: University of Oklahoma Press, 1983. 345 pp., illus., index, $13.95.

Julyan, Robert. *The Place Names of New Mexico*. Albuquerque: University of New Mexico Press, 2000. 385 pp., $21.

Kutz, Jack. *Mysteries and Miracles of New Mexico: Guidebook to the Genuinely Bizarre in the Land of Enchantment*. Corrales, NM: Rhombus Publishing Co., 1988. 216 pp., $7.95.

Lippard, Lucy R. *On the Beaten Track: Tourism, Art, and Place*. New York: The New Press, 1992. 182 pp., $18.95.

Lynn, Sandra D. *Windows on the Past: Historic Lodgings of New Mexico*. Albuquerque: University of New Mexico Press, 1999. 209 pp., $24.95.

Morrow, Baker H., and V. B. Price. *Anasazi Architecture and American Design*. Albuquerque: University of New Mexico Press, 1997. 214 pp., $29.95.

Poling-Kempes, Lesley. *Valley of Shining Stone: The Story of Abiquiu*. Tucson: University of Arizona Press, 1997. 272 pp., $24.99.

Rhodes, Richard. *The Making of the Atom Bomb*. New York: Simon & Schuster, 1986. 886 pp., $17.

Robertson, Edna, and Sarah Nestor. *Artists of the Canyons & Caminos: Santa Fe: Early Twentieth Century*. Layton, Utah: Ancient City Press, 2006. 188 pp., $19.95.

Steele, Thomas J. *Santos and Saints: The Religious Folk Art of Hispanic New Mexico*. Santa Fe: Ancient City Press, 1974. 220 pp., index, $12.95.

Tobias, Henry. *History of the Jews in New Mexico*. Albuquerque: University of New Mexico Press, 1990. 294 pp., $24.

Tobias, Henry. *Jews in New Mexico Since World War II*. Albuquerque: University of New Mexico Press, 2008. 172 pp., $15.

Trimble, Stephen. *Talking with the Clay: The Art of Pueblo Pottery*. Santa Fe: School of American Research Press, 1987. 116 pp., $22.95.

Weigle, Marta. *Brothers of Light, Brothers of Blood: The Penitentes of the Southwest*. Santa Fe: Ancient City Press, 1976. 300 pp., $12.95.

Weigle, Marta, and Kyle Fiore. *Santa Fe and Taos: The Writer's Era 1916–41*. Santa Fe: Ancient City Press, 1982. 229 pp., illus., index, $16.95.

Weigle, Marta, and Peter White. *The Lore of New Mexico*. Albuquerque: University of New Mexico Press/American Folklore Society, 1988. 523 pp., $37.

Wilson, Chris. *The Myth of Santa Fe: Creating a Modern Regional Tradition*. Albuquerque: University of New Mexico Press, 1997. 409 pp., $35.

✳ Literary Works

Anaya, Rudolfo A. *Bless Me Ultima*. Berkeley, CA: Tonatiuh–Quinto Sol International, 1972. 247 pp., $11.95.

Bartlett, Lee, V. B. Price, and Dianne Edenfield Edwards, eds. *In Company: An Anthology of New Mexico Poets After 1960*. Albuquerque: University of New Mexico Press, 2004. 542 pp., $39.95.

Bradford, Richard. *Red Sky at Morning*. New York: Harper & Row, 1968. 256 pp., $8.95.

Cather, Willa. *Death Comes for the Archbishop*. New York: Vintage, 1927. 297 pp., $8.95.

Crawford, Stanley. *Mayordomo: Chronicle of an Acequia in Northern New Mexico*. New York: Anchor Books Doubleday, 1988. 231 pp., $8.95.

Hillerman, Tony, ed. *The Spell of New Mexico*. Albuquerque: University of New Mexico Press, 1976. 105 pp., $9.95.

Horgan, Paul. *The Centuries of Santa Fe*. Santa Fe: William Gannon Publishers, 1956. 363 pp., index, $9.95.

Nichols, John. *The Milagro Beanfield War*. New York: Ballantine Books, 1974. 629 pp., $5.95.

Niederman, Sharon. *Return to Abo: A Novel of the Southwest*. Albuquerque: University of New Mexico Press, 2005. 300 pp., $24.95.

Quade, Kirstin Valdez. *Night at the Fiestas: Stories*. New York: W. W. Norton, 2015. 275 pp., $15.95.

Waters, Frank. *The Man Who Killed the Deer*. New York: Farrar Rinehart, 1942. 217 pp., $3.95.

✳ Local Histories

Chauvenet, Beatrice. *Hewett and Friends: A Biography of Santa Fe's Vibrant Era*. Santa Fe: Museum of New Mexico Press, 1983. 248 pp., illus., index, $16.95.

DeBuys, William. *Enchantment and Exploitation: The Life and Hard Times of a New Mexican Mountain Range*. Albuquerque: University of New Mexico Press, 1985. 394 pp., illus., index, $15.95.

Gregg, Josiah. *The Commerce of the Prairies*. Lincoln: University of Nebraska Press, 1967. 343 pp., index, $9.95.

Hemp, Bill. *Taos Landmarks & Legends*. Los Alamos, NM: Exceptional Books Ltd., 1996. 134 pp., $19.95.

Hordes, Stanley. *To the End of the Earth: A History of the Crypto-Jews of New Mexico*. New York: Columbia University Press, 2005. 499 pp., $40.

Horgan, Paul. *Great River: The Rio Grande in North American History*. Austin: Texas Monthly Press, 1984. 1,020 pp., index, $14.95.

Jenkins, Myra Ellen, and Albert H. Schroeder. *A Brief History of New Mexico*. Albuquerque: University of New Mexico Press, 1974. 87 pp., illus., index, $8.95.

Price, V. B. *The Orphaned Land: New Mexico's Environment Since the Manhattan Project*. Photography by Nell Farrell. Albuquerque: University of New Mexico Press, 2011. 362 pp., $23.

Rudnick, Lois Palkin. *Utopian Vistas: The Mabel Dodge Luhan House and the American Counterculture*. Albuquerque: University of New Mexico Press, 1996. 401 pp., $19.95.

Simmons, Marc. *New Mexico: An Interpretive History*. Albuquerque: University of New Mexico Press, 1988. 207 pp., $10.95.

✳ Photographic Studies

Brewer, Robert, and Steve McDowell. *The Persistence of Memory: New Mexico's Churches*. Santa Fe: Museum of New Mexico Press, 1991. 152 pp., $39.95.

Cash, Maria Romero. *Built of Earth and Song: Churches of Northern New Mexico*. Santa Fe: Red Crane Books, 1993. 184 pp., $11.95.

Clark, William, Edward Klanner, Jack Parsons, and Bernard Plossu. *Santa Fe: The City in Photographs*. Santa Fe: Fotowest Publishing, 1984. 72 pp., $14.95.

Gregg, Andrew K. *New Mexico in the 19th Century: A Pictorial History*. Albuquerque: University of New Mexico Press. 196 pp., index, $15.95.

Nichols, John, and William Davis. *If Mountains Die: A New Mexico Memoir*. New York: Alfred A. Knopf, 1987. 144 pp., $19.95.

Niederman, Sharon. *New Mexico's Tasty Traditions: Recollections, Recipes & Photos*. Santa Fe: New Mexico Magazine, 2004. 215 pp., $26.

Robin, Arthur H., William M. Ferguson, and Lisa Ferguson. *Rock Art of Bandelier National Monument*. Albuquerque: University of New Mexico Press, 1989. 156 pp., index, $29.95.

Varjabedian, Craig, and Michael Wallis. *En Divina Luz: The Penitente Moradas of New Mexico*. Albuquerque: University of New Mexico Press, 1994. 130 pp., $25.

Warren, Nancy Hunter. *Villages of Hispanic New Mexico*. Santa Fe: School of American Research, 1987. 109 pp., $18.

Wilson, Chris, and Stefanos Polyzoides, eds. *The Plazas of New Mexico*. Photography by Miguel Gandert. San Antonio: Trinity University Press, 2011. 337 pp., $48.

✳ Recreation

Anderson, Fletcher, and Ann Hopkinson. *Rivers of the Southwest: A Boater's Guide to the Rivers of Colorado, New Mexico, Utah, and Arizona*. Boulder, CO: Pruett Publishing Co., 1982. 129 pp., illus., index, $8.95.

Kaysing, Bill. *Great Hot Springs of the West*. Santa Barbara, CA: Capra Press, 1984. 213 pp., illus., index, $10.95.

Matthews, Kay. *Cross-Country Skiing in Northern New Mexico: An Introduction and Trail Guide*. Placitas, NM: Acequia Madre Press, 1986. 96 pp., maps, $7.95.

Pinkerton, Elaine. *Santa Fe on Foot: Walking, Running and Bicycle Routes in the City Different*. Santa Fe: Ocean Tree, 1986. 125 pp., illus., maps, $7.95.

Santa Fe Group of the Sierra Club. *Day Hikes in the Santa Fe Area*. Santa Fe: Sierra Club, 1997. 192 pp., index, $8.95.

Ungnade, Herbert E. *Guide to the New Mexico Mountains*. Albuquerque: University of New Mexico Press, 1988. 235 pp., index, $10.95.

✳ Travel

Boyd, E. *Popular Arts of Spanish New Mexico*. Santa Fe: Museum of New Mexico Press, 1974. A color photographic study of the entire spectrum of Hispanic art in the Land of Enchantment.

Chronic, Halka. *Roadside Geology of New Mexico*. Missoula, MT: Mountain Press Publishing Co., 1987. 255 pp., index, $11.95.

Fugate, Frances L., and Roberta B. Fugate. *Roadside History of New Mexico*. Missoula, MT: Mountain Press Publishing Co., 1989. 483 pp., index, $15.95.

Hackett, Charles Wilson. *Revolt of the Pueblo Indians of New Mexico and Otermín's Attempted Reconquest, 1680–1682*. Albuquerque: University of New Mexico Press, 1942.

Henderson, Alice Corbin. *Brothers of Light: The Penitentes of the Southwest*. New York: Harcourt, Brace, 1937. One of the best treatments of the Penitente phenomenon.

Kendall, George. *Narrative of the Texan–Santa Fe Expedition*. Albuquerque: University of New Mexico Press, 1844. Illus., maps. Outlines the beginning of the conflict between Texas and New Mexico that is still evident today, mostly in attitudes.

Knee, Ernest. *Santa Fe, New Mexico*. New York: Chanticleer Press, 1942. An unpretentious, classic photographic study of authentic old Santa Fe charm accompanied by text.

Niederman, Sharon. *Signs & Shrines: Spiritual Journeys Across New Mexico*. Woodstock, VT: The Countryman Press, 2012. 256 pp., $19.95.

Robertson, Edna. *Artists of the Caminos and Canyons: The Early Years*. Santa Fe: Peregrine Smith, 1976. A study of the turn-of-the-20th-century artists in Santa Fe and Taos.

Ross, Calvin. *Sky Determines*. Albuquerque: University of New Mexico Press, 1948. A unique book that covers New Mexico history, weather, art, landscape, and more.

Spivey R. *Maria*. Flagstaff, AZ: Northland Press, 1979. About the famous San Ildefonso Pueblo potter.

INDEX